A Field Guide to Community Literacy

This practical guidebook presents trends, research-grounded strategies, and field-based solutions to challenges of working in community-based literacy initiatives. A comprehensive guide for practitioners, this book addresses best practices for implementing, maintaining, expanding, and evaluating community-based literacy initiatives. The contributors in this volume help readers shift thinking from merely considering, "How can communities support literacy?" to "How can literacy help us create, support, and strengthen communities?"

Organized into four parts – on building community through literacy, program design, case studies from the field, and program evaluation – chapters cover research-based and innovative practices in a diverse range of populations and settings, including family services, adult literacy initiatives, community centers, and tutoring programs. With an abundance of praxis-oriented examples and real-world strategies from top scholars and practitioners, the book serves as a roadmap for essential topics, including funding, writing grant proposals, handling audits, and conducting research within program settings. With templates, models, planning tools, and checklists ready for immediate use, this book is an invaluable field manual for individuals involved in community literacy work, researchers, and students in literacy-oriented courses either at the undergraduate or graduate levels.

Laurie A. Henry is Professor of Literacy Studies at Salisbury University, USA, and Dean of the Seidel School of Education.

Norman A. Stahl is Professor Emeritus of Literacy Education at Northern Illinois University, USA, and President of the Reading Hall of Fame.

i

A Field Guide to Community Literacy

Case Studies and Tools for Praxis, Evaluation, and Research

EDITED BY LAURIE A. HENRY AND NORMAN A. STAHL

Routledge
Taylor & Francis Group

NEW YORK AND LONDON

Cover image: Cheryl Wassenaar

First published 2022
by Routledge
605 Third Avenue, New York, NY 10158

and by Routledge
4 Park Square, Milton Park, Abingdon, Oxon, OX14 4RN

Routledge is an imprint of the Taylor & Francis Group, an informa business

Library of Congress Cataloging-in-Publication Data
A catalog record for this book has been requested

ISBN: 978-1-032-13187-0 (hbk)
ISBN: 978-1-032-11811-6 (pbk)
ISBN: 978-1-003-22804-2 (ebk)

DOI: 10.4324/9781003228042

Typeset in Bembo and Gill Sans
by Apex CoVantage, LLC

Contents

Acknowledgments

We would like to acknowledge our contributing authors; without them and their dedication to the work at hand, this book would not be possible. More broadly we would like to recognize community-based literacy program providers across the globe for their resilience in serving their clientele with unwavering commitment during such unprecedented and difficult times as was brought forward by the coronavirus pandemic.

Additionally, we are grateful for our editor Karen Adler, editorial assistant Emily Dombrovskaya, and their colleagues at Routledge/Taylor & Francis Group for the support of both our first text – *Literacy Across the Community: Research, Praxis, and Trends* – and this complimentary field guide. The continual support we received for these writing endeavors made the experience of publishing with them a true joy. In addition to our academic homes (Salisbury University and Northern Illinois University), we wish to recognize our professional homes (Literacy Research Association and American Reading Forum), which provided the initial venues for us to connect and collaborate. From singing waitstaff at Cafe Italia in Palm Springs to beachside cafés at the Sundial, these organizations provided the time and space for us to engage in the creative thought and visualization that became the basis of our two texts.

Finally, our greatest appreciation is for our spouses who accompanied us on this journey. Their constant support and understanding of the time commitment required to undertake the development of two edited books was unwavering. To Bill and Carolyn, thank you for your love, patience, and encouragement. This book wouldn't be possible without you.

Foreword

Perhaps unsurprisingly, the field of literacy education has a tendency to reify the concepts of *literacy* and of *education*, turning them into *ofcourse-nesses* (Woodside-Jiron, 2004) – unquestioned assumptions that have the power to shape policy, practice, and perception. Reifying literacy in this way results in the privileging of school-based definitions of literacy, in assumptions that formal education is the only (or at least the primary) context in which literacy is learned or developed, and substantial emphasis on skills-based, standardized test scores to determine the supposed literate worth of individuals, families, communities, and even entire nations. The reification of literacy also relegates family and community literacy prac-tices and programs to lesser positions, suggesting they are not "real" lit-eracy or are somehow secondary to the "true" work of literacy education, which *of course* happens in formal schooling. The chapters in this volume, therefore, offer an important antidote to these ofcoursenesses, reminding us that literacy is not simply a set of cognitive skills possessed by individ-uals but also is something that individuals, families, and communities use purposefully out in the world (Barton & Hamilton, 1998; Perry, 2012; Street, 1984). Indeed, this volume collectively asks us to shift our thinking so that we may understand literacy and its relationship with, effects on, and consequences for diverse communities. This volume also invites us to begin reimagining community-based literacy initiatives, as well as the relationship of those programs to both the communities they serve and to more formal educational contexts.

This perspective shift is one I see happening before my very own eyes each summer, as I teach an elective graduate seminar in family and community literacy. The students in this course represent a variety of educational experiences and goals – some students are seasoned K–12 classroom teachers seeking endorsement as a literacy specialist; others seek initial teacher licensure in secondary English language arts; still others have come from programs as diverse as music education, family studies, or teaching English to speakers of other languages. Among all of the assignments I give in my teaching, this course's Family Visit and Community Walk project seems to have the most profound effect on students. In this assignment, students are expected to conduct an in-depth visit with a family that is different from themselves in some meaningful way, such as race/ethnicity, language spoken in the home, religious belief, immigration status, family structure, and so on. During the visit, students are expected to observe the environment (especially if the visit occurs in the family home) and interview at least one adult and one child/youth in the household, with the goal of beginning to understand the family's Funds of Knowledge (González et al., 2005) and their Community Cultural Wealth (Yosso, 2006). For the Community Walk, students visit a publicly accessible site and spend time noting the various texts available, as well as the ways in which people use literacy in that context. Some students choose a site that is connected in some way to the family they visit (e.g., a place of worship attended by the family or other location they frequent), while others might select a place they've visited many times themselves but wish to view with fresh eyes (e.g., the public library or a central bus station) or even an event they might stumble upon (e.g., a Black Lives Matter protest in Louisville, KY in the wake of Breonna Taylor's murder by police). As a result of this assignment, students develop a significantly broadened understanding of the nature of literacy. Their eyes are opened to the myriad of texts and literacy practices that contextualize everyday life in the world (and which are largely ignored in formal literacy teaching). As they retrain themselves to view literacy as more than a set of skills and more than "reading books," they develop profound respect for the ways in which families across all walks of life value and support education and literacy development.

As Zoch and He (2020) observed, requiring educators to develop relationships with families and observe the communities where they serve is an essential element to better preparing teachers to work with culturally and linguistically diverse literacy learners that may help them to counter deficit assumptions and other stereotypes. Almost universally, my students notice that, when interviewed about their literacy practices, families typically only describe the kinds of texts that are sanctioned by schools (i.e., books) and are often hard-pressed to consider their grocery lists, work emails, church newsletters, and Instagram posts as "real" literacy. Students are astonished to discover that families hold such narrow, school-privileged conceptualizations of literacy – forgetting that they, themselves, shared the exact same perspectives only a few short weeks before!

As they observe a familiar community setting with eyes and ears freshly attuned to identify all the texts and practices occurring in that context, students are surprised to discover just how many texts are present in remote areas of a nature preserve or just how much literacy skill and knowledge is required to order their favorite beverage at Starbucks. As they consider these community contexts through the lenses of the various families they've come to know, students are dismayed to notice that texts are almost universally in English – even in neighborhoods where other languages dominate or in locations where signage in other languages should be imperative – or that almost no contexts provide Braille text for the visually impaired. Importantly, students begin to understand that, although the rhetoric around literacy and literacy education is typically one of empowerment, literacy also can be used to exclude some in the community.

And, perhaps most significantly, my students emerge from this assignment questioning the assumptions, expectations, and ideologies – the ofcoursenesses – behind both formal literacy instruction and the vast majority of family and community literacy initiatives in this country. As they consider these experiences in relation to programs, we study in the course, they begin to ask *why* – Why do family literacy programs focus so predominantly on parent-child storybook reading, ignoring the multitude of other ways in which literacy organically happens in the home? Why are schooled definitions of literacy the default in community literacy programs? Why, as St. Clair (2008) noted, are family and community programs so focused on human capital outcomes, such as reading levels attained or GEDs earned, when social outcomes such as enhanced parent-school relationships or greater community networking may be even more powerful for program participants? Why don't the majority of K-12 schools bring diverse family and community literacies, Funds of Knowledge, or Community Cultural Wealth into the classroom as a fundamental part of and basis for curriculum and instruction?

The chapters in this volume offer similar opportunities for practitioners, policymakers, and researchers to thoughtfully reconsider how we think about literacy, how we support literacy development, and how we develop stronger literacy-based connections among families, communities, and both formal and informal educational contexts. In many ways, this important volume helps us shift our thinking from only considering "How can communities support literacy?"; it invites us to also ask "How are literacies and communities deeply intertwined?" and "How can literacy help us create, support, and strengthen communities?"

As you read through this important *Field Guide to Community Literacy*, keep in mind that field guides are most effective when we rise from our armchairs or step away from our desks and consider the guides in relation to the field. I therefore invite you to walk through the communities where you live and work to take a fresh look at the myriad texts and literacy practices that occur in those contexts. I encourage you to connect with families that are different from yourselves in meaningful ways so that you may begin to see literacy practices, Funds of Knowledge, and Community Cultural Wealth that might previously have been hidden to you. In other words, I challenge you to engage in your own Family Visit and Community Walk assignment as a companion to this *Field Guide* – and to use what you discover to change your own thinking and practice with regard to community literacy.

Kristen H. Perry
University of Kentucky

References

Barton, D., & Hamilton, M. (1998). *Local literacies: Reading and writing in one community*. Routledge.

González, N., Moll, L. C., & Amanti, C. (Eds.). (2005). *Funds of knowledge: Theorizing practices in households, communities, and classrooms*. Routledge.

Perry, K. H. (2012). What is literacy? A critical overview of sociocultural perspectives. *Journal of Language and Literacy Education, 8*(1), 50–71.

St. Clair, R. (2008). Reading, writing and relationships: Human and social capital in family literacy programs. *Adult Basic Education and Literacy Journal, 2*, 84–93.

Street, B. (1984). *Literacy in theory and practice*. Cambridge University Press.

Woodside-Jiron, H. (2004). Language, power, and participation: Using critical discourse analysis to make sense of public policy. In R. Rogers (Ed.), *An introduction to critical discourse analysis in education* (pp. 173–205). Lawrence Erlbaum Associates.

Yosso, T. J. (2006). Whose culture has capital? A critical race theory discussion of community cultural wealth. In A. D. Dixson, C. Rousseau Anderson, & J. K. Dinner (Eds.), *Critical race theory in education: All God's children got a song* (1st ed., pp. 181–204). Routledge. https://doi.org/10.4324/9781315870557-17

Zoch, M., & He, Y. (2020). Utilizing community cultural wealth to learn with diverse language communities. *The Teacher Educator, 55*(2), 148–164. https://doi.org/10.1080/08878730.2019.1609639

Introduction

A year ago, we had the privilege to edit the text *Literacy Across the Community: Research, Praxis, and Trends* for Routledge. Its purposes were to present current trends in research and resultant praxis in the field of community literacy, investigate challenges impacting community literacy programs as well as their possible solutions as drawn from research, and document implications for P20 education. We believe that the volume did meet the goals set for it. But as we worked with the talented cadre of both established and emerging scholars, we came to the conclusion that what was needed equally by the field was a text that would serve as a practical guide for established community literacy educators and their program's stakeholders as well as those individuals who are in the midst of designing programs for their respective communities. Hence, the idea of preparing *A Field Guide to Community Literacy: Case Studies and Tools for Praxis, Evaluation, and Research* that presents scholarship related to the praxis of community-based literacy initiatives as explicated through a community action lens was born. Our vision then was that the two volumes together would provide a yin and a yang for the community literacy field as it exists in the third decade of the 21st century.

As such, the purposes for this guidebook are to present current trends in praxis from the field of community literacy, to offer field-based solutions for the challenges impacting community initiatives, and to provide a guide for practitioners who are interested in the best practices for implementing, maintaining, expanding, and evaluating community-based literacy initiatives.

DOI: 10.4324/9781003228042-1

In composing this guidebook, we had the good fortune to collaborate with leading program providers and scholars in the field of community-based literacy to create a practical guidebook that can promote both research-based and innovative practices within community-based literacy programs. These include family services, adult literacy initiatives, community centers, tutorial programs, etc. as supported by a variety of agencies and philanthropic sources (e.g., governmental, non-profit, foundational, etc.). Through this volume we seek to fill a gap in the scholarship related to the praxis of community literacy initiatives across populations (from children to adults), including a variety of societal groups (e.g., immigrants, refugees, indigenous societies, and so forth). Our focus is on providing a field guide *for the field, from the field*.

Our approach for this guidebook is to include first a part that provides a foundation for the field through the examination of the context of community literacy initiatives with an emphasis on the importance of community building. The second part provides chapters that set the stage for designing, implementing, and funding community-based literacy programs. Then there is a part that provides descriptive analyses highlighting multiple case studies illustrating research-based best practices and community-based action research projects undertaken by a variety of literacy providers and associated stakeholders. Finally, the last part of the volume provides practical methods for conducting both formative and summative program evaluations regularly required by program advisory boards and funding agencies. Additionally, there is coverage of qualitative and quantitative research methods for practitioners and scholars who are interested in conducting empirical research. The text concludes with a robust set of appendices included to guide individuals as they develop, implement, and maintain their own programs.

Building Community Through Literacy

Education and literacy in the modern community is so much more than the current options associated with PK–12 public, private, or charter schools. Indeed, these education providers may not accurately represent or even draw from the local community any longer. In so many situations it is now left to the members of a respective community through the community centers, religious organizations, non-profit associations, etc. to put community back into education and education back into the community. The four chapters comprising the first part of this text tackle the very construct of community as well as the role of and relationship to community as it interacts with our current notion of literacy.

Jacobson (Chapter 1) proposes that adult literacy education is marked by conscious community building shaped by the literacy practices and needs of learners. The chapter considers this connection between adult literacy and community building in three distinct ways: 1) the benefits of a collective sense of belonging in a classroom, 2) the role of literacy practices in establishing membership in a community, and 3) literacy education as communal liberation. In each case, adult literacy development and community work are inseparable. Through Bennett's (Chapter 2) historical and contemporary descriptions of initiatives, programs, centers, and schools developed by and within economically, culturally, and linguistically marginalized communities, she demonstrates how communities can provide a form of supplemental education that bridges the gap between what schools offer and the unmet needs of the community's children, particularly in literacy.

The team of Jacobs, Cramer, Mullikin, and Westberg (Chapter 3) share how the National Center for Families Learning (NCFL) has worked to eradicate poverty through education solutions for families. Their chapter presents the NCFL's perspective of family engagement and the models that have emerged from three decades of family-centered work along with compelling evidence of what works for families most in need and what produces positive outcomes. The final work in this part by Cooper-Novack and Nordquist (Chapter 4) considers the ways that both "community" and "the academy" are frequently oversimplified and essentialized in discussions of community literacies; examines their experiences creating and supporting an arts fellowship for refugee and immigrant youth in partnership with a non-profit center, a local literacy center, and a large private university; and explores the ways that both fixed definitions can be troubled to create and portray fluid and shared experiences.

Setting the Stage for Program Design

In the formative stages of the design of any new program, or even the extension of an existing program/service, there are a range of activities that need to be undertaken. Only the financially most well-endowed program need not be overly concerned with the generation of the finances necessary to permit the program to open its doors and deliver services to the community. For so many service providers this need necessitates mastering the art of writing grant proposals and, if successful in obtaining external funding, then mastering all stages of grant management. We suggest that another key component of the preliminary groundwork of program design is conducting a community audit of the local literacy scene to discern the nature of the services currently being delivered. This form of a gap analysis might be taken in mass or with a specific targeted program. Finally, it can be proposed that an action plan (strategic plan) must be formulated for the proposed program and then followed with any necessary revisions through the life span of the project.

We begin with the concept of the community literacy audit as focused on both the community itself and on a specific program provider. Bennett in Chapter 5 covers a technique found in the field of program evaluation, the community literacy audit that allows community members and educators to determine the current unmet literacy needs of that locale and examines the processes and programs available within the community to fulfill these unmet needs. In turn, through the audit, communities and educators can develop and implement initiatives and programs that are designed to bridge the gap between "traditional" schooling and community literacy. In Chapter 6 Wilson discusses how she used an external community audit in West Texas to analyze the services provided by seven of the community literacy programs, from their history to future impact and everything in between. The resultant recommendations for formative actions are provided for other communities who wish to implement similar programs. In Chapter 7 Chambers and Teasdell employ a transformative education perspective in identifying literacy programs available outside the K–12 setting and then describe how these initiatives meet the needs of marginalized populations. This audit features youth and adult literacy programs that provide sustainable practices and equip participants to create, change, and challenge within their worlds. The specific models of instruction along with their benefits provide examples for anyone interested in community uplift through an investment in cultural and social capital.

Next, in Chapter 8, Atkinson, Anderson, Swaggerty, and Rowe describe how communities can utilize a collective impact approach to improve children's literacy learning through a jointly constructed community action plan. Specific examples from one rural southeastern region's effort to improve early literacy from birth to grade three are shared, including recent efforts to meet community needs during the COVID-19 pandemic.

Finally, we shift to a focus on funding for community-based literacy programming. Browning (Chapter 9) introduces the overlooked psychology of understanding how to develop successful grant requests based on researching grant-makers' funding priorities, establishing prewriting communications, and writing every word in a grant request based on your understanding of the funder's decision-making processes. Guidance for identifying potential funding sources and discovering what an agency's priorities for awarding grants are a main focus.

Case Studies from the Field

It would be all but nonsensical to think that a community literacy program located in the Mission District of San Francisco would face the exact same problems or have the exact same needs of a program found in rural Rochelle in Illinois. Still, there is much to be learned from programs situated throughout North America and beyond. While each program is part and parcel of a specific community, so too is it part of the much larger literacy context in which programs face similar challenges, and thus each can benefit from the knowledge of the solutions employed by other community literacy providers in other locales as they overcame similar challenges. Furthermore, while attendance at conferences and Zoom meetings provide a necessary opportunity for the sharing of programmatic activities, the careful analysis of case studies and well-written program descriptions of successful praxis authored by other service providers remains an essential means of disseminating valuable information.

Waldron showcases in Chapter 10 how one community, Flint, Michigan, is using a multi-coordinated, community-wide approach to improve literacy equity, access, and capacity. Specifically, the chapter examines the *Flint Kids Read* campaign undertaken as a multi-partner community effort that includes both an audit of resources and the evaluation of programming and its relationship to children's successful entry and participation in schools. A second example of programming as found in the northeast USA that is presented by Marsh in Chapter 11 describes a non-profit foundation's mission in supporting students with learning differences through individualized instruction with research-based methods. The chapter highlights the organization's relationship to and support of local schools to provide an appreciation for the role the organization plays in supporting students' literacy development. Chapter 12 by Yee focuses on the community literacy practices of two young first-generation Asian immigrant activists in Philadelphia, who, after being politicized by a campaign against school violence, became full-time youth organizers in the Chinese and Vietnamese immigrant communities. Qualitative methods explore the critical literacy practices that develop their critical consciousness and praxis and how, subsequently, they developed afterschool and summer program curricula that reflected their analysis of immigrant youth identities and power differentials in American society.

Within Chapter 13, Hughes explores health literacy as a high-stakes literacy that requires patients to navigate multiple activity systems and engage in a variety of complex literacy practices. The chapter draws on a case study of the literacy practices used by patients with Type 2 Diabetes as they learn to manage their disease. Chapter 14 presents another community-oriented program as Semingson and Bezboruah cover the process of starting and maintaining ("stewarding") a public book exchange as part of the broader Little Free Library program. These authors further discuss the broader free library movement with a focus on possibilities and caveats for getting started and practical steps for establishing little free libraries, with measures to navigate restrictions, rules, and other challenges of maintaining little free libraries.

Montero, Dénommé-Welch, and Henry (Chapter 15) explain that many Indigenous languages continue to be at risk for what linguists describe as *language death* or the time when the last native speaker of the language dies. This chapter explores Indigenous-led, community-based language regeneration initiatives that rely on fluent speakers of the language (e.g., nesting programs and "master-apprentice" models) and initiatives where few or no fluent speakers exist (e.g., digital-assisted language regeneration). Furthermore, the chapter underscores the resources and partnerships necessary to foster sustainable community-based, Indigenous-led language regeneration. With Chapter 16, Cridland-Hughes and Schreuder delve into the 826 National Model with its San Francisco roots and its subsequent national network as a school-community partnership supporting students' passion for writing. 826's literacy initiatives build relationships among local schools, communities, and writers in place-based settings. However, issues unique to 826 (including gentrification and replication impediments in rural areas) reveal sustainability challenges to this urban-based literacy organization. Finally, in this part of the text Flores, Meyer, Tignor, and Massey (Chapter 17) provide a brief history of university-based literacy centers and their transformation over time to increase community outreach and engagement that is followed by a detailed description of the May Literacy Center, a university-based literacy clinic. The chapter focuses on programming for teacher education, community outreach, partnerships, and essential resources.

Evaluating and Researching Community Literacy Programs

While community literacy providers admittedly must focus on the multitude of day-to-day operations associated with serving each client who enters the premises, it can be said that a very important, if not the most important, component of programmatic maintenance is a well-designed and well implemented plan for both formative and summative evaluation. Indeed, the evaluation cycle as implemented across the program life span is the key to a well-run and successful community literacy program regardless of the overall mission and goals of the project.

In addition, literacy providers on the ground floor often believe that the conduct of research is beyond the scope of the program if not equally beyond the competencies of the members of the project team. Yet, we propose that such is not (should not be) the case. Each literacy provider should have a basic understanding of both qualitative and quantitative research methods if only to be able to read critically those articles, chapters, books, web pages, etc. comprising the literature base for the field. But more so, such a competency along with a fundamental knowledge of the stages of evaluation permit the program directors or coordinators to form valuable and lasting partnerships with established educational researchers to tackle collaboratively the range of issues associated with the delivery of a community literacy program.

In Chapter 18, Genareo presents the needs for and purposes of literacy program evaluations. An overview of formative and summative evaluation methods is given, followed by descriptions of four evaluation models: Kirkpatrick model, outcome-based evaluation model, CIPP model, and logic model. Each model description also includes examples of how it could be used within a literacy program evaluation framework. Johnson (Chapter 19) next examines the design and implementation of collaborative and participatory approaches to studying literacy development within community settings. The chapter details the theoretical foundation for community-based qualitative research (CBQR), followed by an in-depth discussion of certain issues pertinent to the design and implementation of community-based studies. Then there is a review of ways that findings from community-based studies are disseminated and how community literacy specialists can evaluate the quality of these studies. Finally, Holt and Zaleski (Chapter 20) describe statistical modeling methods that account for contextual effects, mediating and moderating factors that can capture sociocultural and other environmental relationships to literacy within our communities. The chapter further demonstrates how randomized controlled trials are used in community settings to make causal inferences regarding literacy in the community. Moreover, a flexible class of growth models used to examine developmental change in language and literacy are described. These analytic methods are illustrated with research examples from the literature.

Part One

Building Community Through Literacy

Chapter 1

Adult Literacy and the Work of Community Building

Erik Jacobson

Author Note

Erik Jacobson: https://orcid.org/0000-0002-4367-4780

In contrast to K–12 education, organized into publicly funded buildings that help define neighborhoods for generations, adult literacy education has historically found, repurposed, and created new spaces for students and teachers to work in. Over the decades, this has included secluded forests, churches, spare rooms in public housing, union halls, public libraries, and correctional facilities. The goals of these programs vary, making it difficult to identify something that could be called a "typical" adult literacy program. Rather, the nature of these programs is shaped by the work of the people committed to building them.

For this reason, the concept of community has long been central in discourse about adult literacy, and it is deployed in a number of different ways. For example, adult literacy services are often provided by self-described *community-based* organizations. Here, *community-based* has at least two meanings. First, it implies that the physical location of the organization was established where the people who will use the services live. Second, it implies that the organization will be operated by people who come from the group(s) being served. In a similar fashion, adult literacy programs often identify *community building* as a central goal of their work. However, beyond a shared commitment to the abstract notion of community, the specifics of what community building looks like can vary a great deal. Indeed, conceptions of community building within the field of adult literacy evince key differences in theoretical and pedagogical perspectives.

Adult Literacy Instruction and Being in Community

Adult literacy development is often associated with formal instruction, either in the form of one-on-one volunteer tutoring or class-based instruction provided by teachers. Learners may be working on the fundamentals of decoding and encoding, studying to pass high school equivalency tests, or looking to transition into postsecondary education or vocational training. Students also identify specific skills that they want to develop, such as being able to read a particular religious text, communicating with distant family members, or completing business-related paperwork. Though programs may vary in philosophy and approach, formal instruction is seen as a way of helping adult learners increase their facility with reading and writing.

For this reason, it is common for research into adult literacy instruction to focus on classroom-level factors that can improve outcomes. Beder and Medina's (2001) study of classroom dynamics in adult literacy examined the influence of community, defined as "a collective sense of belonging among the members of the class" (pg. 103). Their results did not conclusively demonstrate that the presence of community supported student progress, but they suggested it was worth further exploration. In fact, others continue to promote the value of having a sense of community in the classroom. For example, Weissner et al. (2010), argue that community, understood as an ethos of mutuality and caring, is essential in adult education programs. The development of supportive relationships between students is thought to create a classroom atmosphere more conducive to learning. Here, community building can be conceptualized as the intentional cultivation and maintenance of this in-classroom feeling of being connected.

Over the past few decades, many adult literacy programs have promoted the centrality of being in community as a guiding principle. For example, the Open Book in New York City (1985–2000) was organized around a collaborative decision-making process that was explicitly intended to give students a role in the running of the program. This approach required a shared sense of responsibility among students and teachers, for the program and for each other. One adult learner in the program explained, "What community means to me – to be there for others and to try and lift each other up when we are down. Life is a community of caring and love and hope. My class is like that" (Gordon & Ramdeholl, 2010, p. 29). A study of adult literacy programs in Japan found a similar sentiment (Jacobson, 2009), with teachers often noting the primacy of developing caring relationships with their students. In fact, such relationships were seen as an end in themselves, rather than just instrumental in helping the learner make progress with regard to developing their literacy skills.

Beyond fostering an ethics of caring, adult literacy programs can also establish or expand groups and networks that people are affiliated with. That is, students may *feel* a sense of community, but they can also *constitute* a community that recognizes itself as such. They are a group of people who share certain goals and have similar needs. Once organized, they can advocate on their own behalf. Adult literacy programs can also create opportunities for people to interact with others who come from different backgrounds, creating diverse networks. For example, volunteer tutoring programs often bring people together across class and racial lines, city-wide programs create multilingual and multicultural classrooms, and prison education projects establish new cohorts within a volatile space.

This experience of being in community with others is not limited to formal adult literacy instruction. For example, in the early 1980s in Cobden, Illinois, a group of Spanish-speaking migrant workers came together to learn English without the presence of a trained teacher (Kalmar, 2001). In the process, they developed their own Spanish to English dictionary, using the Spanish alphabet to capture the sounds of English. Use of this distinct hybrid alphabet (Kalmar, 2001) marked the learners as being members of a very particular speech community, and their collaboration demonstrated the collective sense of belonging that many students and teachers in formal classrooms strive for.

In fact, adult literacy programs have found that this sense of mutual support and nurturing is hard to develop. In Beder and Medina's study (2001), the researchers found that in only a quarter of the classes studied was a sense of community "pervasive." Indeed, even those who were involved in the Open Book believe that the program did not always achieve its goals of collaborative decision making and mutuality in relationships (Gordon & Ramdeholl, 2010, p. 31). Beyond any potential issues with teaching strategy, one reason for this might be the enrollment turbulence (Beder and Medina, 2001) that many programs experience. Across the United States, programs funded by the federal government report that almost 33% of students separate from programs before making progress or meeting their goals (U.S. Department of Education, 2018). Adult literacy learners have been described as "stopping out" of programs, moving in and out of formal instruction as their life circumstances allow (Comings, 2009). In addition, limited resources for public transportation or childcare create situational barriers that make continuing in programs difficult for some learners (Quigley, 1997). This persistent and widespread churn militates against a collective sense of belonging developing in classrooms.

This instability is also present at the program level. Funding waxes and wanes, and the tenuous nature of service provision can create a chaotic situation in which learners may have no guarantee that they will be able to find what they need or that their program will remain open. It may be the case that the fluid nature of adult literacy programs provides for the creation of new communities that are more liminal in nature. The potential for being in community is always there, leading generations of students, tutors, and teachers to aim for it, but it is difficult to fully realize or stabilize. This in turn limits the ability of adult learners to advocate for services. Without well-established, expansive networks, learners are left vulnerable to shifting political winds that bring budget cuts and reduced access to education. In this situation, community building then becomes a type of triage – a constant attempt to increase the size of the population that is aware of and committed to supporting adult literacy instruction.

Adult Literacy Practices and the Nature of Community Membership

Outside of formal instruction, adults also develop new literacy skills and refine existing ones while engaged in daily life activities. They also learn new literacy practices, understood as distinct ways of using reading, writing, and other semiotic resources that are shaped by broader social forces (Barton and Hamilton, 2000). The nature of these practices has been a key feature of literacy studies that look at reading and writing in specific cultural (Heath, 1983), historic (Graff, 1991), and socio-economic (Purcell-Gates, 1995) contexts. These contexts influence the goals adults have for reading and writing and determine what access adults have to the resources they need to meet those goals.

This more ethnographic approach to understanding adult literacy development is often focused on identifying the types of reading and writing practices that mark somebody as a member of a particular community, understood mainly as a group of people connected by a shared interest, activity, affiliation, identity, or status. For example, Richardson's (2003) work examines how African American women use particular literacy practices to assert their gendered ethnic identity. Kalman (1999) studied the literacy practices of scribes working in Mexican town squares, highlighting what they need to do in order to establish their status as experts for potential customers. Bushnell (1990) explored how graffiti was used in the Soviet Union to make internal feelings of dissent public. To be considered a member of something like an informal guild or dissident group, adults need to be capable of following the shared routines and meeting sometimes unstated expectations.

The existence and nature of these literacy practices may not always be transparent to those participating in a community they are associated with. Often, it is through an adult struggling to master these practices that the contours of a given community's understanding of the use of print is made clear. For example, Perry's (2009) work highlights how refugees in the United States who are literate in English may still struggle to understand the use of a particular text and the nature of common text genres in their new contexts (e.g., K-12 school communication). Eubank's (2017) work explores how some adults have difficulty navigating welfare and healthcare bureaucracies that demand ever increasing facility with digital platforms. Their struggle with new literacy demands place them outside of one community (those who can access care and support) and into another (those whose literacy skills and practices make them vulnerable). Those easily accessing resources due to their facility with certain literacy practices may not be aware of their own privileged position or even of what they are doing to gain that access.

Adults' developing literacy practices can also be associated with the creation of new communities. For example, the development of internet culture was influenced by the establishment of online forums and chat rooms. This involved experiments with new types of reading and writing that fostered emergent virtual networks. In a previous generation, access to cheap mimeographing allowed for the creation and dissemination of new types of texts, such as zines, that were associated with groups that had common interests (Eichhorn, 2016; Guzetti, 2018). Often, the development of new technology-related literacy practices comes out of necessity. For example, out-of-status adults in the United States needed to determine which text messaging services are more likely to be secure, as it is essential for their safety. As with graffiti, understanding where to write is just as important as understanding what to write. Given a shared vulnerability, this is a lesson that is often disseminated as soon as it is learned.

Williams (1976) famously suggested that *community* is one of the few words that has no negative connotations. However, establishing a community understood as a group of intentionally affiliated people necessarily demands leaving others out of that group. So, while the idea of community may generally be seen in a positive light, history demonstrates how the concept of adult literacy can be used as a means of exclusion and oppression. For example, after the Civil War in the United States, literacy tests for voting limited the franchise of emancipated African Americans. Literacy acted as a de jure means of segregation, marking African Americans as second-class citizens. Also in the United States, the Immigration Act of 1917 included "illiterates" in the list of those barred from entering (joining alcoholics, anarchists, and the mentally ill, among others). Disparaging their literacy skills was a rhetorical device used to paint immigrants more broadly as a dangerous and unwanted *other* (NeCamp, 2014).

This same dynamic has also been noted in contemporary politics. For example, in UK politics, adult immigrants' language and literacy skills are used to question their rights to remain in and participate in society (Simpson, 2015). As another example, in 2018, Kentucky announced that it would create health and financial literacy tests for Medicaid recipients who could not fulfill the recently introduced work requirement. Given persistent concerns about low levels of health literacy (Ylitalo et al., 2018) and financial literacy (Hung et al., 2009), these types of gatekeeping policies would prevent large numbers of people from accessing Medicaid – surely the intention, rather than an unexpected outcome. In keeping with historical precedent, here adult literacy helps to define ideas of community membership, particularly who is qualified and deserving of resources and access to the commons.

Adult Literacy Praxis and Communal Liberation

Faced with exclusion and oppression, adult learners have long looked to their own literacy development as a means to reshape and redefine the nature of the communities (spatial, sociopolitical, socio-economic) that they are living in. African Americans who had been enslaved and forbidden to become literate risked their own lives to learn to read and write and to teach others to do so. These smuggled literacy practices were a key part of their resistance and struggle for emancipation. This legacy continued throughout the 20th century, as developing literacy was an essential element of the civil rights movement. One example is the work of Septima Clark, Bernice Robinson, and the Citizenship Schools in the late 1950s. This effort taught adult learners about their rights as citizens, developed their literacy skills, and facilitated registering to vote. Thousands of adults who went through the program became teachers and leaders in their localities, connecting adult literacy with political mobilization.

This type of activity is often described as popular education, understood as people's self-directed educational efforts tied to social change agendas. Rather than the focus on the development of a given adult's literacy skills in isolation or to treat literacy as an end in itself, popular education views literacy as a means to achieve a goal the community has identified as important. It may include work on fundamental literacy skills like decoding and writing, but it is focused upon the development of literacy skills and practices that have implications for political activity (such as organizing, petitioning, and distributing information). Adult literacy development conceptualized as political praxis views liberation as an ongoing, collective process (Hurtig & Adams, 2010), rather than an individualistic or atomized activity.

Communal liberation efforts that include adult literacy development can take place at different scales, from small neighborhood groups to national projects. For example, in the 1950s, French colonial authorities supported the development of literacy in Vietnamese because they believed that it would provide a bulwark against Chinese influence. However, the Vietnamese people utilized this newly developing native language literacy as a key part of their anticolonial efforts against the French occupiers (Anderson, 1995). Other countries emerging from occupation or undergoing revolutionary change have also introduced large-scale adult literacy campaigns designed to both provide education and create a new sense of solidarity (e.g., Angola, East Timor, Cuba, Guinea-Bissau). During the Sandinista National Literacy Crusade in Nicaragua (in 1980), 100,000 literacy workers helped over 400,000 people to read and write. The vice minister of education at the time suggested that this campaign was "a political project with pedagogical implications, not a pedagogical project with political implications" (Brookfield & Holst, 2011, p. 78). These types of efforts use adult literacy work as a means to reshape the populace's understanding of themselves as a national community.

As with the civil rights struggle in the United States, adult literacy campaigns have also served as a means for oppressed minorities to gain recognition as equal members of the larger society. For example, in Japan, the Buraku community have long been discriminated against in education, marriage, and employment, in part because of ascribed inherited impurity due to the professions of their ancestors. In the late 1950s and early 1960s, Buraku mothers came together to initiate adult literacy classes for themselves, having realized their own limited literacy skills were preventing them from fully advocating for their children (Asano, 1990). Over the decades, the number of Buraku Liberation adult literacy classes expanded and became an essential part of the larger political struggle to change their social and legal status. These adult literacy learners were committed to changing the discriminatory conditions that led to their own poor educational outcomes. By fighting for education and liberation, adult literacy students were activists for a new Japanese polity.

These Buraku adult literacy classes found some success. Anti-Buraku prejudice remains, but it is now in a somewhat attenuated form, and educational and employment outcomes have improved. This was possible because adult literacy activists were part of a larger Buraku rights movement. Although this tradition is an inspiring one, it is important to not romanticize or overstate the power of adult literacy programs. From abolition to civil rights to immigrants' rights, adult literacy work has played an important role in societal change, but it has not been a force in isolation. Not all large-scale campaigns have been successful in either increasing the literacy skills of large numbers of people or dismantling exclusionary structures. Adult literacy programs can't reshape sociopolitical or socio-economic relations removed from larger political developments.

Implications

As suggested earlier, the concept of community is deployed in the field of adult literacy in a number of ways. For that reason, those who are committed to connecting their teaching practice to community building need to continually ask these questions (among others).

A) What Are the Learners' Goals?

Adult literacy development should not be understood as limited to the fundamental aspects of learning to encode and decode. Rather, adult literacy development continues well past initial fluency, as adults learn to accomplish literacy-related tasks in multiple contexts and with diverse audiences. They also need to gain mastery of various genres and registers in order to establish membership in communities they want to join. Indeed, for the last few decades there has been a push for contextualized curricula – lessons and materials that are built on the real-world needs and goals of learners. Research suggests that this approach makes it more likely that adults will take up new literacy practices outside of the classroom (Purcell-Gates et al., 2002). However, teachers cannot unilaterally decide what constitutes a contextualized activity – only the learner can determine whether or not the classroom activity connects their lives in a meaningful way (Dirkx et al., 1999).

B) Where Are Teaching and Learning Taking Place?

Only a limited number of adults enroll in adult literacy programs to increase their skills or learn new literacy practices, so the majority of literacy development happens informally, alongside others who can act as mentors or who are learners themselves. For example, research suggests that adults learning to read, write, and work with digital resources prefer to be with family and friends who can show them the ropes rather than with teachers in a classroom (Selwyn et al., 2006). This informal community-based learning relies upon access to necessary materials (e.g., connectivity, library books, etc.), so we need to ensure there is efficient and equitable distribution of resources to the various places in the community where adults are focused on their own literacy development. Because the community of adult literacy learners extends beyond the classroom, formal instruction should not be supported at the expense of informal teaching and learning.

C) Which Side Are You on?

At the classroom level, recognizing the communal nature of community building means that teachers have to be clear about their own praxis. The desire to help students fully realize their own agency cannot lead to negating that agency in the process – this is the problem at the heart of critical pedagogy. Learners need to lead conversations that concern them. As VALUE, a national adult literacy advocacy organization founded and operated by adult literacy learners, often proclaims, "Nothing about us without us." Thus, the role of teachers in efforts to use adult literacy for community building can be complicated, especially for those who may share the goals of a given group but do not have membership status. What is the nonmember's role in the struggle and therefore the educational project? hooks (2000) suggests that teachers need to base their practice on the idea of solidarity. She explains:

> Solidarity is not the same as support. To experience solidarity, we must have a community of interest, shared beliefs and goals around which to

unite, to build Sisterhood. Support can be occasional. It can be given and just as easily withdrawn. Solidarity requires sustained, ongoing commitment.

(hooks, 2000, p. 66; cited by Walia, 2013, p. 132)

Rather than supporting communities they care about but are not members of (on the basis of race, gender, class, sexuality, etc.), teachers who embrace a praxis of solidarity contribute to the creation of new communities grounded in a common struggle. If the students in your class declare, "Estamos en la lucha," they are presenting an opportunity to identify the shared beliefs and goals that makes solidarity possible. Indeed, you can only say estamos if you are really en la lucha.

References

Anderson, B. (1995). *Imagined communities.* Verso.

Asano, T. (1990). Buraku literacy movement. In Buraku Liberation Research Institute (Ed.), *The literacy work and discrimination in Japan* (pp. 2–8). Kaihou Shuppan Sha.

Barton, D., & Hamilton, M. (2000). *Local literacies.* Routledge.

Beder, H., & Medina, P. (2001). *Classroom dynamics in adult literacy education.* The National Center for the Study of Adult Learning and Literacy. https://doi.org/10.1037/e305502004-001

Brookfield, S., & Holst, J. (2011). *Radicalizing learning.* Jossey-Bass.

Bushnell, J. (1990). *Moscow graffiti.* Unwin Hyman.

Comings, J. (2009). Student persistence in adult literacy and numeracy programs. In S. Reder & J. Bynner (Eds.), *Tracking adult literacy and numeracy skills* (pp. 160–176). Routledge.

Dirkx, J. M., Amey, M., & Haston, L. (1999). Context in the contextualized curriculum: Adult life worlds as unitary or multiplistic? In A. Austin, G. E. Nynes, & R. T. Miller, *Proceedings of the 18th Annual Midwest Research to Practice Conference in Adult, Continuing and Community Education* (pp. 79–84). University of Missouri at St. Louis.

Eichhorn, K. (2016). *Adjusted margin: Xerography, art, and activism in the late twentieth century.* MIT Press. https://doi.org/10.7551/mitpress/10057.001.0001

Eubanks, V. (2017). *Automating inequality.* St. Martin's Press.

Gordon, J., & Ramdeholl, D. (2010). "Everybody had a piece . . ." Collaborative practice and shared decision making at the Open Book. In D. Ramdeholl,

T. Giordani, T. Heaney, & W. Yanow (Eds.), *The struggle for democracy in adult education* (pp. 27–35). Jossey-Bass. https://doi.org/10.1002/ace.388

Graff, H. (1991). *The literacy myth.* Transaction Publishers.

Guzetti, B. (2018). Diverse men making media: Creating cultural (re)constructions of gender and race. In B. Guzetti, T. Bean, & J. Dunkerly-Bean (Eds.), *Literacies, sexualities and gender* (pp. 193–207). Routledge. https://doi.org/10.4324/9780429458514-16

Heath, S. B. (1983). *Ways with words.* Cambridge University Press. https://doi.org/10.1017/CBO9780511841057

hooks, b. (2000). *Feminist theory: From margin to center.* South End Press.

Hung, A., Parker, A., & Yoong, J. (2009). *Defining and measuring financial literacy.* Rand Corporation. https://doi.org/10.2139/ssrn.1498674

Hurtig, J., & Adams, H. (2010). Democracy is in the details: Small writing groups prefiguring a new society. In D. Ramdeholl, T. Giordani, T. Heaney, & W. Yanow (Eds.), *The struggle for democracy in adult education* (pp. 15–25). Jossey-Bass. https://doi.org/10.1002/ace.387

Jacobson, E. (2009). Community building as an instructional goal in Japanese adult basic education. *Adult Basic Education and Literacy Journal, 3*(3), 161–170.

Kalman, J. (1999). *Writing on the plaza.* Hampton Press.

Kalmar, T. (2001). *Illegal alphabets and adult biliteracy.* Lawrence Erlbaum. https://doi.org/10.4324/9781410605726

NeCamp, S. (2014). *Adult literacy and American identity.* Southern Illinois University Press.

Perry, K. (2009). Genres, contexts, and literacy practices: Literacy brokering among Sudanese refugee families. *Reading Research Quarterly, 44*(3), 256–276. https://doi.org/10.1598/RRQ.44.3.2

Purcell-Gates, V. (1995). *Other people's words.* Harvard University Press.

Purcell-Gates, V., Degener, S., Jacobson, E., & Soler, M. (2002). The impact of authentic adult literacy instruction on adult literacy practices. *Reading Research Quarterly, 37*(1), 70–92. https://doi.org/10.1598/RRQ.37.1.3

Quigley, A. (1997). *Rethinking literacy education: The critical need for practice based change.* Jossey-Bass.

Richardson, E. (2003). *African American literacies.* Routledge. https://doi.org/10.4324/9780203166550

Selwyn, N., Gorard, S., & Furlong, J. (2006). *Adult learning in the digital age.* Routledge. https://doi.org/10.4324/9780203003039

Simpson, J. (2015). English language learning for adult migrants in superdiverse Britain. In J. Simpson, & A. Whiteside (Eds.), *Adult language education and migration* (pp. 200–213). Routledge. https://doi.org/10.4324/9781315718361-16

U.S. Department of Education, Office of Career, Technical, and Adult Education (2018). *Adult education and family literacy act of 1998: Annual report to congress, program year 2015–16.* U.S. Department of Education. https://www2.ed.gov/about/offices/list/ovae/pi/AdultEd/aefla-resource-guide.pdf

Walia, H. (2013). *Undoing border imperialism.* AK Press.

Weissner, C. A., Sheared, V., Lari, P., Kucharczyk, S. Z., & Flowers, D. (2010). Creating and re-creating community. In C. Kasworm, A. Rose, & J. M. Ross-Gordon (Eds.), *Handbook of adult and continuing education* (pp. 431–440). Sage.

Williams, R. (1976). *Keywords: A vocabulary of culture and society.* Croom Helm.

Ylitalo, K., Meyer, M., Lanning, B., During, C., Laschober, R., & Griggs, J. (2018). Simple screening tools to identify limited health literacy in a low-income patient population. *Medicine, 97*(10). Published online March 9th, 2018. https://doi.org/10.1097/MD.0000000000010110

Chapter 2

The Community as Educator

Historical and Contemporary Responses by Economically, Culturally, and Linguistically Marginalized Communities to the Colonization of Literacy in Education

Ann M. Bennett

Author Note

Ann M. Bennett: https://orcid.org/0000-0001-6637-9824

Introduction

Contemporary educational policy seeks to ensure that all children receive instruction in literacy that follows appropriate childhood and adolescent development and equitable access to the resources necessary for this instruction. One only need examine the most recent report on reading from the National Assessment of Educational Progress (NAEP) to know that current policy is failing in this regard (National Center for Education Statistics, NCES, 2019). Consistently, we see that economically, culturally, and linguistically marginalized (ECLM) students demonstrate proficiency in reading that is considered to be well below that of their more advantaged peers (NCES, 2019).

DOI: 10.4324/9781003228042-4

The "underachievement" of ECLM students is often tied to majoritarian deficit beliefs about their own families and the communities in which they live, as opposed to the schools that they attend. These external factors to schooling often include parental language, parental aspiration, neighborhood culture, violent crime, unemployment, family or neighborhood ethos, and material poverty (Smyth & Wrigley, 2013; Tatum, 2009). Despite the overwhelming deficit discourses typically associated with these communities, it is the individuals in these communities who provide a form of supplemental education that bridges the gap between what the school offers and the unmet needs of the community's children, particularly in literacy.

ECLM communities have been establishing community literacy programs throughout the 19th and 20th centuries in an effort to counter the educational inequities that their children face(d) in American schools. The Mexican communities of the Southwest United States created *escuelitas* where their children were taught in both Spanish and English. This allowed the children to practice their English skills outside of formal schooling while still retaining and remaining connected to Spanish culture as a form of resistance to English-only practices (Barrera, 2006; Blanton, 2007; Salinas, 2001). Indigenous and First Nations[1] communities throughout North America, whose ancestral lands were claimed and unceded by the United States and Canada, have engaged in language reclamation both formally and informally to ensure that their literacy (and cultural) practices continued despite historically forced assimilation (Castagno & Brayboy, 2008; Hinton, 2011, 2013; Lomawaima & McCarty, 2006; McCarty & Nicholas, 2014). Finally, the Children's Defense Fund Freedom Schools were established as a cultural and literacy summer enrichment program designed to provide Afro-centric academic programming in communities where this kind of programming did not exist or would be cost prohibitive (Children's Defense Fund, 2021; Groenke et al., 2011). Through the creation of these schools and programs, members of these communities sought to ensure that their children were not simply subjected to the curriculum within "traditional" schooling in the United States.

Given that modern day curriculum often values and is biased toward "mainstream styles of speaking, writing and behaving" (Spears-Bunton & Powell, 2009, p. 7), which typically equates with a societal and educational structure that seeks to reproduce middle-class Whiteness (Bennett, 2015), schools position ECLM students at a disadvantage. It is through initiatives and programs created by the community in which they live that the children can take back ownership of their own literacy development and fulfill their unmet needs.

Historical Overview of Community Literacy

Before one develops literacy curricula, one should consider the history of community literacy within ECLM communities. ECLM communities have conducted informal and formal community literacy audits and determined the specific needs of their children in response to the unmet needs created by "traditional" and inequitable schooling in the United States. For many ECLM communities, community literacy means retaining or rebuilding what has been lost through colonization within education.

Escuelitas

As early as the 19th century, the Mexican community of the Southwest United States responded to inequitable education through the development of *escuelitas*, or little schools (Barrera, 2006; Blanton, 2007; Salinas, 2001). English was the predominant language used in schools in the United States, and it was forced upon the Mexican children who attended those schools by educators who spoke no Spanish and were not prepared to educate children who did not speak English (Barrera, 2006). In turn, the Mexican children were forced to speak and learn in English. This forced assimilation served two functions. First, it placed Mexican language and culture in an inferior position to that of the English language and mainstream culture in the United States (Barrera, 2006; Blanton, 2007; Salinas, 2001). Second, it used literacy as "a gatekeeping function, determining whether and how far students progress through the educational system" (Lucas & Schecter, 1992, p. 87), which necessitated Mexican children learn English if they wanted to "succeed" within this system. Community *escuelitas*, which were often one-room schoolhouses, educated Mexican children in both Spanish and English and utilized teachers who were educated in Mexico (Barrera, 2006). Less formal *escuelitas* developed in the homes of women and were set up as a form of preschool (Barrera, 2006). Regardless of how the *escuelitas* were designed, they served one primary purpose: to ensure the preservation of the Mexican language and identity as a form of resistance to English-only practices (Barrera, 2006; Blanton, 2007; Salinas, 2001).

The *escuelita* Colegio Altamirano was founded in 1897 and operated until 1958 in Hebbronville, Texas (Barrera, 2006; Salinas, 2001). The middle-class Tejano families living in Hebbronville desired a school that would provide their children with an education that encompassed both their native language and culture, as well as the requirements placed upon their children by local

English-only schools (Barrera, 2006; Salinas, 2001). Salinas (cited in Barrera, 2006) stated that "the insistence on maintaining a separate private school served as a powerful stand against assimilation and acculturation at the same time that the school provided the requisite educational opportunities that would ensure a place for Tejano children in mainstream Anglo society and public schools" (p. 39).

The Mexican communities of the Southwest United States determined that what was most important for their children was to maintain their cultural identity and language (Barrera, 2006; Blanton, 2007; Salinas, 2001). The communities did not necessarily disagree with the schooling that was offered by local and state governments (Barrera, 2006; Salinas, 2001). However, this schooling sought to efface the identities of their children, and, in turn, it needed to be supplemented by the community itself (Barrera, 2006; Blanton, 2007; Salinas, 2001).

Language Reclamation Initiatives

The Indigenous and First Nations communities of the United States and Canada have focused their community literacy initiatives on language reclamation. According to McCarty and Nicholas (2014), "Language reclamation includes *revival* of a language no longer spoken as a first language, *revitalization* of a language already in use, and *reversal of language shift* . . . to describe the reengineering of social supports for intergenerational mother tongue transmission" (p. 106; emphasis in original). The intention behind reclaiming language is not just to ensure the continuance of Indigenous and First Nations languages, but it is also to ensure the perpetuation of Indigenous and First Nations cultures and self-determination (Castagno & Brayboy, 2008; Hinton, 2011; Lomawaima & McCarty, 2006). For centuries, the education provided to Indigenous and First Nations children by national, state, and local governments has sought to "erase and replace" (McCarty & Nicholas, 2014, p. 107) their language and culture with middle-class Whiteness (Castagno & Brayboy, 2008; Hinton, 2011). In response, Indigenous and First Nations communities have examined the resources available in their communities and used those resources to develop language reclamation both in and outside of schools (Castagno & Brayboy, 2008; Hinton, 2013; Lomawaima & McCarty, 2006; McCarty & Nicholas, 2014).

One such example is that of the efforts to reclaim the Kanienkeha language by the Kanien'kehaka people, also known as the Mohawk people.

In 1970, a group of Kanien'kehaka parents wanted to ensure that their children learned the Kanienkeha language. The parents were able to convince the local elementary school to teach Kanienkeha for 15 minutes each day (McCarty & Nicholas, 2014). Using the resources available in the community, the program persisted for several years and was eventually expanded after the University of Quebec established a Native-language teacher education program. What started as 15 minutes a day of instruction evolved into a writing system and curriculum developed by Kanien'kehaka student teachers. After a bill was passed in Quebec that made French the sole official language, the Kanien'kehaka established two community schools, Kahnawake Survival School and the Kanien'kehaka Raotitiohkwa Cultural Center, to continue Kanienkeha language instruction. The community schools reversed the trend of language loss by the younger generations in the Kanien'kehaka community (McCarty & Nicholas, 2014).

According to Castagno and Brayboy (2008), the most critical element of schooling for Indigenous and First Nations youth is attention to local contexts. The specific needs of communities and their cultures must be at the forefront of education, as this ensures the self-determination of Indigenous and First Nations people (Castagno & Brayboy, 2008; Lomawaima & McCarty, 2006; McCarty & Nicholas, 2014). Ironically, the rise of culturally responsive education has not provided this to Indigenous and First Nations people due to the standardization of the idea across ECLM communities (Castagno & Brayboy, 2008).

The Children's Defense Fund Freedom Schools

For the Black community in the United States, schooling has been consistently contentious since even before the official founding of the country. One of the first examples of deficit thinking in education policy was directed at the Black community through the passage of compulsory ignorance laws, which prevented slaves from receiving an education, particularly in the area of literacy (Bennett, 2015; Valencia, 1997). Even after compulsory ignorance laws were declared illegal in 1868, the belief that Black children needed to be excluded from education with white children persisted (Bennett, 2015; Menchaca, 1997). When schools were ordered to integrate following the *Brown v. Board of Education* (1954) decision, a new problem emerged for the Black community. In particular, Black educators who had been educating Black children in segregated schools were removed from their positions in favor of white educators. Schools argued that Black students would receive a better education from white educators (Templeton et al., 2021) and, as a result, removed the Black community from the education of Black Children.

Following the Mississippi Freedom Summer of 1964, the Children's Defense Fund Freedom Schools (CDFFS) movement began. Founded by Marian Wright Edelman, the CDFFS program seeks to aid Black youth in "fall[ing] in love with books" through cultural and literary enrichment (CDFFS, 2010). The program often occurs in Black communities where similar programming does not exist or lacked the funding to be established (Children's Defense Fund, 2021; Groenke et al., 2011). Through Afro-centric programming, literacy, and civic engagement, the CDFFS seeks to end the disparity between the Black community and their more advantaged peers in accessing reading during the summer, which can create learning loss that can lead to even greater disparities (Children's Defense Fund, 2021). In 2020, 77% of program attendees were able to avoid summer learning loss (Children's Defense Fund, 2021).

According to Jeffries (2019), the successful education of Black youth is possible if the community "push[es] together toward amelioration of the academic, disciplinary and other disparities in education that continue to plague students of color in our nation's contemporary public schools" (p. 61). Programs like the CDFFS represent just one approach to working toward this amelioration. *Escuelitas*, language reclamation, and culture-centric summer programming all exist as a form of resistance to "traditional" schooling in favor of community literacy.

Conclusion

Communities in the United States have been serving as educators for their children for centuries. Unfortunately, this has occurred due to "traditional" schooling not meeting the needs of ECLM children. Indeed, community literacy programs are meant to address the inequities that children experience in a classroom that is intended to educate *all children*. From Mexican *escuelitas* to Indigenous and First Nations language reclamation schools to the CDFFS, responses to inequity have been to rely on the ethos and identity of the community as the foundation for learning. Reducing the curriculum, applying standardized pedagogies, and measuring achievement through high-stakes testing (Au, 2007; Berliner, 2011), commonly referred to as the "back to basics" approach in the United States, is in stark contrast to this foundation. If we truly wish to educate *all children*, we must recognize the humanity of both the children and the communities in which they live by honoring alternative ways of knowing and learning.

Note

1. The terms Indigenous and First Nations are used throughout this chapter. However, these two terms should not be considered representative of all the tribal nations found in both the United States and Canada. The author recognizes the right of self-determination and understands that Alaska Native, American Indian, American Native, Native, Native American, and Métis may be the preferred terms of a tribal nation in addition to specific terms used within a tribal language.

References

Au, W. (2007). High-stakes testing and curricular control: A qualitative meta-synthesis. *Educational Researcher, 36*(5), 258–267. https://doi.org/10.3102/0013189X07306523

Barrera, A. (2006). The "little schools" in Texas, 1897–1965: Educating Mexican American children. *American Educational History Journal, 33*(2), 35–45.

Bennett, A. M. (2015). *Deficit discourse, literate lives: Success narratives of Black youth* (Publication No. 3493) [Doctoral dissertation, The University of Tennessee]. Tennessee Research and Creative Exchange.

Berliner, D. (2011). Rational responses to high stakes testing: The case of curriculum narrowing and the harm that follows. *Cambridge Journal of Education, 41*(3), 287–302. https://doi.org/10.1080/0305764X.2011.607151

Blanton, C. K. (2007). *The strange career of bilingual education in Texas, 1836–1981.* Texas A&M University Press.

Castagno, A. E., & Brayboy, B. M. J. (2008). Culturally responsive schooling for Indigenous youth: A review of the literature. *Review of Educational Research, 78,* 941–992. https://doi.org/10.3102/0034654308323036

Children's Defense Fund. (2021). *CDF freedom schools.* Children's Defense Fund. www.childrensdefense.org/programs/cdf-freedom-schools/.

Children's Defense Fund Freedom Schools. (2010). *Summer integrated reading curriculum guide* (Vol. 12). Children's Defense Fund Freedom Schools.

Groenke, S. L., Venable, T. E., Hill, S., & Bennett, A. (2011). Not your typical summer enrichment program: Reading young adult literature in freedom schools. *The Alan Review, 38*(3), 29–36. https://doi.org/10.21061/alan.v38i3.a.4

Hinton, L. (2011). Revitalization of endangered languages. In P. K. Austin & J. Sallabank (Eds.), *The Cambridge handbook of endangered languages* (pp. 291–311). Cambridge University Press. https://doi.org/10.1017/CBO9780511975981.015

Hinton, L. (2013). *Bringing our languages home: Language revitalization for families*. Heyday Books.

Jeffries, R. (2019). *Queen mothers: Articulating the spirit of Black women teacher-leaders*. Information Age Publishing.

Lomawaima, K. T., & McCarty, T. L. (2006). *"To remain an Indian": Lessons in democracy from a century of Native American education*. Teachers College Press.

Lucas, T., & Schecter, S. R. (1992). Literacy education and diversity: Toward equity in the teaching of reading and writing. *The Urban Review, 24*(2), 85–104. https://doi.org/10.1007/BF01239354

McCarty, T. L., & Nicholas, S. E. (2014). Reclaiming Indigenous languages: A reconsideration of the roles and responsibilities of schools. *Review of Research in Education, 38*(1), 106–136. https://doi.org/10.3102/0091732X13507894

Menchaca, M. (1997). Early racist discourses: The roots of deficit thinking. In R. R. Valencia (Ed.), *The evolution of deficit thinking: Educational thought and practice* (pp. 13–40). Routledge Falmer.

National Center for Education Statistics. (2019). Nation's report card. National Assessment of Educational Progress. *Office of Educational Research and Improvement*, U.S. Department of Education.

Salinas, C. (2001). El Colegio Altamirano (1897–1958): New histories of Chicano education in the Southwest. *The Educational Forum, 65*(1), 80–86. https://doi.org/10.1080/00131720008984465

Smyth, J., & Wrigley, T. (2013). *Living on the edge: Rethinking poverty, class, and schooling*. Peter Lang Publishing, Inc.

Spears-Bunton, L. A., & Powell, L. (2009). *Toward a literacy of promise: Joining the African American struggle*. Routledge.

Tatum, A. (2009). *Reading for their life: (Re)Building the textual lineages of African American adolescent males*. Heinemann.

Templeton, T., White, C., Peters, A. L., & Horn, C. L. (2021). *A QuantCrit analysis of the Black teacher to principal pipeline* (Working paper no. 102–21). University of Houston Education Research Center.

Valencia, R. R. (1997). Conceptualizing the notion of deficit thinking. In R. R. Valencia (Ed.), *The evolution of deficit thinking: Educational thought and practice* (pp. 1–12). Routledge Falmer. https://doi.org/10.4324/9780367855581-1

Warren, E., & Supreme Court of the United States. (1953). U.S. Reports: *Brown v. Board of Education*, 347 U.S. 483 [Periodical] Retrieved from the Library of Congress https://www.loc.gov/item/usrep/347483

Chapter 3

Family Engagement
Results That Matter From the National Center for Families Learning

Kim Jacobs, Joshua Cramer, Wendee Mullikin, and Laura Westberg

Author Note
Kim Jacobs: https://orcid.org/0000-0002-4956-5008
Joshua Cramer: https://orcid.org/0000-0002-8504-8390
Wendee Mullikin: https://orcid.org/0000-0002-8705-9253
Laura Westberg: https://orcid.org/0000-0002-1036-3601

Thirty Years of Evidence and Practice

Research on children's success in school points to the importance of the family in children's development and academic achievement (Christenson & Reschly, 2009). We also know that, when parents are actively involved in their children's education, their children do better in school (Eccles & Harold, 1996; Epstein, 1995; Epstein & Dauber, 1991; Henderson & Berla, 1994). Henderson and Berla (1994) said the most accurate predictor of a student's achievement is the extent to which that student's family can create a home environment that encourages learning, express high expectations for their children's academic attainment and future careers, and become involved in their children's education at school and in the community. Robinson and Harris (2014) noted the importance of parent involvement for setting the stage for academic success (p. 199). The education reform shift that occurred in the 1980s laid the groundwork for the family literacy movement, designed to attack both poverty and low literacy issues. With student achievement at the nation's forefront, legislators and educators began to look at parental involvement to help children reach higher academic standards.

Historically grounded in comprehensive, four-component family literacy services, National Center for Families Learning (NCFL) designed programs steeped in evidence-based practices to support families most in need. NCFL's approach for working with families emphasizes equity by matching the intensity of the service with the intensity of the need. This model is a proven approach for practitioners – at all levels – to engage families in literacy activities within their communities. As a result of early innovations and applications, generations of families have achieved their self-selected goals and experienced previously unrealized opportunities. The success of families has strengthened the communities in which they live, work, and learn.

Funding and programming built early in the family literacy movement sustained and innovated the model.

- 1985: Parent and Child Education (PACE) legislation was enacted in Kentucky. This foundational program provided the needed data and successful family outcomes for further development of family literacy services.
- 1988: William R. Kenan Charitable Trust programming began. In the first two years, more than 300 families were served, and, two years after exiting the program, most self-reported educational success for both adults and children (Jacobs, 2019).
- 1988: Even Start Program launched and eventually expanded through federal legislation, supported by Congressman William F. Goodling and Senator Paul Simon. It lasted until 2012; its purpose was "(1) to help parents become full partners in the education of their children; (2) to assist children in reaching their full potential as learners; and (3) provide literacy training for their parents" (Soliman, 2018).

Today at least 18 federal programs (11 in the U.S. Department of Education, 6 in the U.S. Department of Health and Human Services, and 1 in the Bureau of Indian Education) include family literacy in the legislation as an allowable expenditure (Clymer et al., 2017, p. 1). In 1990, NCFL partnered with a federal agency, Bureau of Indian Affairs (BIA), to pilot Family and Child Education (FACE) in six BIA-funded elementary schools. Like Even Start, FACE built from the principles of the PACE and Kenan models. FACE is one of the longest standing federally funded early childhood programs in the nation. Since the implementation of the initial pilot program 30 years ago, American Indian families across the nation have benefited from the program's impact. Data collected over the course of the program years tell the story:

- Elementary students score higher on reading and math assessments.
- Caregivers are more engaged in children's learning and believe that FACE participation has a large impact on increasing children's interest in learning.
- FACE children with learning differences are better prepared for kindergarten.
- FACE children significantly and meaningfully increased language development.
- American Indian culture and language is infused throughout the FACE programs.
- FACE adult learners demonstrated reading and math gains, increasing reading and math scores (Yarnell et al., 2018).

In 1991, Toyota's donation to NCFL established the first Toyota-funded family literacy programs, supporting the implementation of family literacy programs in 15 cities across the United States. This generous support created a pattern for innovation and future expansion of family literacy programming for years to come. Over the years, these programs have reported:

- An increase in children's reading scores and in parenting adults' support of children's literacy activities.
- Increased caregiver engagement in children's educational processes (Levesque, 2013, 2017).
- Improved attendance of children when families attend family literacy programming (Levesque & Scordias, 2018).
- Significant gains in English language acquisition (Levesque, 2017).

Even after 30 years of innovation, programming has not strayed far from the original course of four essential and integrated components of family literacy – because it works.

The NCFL Intervention Model

Out of these three decades of work, NCFL has identified a unique approach to family engagement. This three-tiered intervention (Jacobs et al., 2018) coincides with the intensity and duration of services needed and desired by families, driven by family, academic, and community-focused goals (see Figure 3.1).

Built out of the NCFL ground-level work with families, the models are based on evidence, founded in results from third-party evaluations and research projects, and informed by knowledge gained over time by listening to families and observing programs through technical assistance. The intervention spans programming with a community-wide approach, as well as highly intensive programming to support families in reaching their goals.

Family Literacy (Tier 3)

NCFL's signature model, Family Literacy, is explicit and adheres to the federal definition of family literacy services. Family Literacy requires integrated elements of implementation not found in other family engagement programs.

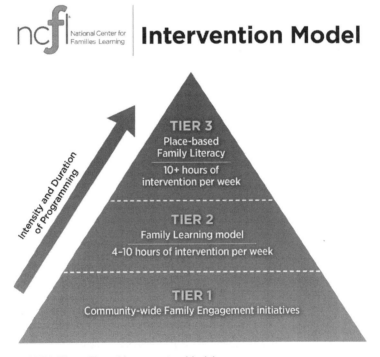

Figure 3.1 NCFL's Three-Tiered Intervention Model

These elements are critical to programming success influencing outcomes for programs and results for families.

The four components of a comprehensive Family Literacy program reflect those developed in the original PACE and Kenan Program models and outlined in the federal definition of family literacy services. These components, plus their intentional integration, set the standard for high-quality services then and continue to be the distinguishing hallmark of a true Family Literacy program today.

At its core, Family Literacy services integrate the four essential components of:

- Adult Education
- Children's Education
- Parent Time
- Parent and Child Together (PACT) Time®

Component Integration

Family Literacy is complex; component integration is the key to successful program implementation. The terminology *comprehensive family literacy services or programs* means the complete and integrated inclusion of the four components. *Integrated* refers to a program design that deliberately coordinates learning activities and experiences, as well as lesson planning and team coordination, across all four components.

Each of the four components of a comprehensive Family Literacy program has distinct goals, elements, and purposes. Standing alone, all four of these components can function independently and can produce results for individuals – parents or children. Quilted together into a cohesive and interwoven program of practice, families make lasting – and stronger – gains together.

According to Andrew E. Hayes, the program evaluator for the original Kenan model programs, "it is critical to note that the model design was not conceived as four separate parts. Each of these parts did serve separate purposes, but to meet the design principles and to achieve the intended goals, the parts must be integrated by a . . . process that took learning experiences beyond the separate parts" (Jacobs, 2019, pp. 66–67).

The following example, based on the concept of sorting objects, can be implemented as noted:

- The concept is shared in a Parent Time session, so parents understand what their children are learning. What is sorting and what do children learn by sorting objects?

- During Adult Education, the teacher may apply sorting objects to a math lesson for adult learners or help them apply the concept to their own lives.
- During PACT Time, parenting adults observe how well their children sort objects and support them by modeling or providing guidance. Let's put the blue beads in the blue box, the red beads in the red box.
- Caregivers move this knowledge into out-of-school, self-selected spaces. Let's sort laundry. Can you put the colors in different piles?
- Soon after the experience, caregivers reflect on the process and their understanding of the learning and discuss possible improvements for next time.

None of this begins without staff having discussions with parenting adults about their goals for their children and what is currently pertinent to their lives. Initially, the concept of children sorting items may have stemmed from a Parent Time session where caregivers expressed concern that children needed more practice in this area.

As programs evolve to meet the needs of families and communities, this integration deepens to create more complex connections across the components and into the home. This requires cross-training and teamwork among the instructional staff – particularly in program design and curriculum implementation.

The Family Literacy model is the gold star of high-impact family engagement and the most intensive type of family program designed to help families thrive. The model requires ten or more hours of intervention per week conducted over a considerable period of time.

Family Service-Learning

Family Service-Learning takes place in some Family Literacy programs and all Family Learning (tier 2) programs. It was created in response to the need for authentic project-based learning across NCFL programs. As families became more confident and stable through program participation, they often began to look beyond their personal family goals and needs to those of their own communities and the changes they would like to see there.

This six-step process called Family Service-Learning (Cramer & Toso, 2015) is woven through the fabric of Family Literacy and Family Learning. It is an intergenerational approach to deeper learner engagement that puts underserved families in a position to identify and address challenges in their communities. Throughout the process, families utilize technology and digital resources in meaningful ways to carry out the project. A deliberate focus on building and leveraging social capital also yields power for adult participants working to gain employment and advocacy skills that will sustain their families.

Both Family Literacy and Family Learning programs largely target low-income populations, which may suggest why the Family Service-Learning process has transformative power on participants. While service-learning opportunities historically tend to be reserved for K–12 and university students, learners from under-resourced groups have demonstrated increased positive outcomes over their peers (Miller et al., 2015; Ellerton et al., 2015). Engaging the whole family in the process provides opportunities for skill building for very young children (Fair & Delaplane, 2015), K–12 students (Furco, 2013), and adults (Kelly, 2013).

Through independent evaluation of the process and the family learning model, The Goodling Institute for Research in Family Literacy found that participants gained experience with key employability skills through this contextualized learning experience (Toso & Krupar, 2016). As a result, NCFL intentionally supports programs implementing the Family Service-Learning process to incorporate a focus on developing goals identified by the Perkins Collaborative Research Network in the Employability Skills Framework (U.S. Department of Education, 2015).

Several examples of successful NCFL Family Service-Learning projects and their impacts on families have recently emerged, as reported in an NCFL internal document (NCFL, 2019).

- In NCFL Family Learning programs funded by the Kellogg Foundation, 196 parents and 211 children participated in 12 Family Service-Learning projects in programs from Oregon to New York City.
- In Dallas, three program sites tackled community issues.
- A cohort of 15 families with middle school students at the Toberman Neighborhood Center in San Pedro, California, participated in several Family Service-Learning projects.
- In Louisville, 385 parents and 540 children participated in Family Service-Learning in 2018–2019. Families spent a total of 414 hours planning, developing, and carrying out 32 projects at 7 Family Learning sites in the city.

Some common themes mentioned by participants include:

- Became more knowledgeable about and increasingly involved in their community,
- Felt empowered to make a difference in their communities and proud of their accomplishments,
- Expanded their social networks,
- Positive social-emotional development, and
- Increase of personal skills such as communication, organization, and team-work.

Many reported that through their participation in Family Service-Learning projects getting to know others living in their communities created new kinships. As a result, the community became more trusting and safer.

Family Learning (Tier 2)

Through years of implementing family literacy programs across the nation, NCFL honed its insights into effectively operationalizing two-generation education solutions. The partnership with Toyota enabled NCFL to engage in continuous improvement of the model in laboratories of learning at a wide variety of partner organizations. Families in more than 420 program sites have benefitted from Toyota's promotion of family literacy and learning. The most recent collaboration – Toyota Family Learning – rose from knowledge gained over three decades of Family Literacy implementation coupled with a desire to meet families where they are.

NCFL Family Learning was envisioned as Family Literacy beyond the classroom walls – offering this model in locations beyond traditional classroom settings because "families who have become disenchanted by formal educational institutions may be more likely to trust their physical and digital neighbors rather than individuals representing education or community service agencies" (Cramer, 2015).

The Family Learning model supports families learning together anytime, anywhere. A deliberate theory of change underlies this model and yields a variety of outcomes. Family Learning helps parents build skills through Parent Time adult skill-building sessions, affirming and building on their role as their child's earliest teacher. Parenting adults and children come together to learn through Parent and Child Together (PACT) Time® in a variety of contexts.

Results from NCFL Family Learning program evaluations clearly show increases in family engagement that lead to positive caregiver outcomes. An independent evaluation from the Goodling Institute showed a 90% increase in family engagement in education, 20% increase in family literacy activities within the home and community, and an increase in leadership skills and social capital for families (Cramer & Toso, 2015). In terms of adult goal attainment, 75% of caregivers improved their English language skills, 47% upgraded their skills to keep their current job, and 21% earned a GED certificate or high school diploma (Cramer, 2016).

This theory of change spreads opportunity to adults, their families, and their peers in the program. However, the full realization of the theory is its capacity to catalyze compounding change. To end the generational cycle of poverty in families, family learning programs help parenting adults build skills and learn how to pass them on explicitly to their children. Families engage others in the community through Family Service-Learning projects. Over time, these families move from their self-perception of invisible and voiceless residents to engaged and confident community members and leaders. This change has the potential to transform communities – and indeed the nation.

The Impact of Social Capital

Along with families participating in service-learning projects, the ability to translate social capital into capital assets through the direct engagement of empowered caregivers is a major focus for Family Learning programs.

An important product of building family networks is the creation of social capital. As adults increasingly desire to move toward their full potential, newly developed social capital can influence myriad benefits. In *Foundations of Social Theory*, Coleman (1990) defined social capital as a resource that comes from relationships that can be leveraged as a capital asset.

Social capital is: "not a single entity, but a variety of different entities having two characteristics in common; they all consist of some aspect of a social structure, and they facilitate certain actions of individuals who are within the structure" (Coleman, 1990, p. 302).

Social capital can also be exchanged for favors or new information (Resnick, 2001). Social capital is lodged within relationships. Ricardo Stanton-Salazar (2001) defined social capital as "relationships and networks that transmit vital forms of resources and institutional support that enable young people to become effective participants within mainstream institutional spheres, particularly the school system" (p. 20). Over the last decade, the importance of social capital has transcended dispute and propelled it into a field of its own (Kwon & Adler, 2014).

The ability to translate social capital into economic and educational capital through the direct engagement of caregivers is a major focus for Parent Time activities. As adults and families move through a Family Learning program, they will have new opportunities to leverage their online and offline networks to reach their personal academic and economic goals. Recent evidence suggests that digital social networks create an easy opportunity for the exchange of social capital, especially if one's network is actively managed (Ellison et al., 2014).

Family Engagement (Tier 1)

The least intensive in terms of parenting adults' commitment in the NCFL model is the tier 1 intervention level. Family Engagement programming includes cross-generation learning opportunities, events, activities, and strategies that support children's academic achievement and sometimes caregiver education, but not adult skill-building based on goal setting. Program supports provided are often less intensive and of shorter duration than Family Literacy or Family Learning programs.

High-quality family engagement programs have purpose, goals, and support outcomes. Not all families need or desire the intensity of commitment a Family Literacy (tier 3) or Family Learning (tier 2) program requires; however, many caregivers still want support when it comes to their children's development. Many organizations provide high-quality family engagement events or opportunities that are open-ended and allow parenting adults to lead the way and choose how to be involved. Families decide what works best for them according to their needs, goals, and desires to move their family forward or perhaps to better their community.

Whatever path a school or community-based education organization may take to engage families, NCFL recommends some minimum principles of high-quality family engagement.

Programming or content should:

- Target the needs voiced by families, including their cultural and linguistic needs and those of the communities in which they live,
- Be evidence-based and include practices that show promise,
- Connect families to their children's school or community-based education programs,

- Focus on children's academics, oral language or vocabulary development, and/or reading and literacy development,
- Connect families to a greater community-wide network, and
- Advocate for caregiver inclusion, input, and leadership.

Say & Play With Words is a city-wide effort to intervene at a critically early age to ensure every child enters kindergarten ready to learn. This program reaches families that may prefer an opportunity of shorter duration in high-need areas of the community. NCFL works with local partners in Louisville to implement the parent groups and playgroups with families in their agencies. The program is conducted with 8–12 families in one-hour weekly groups for 10 weeks.

The goal of this program is to increase the capacity and capability of local agencies to implement evidence-based early language practices with families and to increase the abilities of families to talk more with their children, engage them in conversation, and to target conversation to family routines and events. Long-term impacts are to improve young children's language abilities and ensure readiness for kindergarten and reading proficiency in the primary grades. Caregivers improve self-efficacy, engagement in their children's learning, and social capital. Family engagement opportunities vary within communities, ideally created and driven by the needs and goals of families who live, work, and participate in those communities.

Collective Impact: Strengthening Entire Communities, Systems, and States

When the full intervention model comes together, whether in a small community or throughout a state, the power of multigenerational learning magnifies. NCFL has embarked on a deeper level of impact in communities by joining forces with local entities for collective impact – operating on the principle that no single agency or non-profit foundation can independently resolve community issues. The value of collective impact makes possible the deeper dive into issues and helping families solve problems important to them and their community.

For example, NCFL worked in the city of Detroit, Michigan, to combine services and work with local agencies and partners – as well as multiple funders – to impact families and programs in numerous ways. With multiple agencies working toward the same end – to support vulnerable families with Family Literacy programming – children and families made substantial gains. Caregivers felt more capable and competent to support their children's learning at school and at home. A focus on children's attendance resulted in Family Literacy students who attended school at a rate of 10% above the public school average. Children with parenting adults enrolled in Family Literacy programs made significant gains in reading levels and in reading proficiency (Levesque & Scordias, 2018). These programs leveraged the successes of parents to focus on intentional collaborations and blending of funding. Donna Cielma, then-director of children, youth, and families at Southwest Counseling Solutions in Detroit, believed the collective impact approach was essential for family and program outcomes. "With this significant increase in parents' convictions that their children would have the skills to support that level of academic success, we were able to attract additional funding. Our program has become self-sustaining with additional support, including money from six private funding sources." Cielma added that,

> We could not have done this without Toyota funding and outside evaluation. With this program, we saw dramatic increases in the number of families and parents who learned to speak English and started to participate in their children's academic lives and their own. Funders were attracted to the success of our program and are supporting its expansion.
>
> Jacobs, 2019, 165–166

Currently, NCFL is aligning programs and services across the cities of Louisville and Dallas by targeting the needs of the respective communities. Louisville's collaboration of tier 1–3 family engagement services include: four-component Family Literacy programs in urban and immigrant areas of the city; a Title I focus in Jefferson County (Louisville) Public Schools; book distributions; and early childhood initiatives such as play groups, professional development, and coaching for teachers.

In 2019, *Family Learning Community Dallas* became the latest Toyota-supported initiative, bringing a city-wide approach to communities in Dallas. NCFL, local Dallas organizations, and community leaders have committed to help more families reach economic self-sufficiency through a comprehensive family learning system. The approach encompasses a three-pronged strategy that includes literacy-focused coalition building, parent leadership, and replicating model family learning sites to meet the needs of the community. These parent leadership institutes determine a problem, perform root-cause analysis, and develop a solution before using their collective voice to advocate for their community's needs – such as increasing free/low-cost art and cultural extra-curriculars for students, ensuring playground equipment is accessible for children of all abilities, and health and safety initiatives.

Summary

The NCFL three-tiered family engagement intervention model provides a guide for schools and community education services to use when determining intervention levels with families – ensuring that the intensity of services provided to the families matches the intensity of their need.

Over 50 years of research links the various roles families play in children's education, including supporters of learning, encouragers of grit and determination, models of lifelong learning, and advocates of proper programming and placements for their children (Mapp & Kuttner, 2013).

Comprehensive family literacy and family learning programs are the most intensive family engagement programs available. In addition to building and supporting comprehensive Family Literacy programs, NCFL is a leader for the implementation and replication of best practices in high-quality family engagement across America.

NCFL supports the three-tiered family engagement model as a guide for schools and community education services when determining intervention levels with families. Based on our 30-year experience of working with families, we see Family Literacy and Family Learning models as the family intervention models most likely to move families out of poverty and onto a pathway of positive family engagement, academic achievement, and employability. In turn, families thrive and celebrate their unique contributions to their communities and to society.

References

Christenson, S. L., & Reschly, A. L. (Eds.). (2009). *Handbook of school-family partnerships*. Routledge.

Clymer, C., Toso, B. W, Grinder, E., & Sauder, R. P. (2017, January). *Changing the course of family literacy*. Policy Paper. Goodling Institute for Research in Family Literacy, Penn State University. https://ed.psu.edu/goodling-institute/policy/changing-the-course-of-family-literacy

Coleman, J. (1990). *Foundations of social theory*. Harvard University Press.

Cramer, J. (2015). *Background knowledge: Theory of change*. National Center for Families Learning. Unpublished document.

Cramer, J. (2016). *From theory to outcomes: NCFL's two-generation movement for families*. National Center for Families Learning. http://familieslearning.org/pdf/NCFL_Theory-to-Outcomes-brief-2016.pdf

Cramer, J., & Toso, B. W. (2015). *Family service learning brief*. National Center for Families Learning and the Goodling Institute for Research in Family Literacy. http://familieslearning.org/pdf/NCFL-FSL-brief_F3.pdf

Eccles, J. S., & Harold, R. D. (1996). Family involvement in children's and adolescents' schooling. In A. Booth & J. F. Dunn (Eds.), *Family school links* (pp. 3–34). Lawrence Erlbaum Associates.

Ellerton, S., Di Meo, C., Pantaleo, J., Kemmerer, A., Bandziukas, M., & Bradley, M. (2015). Academic service learning benefits diverse, urban community college students. *Journal for Civic Commitment, 23*, 1–17.

Ellison, N. B., Vitak, J., Gray, R., & Lampe, C. (2014). Cultivating social resources on social network sites: Facebook relationship maintenance behaviors and their role in social capital processes. *Journal of Computer-Mediated Communication, 19*, 855–870. https://doi.org/10.1111/jcc4.12078

Epstein, J. (1995). School/family/community partnerships: Caring for the children we share. *Phi Delta Kappan, 76*(9), 701–712.

Epstein, J. L., & Dauber, S. (1991). School programs and teacher practices of parent involvement in inner-city elementary and middle schools. *The Elementary School Journal, 91*(3), 279–305.

Fair, C., & Delaplane, E. (2015). "It is good to spend time with older adults. You can teach them, they can teach you": Second grade students reflect on intergenerational service learning. *Early Childhood Education, 43*(1), 19–26. https://doi.org/10.1007/s10643-014-0634-9

Furco, A. (2013). A research agenda for K-12 school-based service-learning: Academic achievement and school success. *International Journal of Research on Service-Learning and Community Engagement, 1*(1), 11–22.

Henderson, A. T., & Berla, N. (Eds.). (1994). *A new generation of evidence: The family is critical to student achievement*. National Committee for Citizens in Education. (ERIC Document No. ED375968). https://files.eric.ed.gov/fulltext/ED375968.pdf

Jacobs, K. (2019). *Grit, grace, and gratitude: A thirty-year journey*. National Center for Families Learning.

Jacobs, K., Cramer, J., Noles, T., & Lovett, P. A. (2018). *Defining our work: Families learning together*. National Center for Families Learning. www.familieslearning.org/uploads/media_gallery/NCFL-Defining_Our_Work_F3.pdf

Kelly, M. J. (2013). Beyond classroom borders: Incorporating collaborative service learning for the adult student. *Adult Learning, 24*(2), 82–84. https://doi.org/10.1177/1045159513477844

Kwon, S., & Adler, P. S. (2014). Social capital: Maturation of a field of research. *The Academy of Management Review, 39*(4), 412–422. https://doi.org/10.5465/amr.2014.0210

Levesque, J. (2013). *Toyota family literacy program research project: Meta analysis of the studies of high performing family literacy programs.* National Center for Families Learning. www.familieslearning.org/pdf/TFLPSynthesis.pdf

Levesque, J. (2017). *The collective impact of social innovation on a two-generation learning program with Hispanic/Latino families in Detroit.* National Center for Families Learning. www.familieslearning.org/pdf/NCFL-Collective-Impact-Brief.pdf

Levesque, J., & Scordias, M. (2018). *Southwest Solutions, Corporation for National Service, Social Innovation Project, English language learners Family Literacy project.* Impact study and final report. United Way for Southeast Michigan.

Mapp, K., & Kuttner, P. (2013). *Partners in education: A dual capacity-building framework for family-school partnerships.* Southwest Educational Development Laboratory. www.sedl.org/pubs/framework/FE-Cap-Building.pdf

Miller, J., Berkey, B., & Griffin, F. (2015). International students in American pathway programs: Learning English and culture through service-learning. *Journal of International Students, 5*(4), 334–352. https://files.eric.ed.gov/fulltext/EJ1066262.pdf

National Center for Families Learning (NCFL). (2019). *Internal data.* Unpublished.

Resnick, P. (2001). Beyond bowling together: Socio-technical capital. In J. Carroll (Ed.), *HCI in the new millennium* (pp. 647–672). Addison-Wesley.

Robinson, K., & Harris, A. L. (2014). *The broken compass: Parental involvement with children's education.* Harvard University Press.

Soliman, J. (2018). The Even Start Family Literacy Program: The rise and fall of family literacy and the need for its return. *The Georgetown Journal on Poverty Law & Policy, XXV*(3), 427–450. www.law.georgetown.edu/poverty-journal/wp-content/uploads/sites/25/2019/02/25-3-The-Even-Start-Literacy-Program.pdf

Stanton-Salazar, R. (2001). *Manufacturing hope and despair: The school and kin support networks of U.S. – Mexican youth.* Teachers College Press.

Toso, B. W., & Krupar, A. (2016). *Building employability skills in family literacy programs: Lessons from the Toyota Family Learning Program* (Practioner's Guide

#7). Goodling Institute for Research in Family Literacy. https://ed.psu. edu/goodling-institute/professional-development/practitioners-guide-7-1

U.S. Department of Education, Office of Career, Technical, and Adult Education, Division of Academic and Technical Education. (2015). *Perkins collaborative resource network employability skills framework*. https://cte.ed.gov/ initiatives/employability-skills-framework

Yarnell, V., Lambson, T, & Pfannenstiel, J. (2018). *BIE Family and Child Education Program 2017 Report*. Research & Training Associates, Inc. https://www.bie. edu/sites/default/files/documents/idc2-084604.pdf

Chapter 4

Unsettling Community and University

Finding Fluidity in Community Literacies and the Academy

Gemma Cooper-Novack and Brice Nordquist

Author Note

Gemma Cooper-Novack: https://orcid.org/0000-0001-8052-0468

Brice Nordquist: https://orcid.org/0000-0003-0376-8421

The Community and the Academy

In *Community Literacy and the Rhetoric of Public Engagement*, Flower (2008) sketches her influential framework for community partnership and social transformation from its "most obvious" starting point: "what is the 'community' of community literacy"? (p. 10). For Flower, "the most significant feature of a community is not what or where it is (with its shifting features and overlapping boundaries) but how it functions" (p. 10). Flower represents a community constituted through interactions of "community folk, urban teens, university students and professors" employing "multiple literacies and diverse discourses" to "name and solve problems together" (p. 19). In this depiction, Flower's community isn't held together by shared identity, affinity, or space-time but instead through a pursuit of social change through literate practice.

However, while the identities, affinities, and practices of Flower's community are dynamic and diverse, her representations of it in space-time turn out to be relatively consistent. The urban neighborhood in Pittsburgh, and specifically a "settlement house . . . not a classroom" in this neighborhood, is "the soul of 'community' literacy, its reason for being, and the voice it seeks to amplify" (p. 17). In this way, the *where and when* of community turns out to be much more stable and consequential than Flower suggests earlier.

Participating in a similar positioning of "community," the *Community Literacy Journal (CLJ)* – publishing scholarship from fields as diverse as literacy education, rhetoric and composition, communication, English studies, and gender studies – defines community literacy as "including multiple domains for literacy work extending *beyond* [emphasis added] mainstream educational and work institutions" (*Community Literacy Journal*, n.d.). While these forms of literacy work also take place within institutions of formal education, the journal's defining concept of *community literacy* hinges on its operation *beyond* or *outside* schools or the academy (Doggart et al., 2007; Hansen, 2009.) And so, while community is conceptualized as complex, dynamic, and heterogenous, in Flower, the *CLJ*, and other influential work in the field, one thing seems clear: the community is to be found somewhere outside the bounds of academic spaces.

Perhaps as a result of the separation of "community" and "institutions of formal education," few works of academic community-literacy-based scholarship choose to represent the academy as a complex, dynamic, and heterogenous actor within spaces of community work. Much of the work on community literacy lets *the academy* go undefined once it enters *the community* and, likewise, lets *the community* go undefined where it overlaps with *the academy*. While a number of writers exploring the questions of community literacy and student roles therein examine the internal workings of the university and its impact on student and faculty practices, including the increasing corporatization of the university as an institution – from Peck et al. (1995) to Mutnick (2018) – the question of what the university represents *within a community literacy project* often remains unanswered. Those coming from the academy must see the multiplicities of communities in community literacy, but the multiplicities of the academy and entanglements of academy and community rarely survive all the way to the academy's dialogue with the community. The end result is that the academy becomes, in portraying "community work" or "community literacy," obfuscated via its hegemonic omnipresence. We might question the work of individuals in the academy, but the role of the college or university in these partnerships is monolithic. For instance, when Peck et al. (1995) define a community/literacy partnership, they focus on defining the complexity of *the community*, assuming their readers know the meaning of *the university* (p. 200). In asking "how university knowledge fares when it is walked out into the world" (Peck et al., 1995, p. 219), university knowledge, while perhaps vulnerable, becomes monolithic. The possibility that different university knowledges might fare differently doesn't enter the rhetoric.

Those who do make visible a definition of the academy tend to view themselves as outside of its structure based on community by identity or affinity. One example may be seen in Martinez (2014), who uses the counterstory of composite figure Alejandra's experience to exemplify the outsider position of Latinx students and scholars in an academy that enforces oft-unspoken expectations of cultural uniformity. Through such a lens, the academy becomes, if not inimical to, then certainly opposed to, the needs of the identity-based community in question; academic "community work," then, becomes primarily extractive. Parks (2014) says that in community literacy work at universities, "in the effort to theorize the political impact of such work, the need to *actually* [emphasis added], change the systemic exploitation of distressed communities has been elided" (p. 507). Here the university's projects of community literacy take from the community. The academy extracts in these frameworks from marginalized labor and from those communities it uses to create more prestigious and social (at the expense of the political, per Parks) research. Whether hegemonically undefined or defined as exclusively extractive, "the academy" is frequently essentialized in the body of community literacies research. In this chapter, we explore the ways this essentialization, like the oversimplification of "the community," might limit the potential of community-academy partnerships.

Given our own uneasy and conflicted positions as academic writers and researchers situated in communities of identity, place, and practice, we are committed to using this chapter to explore how (and if) academic practitioners of community literacy can write about the constellation of processes constituting a community in ways that acknowledge the entwinements of academic and community selves and literacies. We consider anthropological theorist Fabian's (2002) distinction between reflexive and reflective stances in ethnographic writing useful for the pursuit of this question. While reflection seeks to eliminate subjectivity by hiding the observer, reflexion requires academic practitioners of community literacy to "present (make present) our past experiences to ourselves" and thereby acknowledge our relationship to the "presence of others precisely inasmuch as the Other has become content of our experience . . . *Somehow we must be able to share each other's past in order to be knowingly in each other's present* [emphasis added]" (p. 91–92). To reveal and better understand our presence in each other's and in our community partners' pasts across communities of identity, place, and practice, and subsequently, the enduring presence of others in our writing, we now turn to methods of collective autoethnography and co/autoethnography.

Site and Methods

Our reflexive praxis in this chapter focuses on our work at the Center, a local learning center that offers educational and community programs for recent immigrants and refugees to our city, which has been a hub of refugee resettlement for the last 50 years. For a decade, the Center has been tailoring youth and adult language and literacy instruction to the goals and needs of this population in the neighborhood and across the city. The Center serves approximately 150 individuals per week through adult English language classes, computer training, financial literacy workshops, college prep classes, individual and small group tutoring, and a range of arts and media-based projects. Several characteristics make the Center unique among non-profit educational organizations in the city: First, it is a family literacy center, where immediate and extended families come together to learn, receive individuated support, and return home to continue to strengthen each other's literacy and language skills; second, it approaches learners as replete with linguistic and cultural resources, rather than deficient in English and in need of remediation and acculturation; finally, the Center operates with an understanding of the interconnected nature of the material, physical, and educational needs of refugees, immigrants, and others across the city.

We have both volunteered for a number of years at the Center, in a range of roles, from writing tutor to theater teacher to board member, as detailed later; our work built up to Brice's cofounding and codirection, with Gemma's collaboration, of a fellowship program for resettled refugee youth artists that built an extensive partnership between the Center – a small non-profit organization with a deeply global orientation – and the university where we both work. As we explore the development of this program through critical co/autoethnographic methods later, we consider our own roles in challenging the traditional ways of defining, theorizing, and experiencing community literacies and in considering the nuances of the role the academy, beyond its assumed hegemonic boundaries, plays in our work and the work of our colleagues in the fellowship program.

Through the methodological orientations of critical co/autoethnography (Coia & Taylor, 2009; Taylor et al., 2014; Holman Jones, 2016), we seek to understand our various roles in community-based literacy programming at the Center through the lens of "creating shared time" (Fabian, 2002, p. 31). We used co/autoethnographic methods to anchor our data in dialogue, interviewing each other about our experiences with writing and belonging at the Center over time. We coded and analyzed transcripts of these conversations with a focus on how each of us understands and experiences *the academy* and *the community* while continuing to draw both of our memories, histories, and knowledges into conversation while building the analysis together. In some ways we are taking what might be called a "conservative approach to the method" of autoethnography (Duncan, 2004, as cited in Wall, 2006), in that we set these depictions of our personal experiences and reflections very much in the context of "traditional" formulations of scholarship. However, as community writing educators who are white and affiliated with a university that has great power in our region, we want to clarify how experiences like ours are regularly written in a manner that denies the complexity of the university. Holman Jones explains that "[i]n critical autoethnography, theory is a *language available to us* [emphasis added], as we write our stories" (2016, p. 234). We came to writing this chapter as a manifestation of our shared and divergent experiences with writing and the Center in part because we were both eager to find the theoretical language that would allow us to understand our experiences, particularly our shared frustration with what we saw as the careless use of the word "community" in university narratives of education and in our respective disciplines (writing studies and literacy education). Co/autoethnographic methods support our interrogation of singular representations of community and academy by examining the awkward relationships not only between individual experience and social context – as all autoethnography does (Holman Jones, 2016) – but also between our two distinct experiences and how each of us understands our own and each other's.

Autoethnography, as a method, allows us to exist in relationship with the structures of power in which we maneuver (for instance, whiteness; university hierarchies; nationality and citizenship), acknowledging and engaging with particular aspects of our privilege and positionality while compelling us not to center it, since autoethnography requires a constant shifting between self and social context. Co/autoethnography, by turn, adds still another station in this constant shifting, our focus on each other's experiences in these contexts.

Both of us, as a professor and a doctoral candidate, have historically hesitated to consider ourselves part of the academy, particularly in the context of our work with the Center. At first, Gemma exaggerated her dismissal of her university connection at the Center: "I won't claim the university because the university doesn't claim me" (G. Cooper-Novack, personal communication, August 27, 2019). While there may be some truth in this regarding the general practices of universities and graduate student labor and laborers, to say that the university doesn't claim its graduate students – and particularly the "community work" of its graduate students – is a disingenuous stance. As a first-generation college student, Brice initially thought of his work at the Center, which began during the first semester of his professorship, as a means of escape from the unfamiliar culture and often-abstracted labor of the academy. But this positioning has always been only partially accurate, as aspects of the academy inevitably become familiar, for better or worse, to people who spend most of their adult lives learning to navigate and succeed in academic institutions. In these ways, the questions we found ourselves asking in attempting to blend the extractive and hegemonic views of the academy were focused on what we meant by "the university" or "the academy" and our own relations to it and the impact of such a place or context and its relations on the Center. These questions have become all the more essential as our colleagues in the fellowship program, particularly adolescent youth artists and intellectuals, came to move more and more fluidly between the supposed boundaries of academy and community.

The Narratio Fellowship

To trace out the relationships among practices and structures that constitute university and community spaces and selves, we focus the remainder of this chapter primarily on the case of the Narratio Fellowship, a collaboration between the Center, our university, and Narratio, a global storytelling and publishing platform for displaced youth. The program was created and is directed by Brice and Narratio founder Ahmed Badr (2020), an Iraqi refugee and poet resettled in the U.S. Gemma joined the program in its first year as an assistant director and cofacilitator and has since moved into a project manager role, coordinating the activities of a growing number of youth fellows, artists, facilitators, and collaborators.

Now in its third year, the Narratio Fellowship brings artists with refugee or immigrant backgrounds together with resettled refugee youth to explore and represent a full range of their own histories and experiences through various modes of artistic expression. The program includes a month-long series of storytelling workshops designed around the artist's media of choice, culminating in a trip to New York City, a performance at the Metropolitan Museum of Art, and workshops at various prestigious organizations in the city. Following the summer program, fellows continue to work with artists and collaborators to design and facilitate workshops, performances, and exhibits at local community centers, libraries, galleries, and schools.

We developed the program in response to challenges in representations and understandings of refugee experience. First, the program seeks to combat the pervasive vilification of refugees and immigrants in an age of nationalistic rhetoric and policy and federally sanctioned xenophobia by elevating the voices of refugee and immigrant youth eager to share their stories on their own terms. Second, the program seeks to complicate representations of refugee experience focused solely on the consequences of war, poverty, and displacement. While these violences must not be forgotten, the program offers space for youth to explore and represent a fuller range of their experiences, including but not limited to displacement and resettlement. Finally, the program challenges assimilationist discourses, particularly in education, focused on "overcoming" linguistic "deficiencies" in pursuit of full integration and socio-economic mobility. The work composed through the Narratio Fellowship tells stories and makes meanings across languages and modes. Through their composing, performance, and publication processes, fellows are encouraged to make meaning with all the linguistic, semiotic, and cultural resources at their disposal. In this way, the program approaches and presents refugee youth as cultural agents.

Showcasing the cultural agency of resettled youth is the driving force of our collaboration with the Metropolitan Museum of Art. In each iteration of the program, cohorts of refugee youth work with project directors, facilitators, and artists-in-residence to reimagine objects in the Met's collections through artistic expression. Over the course of the program, fellows trace and represent connections between objects and their own personal and ancestral histories and, thereby, reveal and fill absences in the museum's readings of histories and cultures. In this way, the program works to reframe representations, offset prejudices, and expand the bounds of what is deemed worthy of attention by official purveyors of cultural value. Beyond their cultural interventions at the Met, fellows have shared their work with a diverse range of global and local audiences. Fellows' poems from our inaugural 2019 cohort are also published in Badr's 2020 book, *While the Earth Sleeps We Travel*.

In addition to its arts-based storytelling activity, the program provides youth fellows at educational transition points – from high school to community college or from either to four-year institutions – with academic mentorship and advising through partnerships with local schools, universities, and resource centers. Over the course of the year-long program, we conduct college essay writing workshops, respond to application materials, connect fellows to faculty and staff of prospective programs of study, arrange meetings with financial aid counselors, consult on course schedules, and work to meet fellows' needs for educational support. With the help of this component of the program, many Narratio Fellows have become thriving undergraduate students at four-year colleges and universities across the region and country, including our university. This movement of fellows across multiple contexts of our shared lives and work emerges as a key theme in our co/autoethnographic account later.

Brice and Gemma both came to the work of the Narratio Fellowship after years of engagement with the Center involving multiple and ongoing literacy and arts-based programs. Brice began his work with the Center as a literacy volunteer soon after joining the Syracuse University faculty. "[The Center] was really the only place that seemed to believe that I was just wanting to volunteer, because there was so much saturation from [the University] into these [literacy] centers" (B. Nordquist, personal communication, August 30, 2019). Gemma, similarly, began her work with the Center as a volunteer during her second year of graduate studies. "[A]fter my first full semester under Trump, knowing that I lived in a city with very extensive refugee populations and refugee support, I felt like I wanted to be doing something that supported refugees and immigrants" (G. Cooper-Novack, personal communication, August 27, 2019).

When each of us started at the Center, our connection to the University was made eminently visible to us through the expectations and assumptions of everyone we worked with, from administrative staff to adult language learners and youth. This was particularly true given that both of us are white, US-born, and monolingual English speakers, all of which placed us outside of the mainstream of the Center and linked us more to the Center's long history of short-term university-based volunteers. However, we both, to a degree, sought to create separation between our identities in spaces of the Center and the university. As such, we bridged hegemonic and extractive frameworks of the university but in a manner that benefitted neither us nor those we were working with. Of course, we were, in truth and in practice, university-affiliated. We failed to engage with the university as a complex system, to acknowledge that we might be university-affiliated while still aiming to decrease the extractive frame of our work. The university, in all its multifacetedness, has the potential to both benefit and harm those with whom we were working (and ourselves) – in fact, it has the likelihood of doing both simultaneously. If we were to live and inhabit this complex definition and practice of the academy and make a conscious attempt to turn from these potential harms, we would be able to provide more as volunteers and educators to members of the Center's community.

From the beginning, the structure of the Narratio Fellowship forced us to come to terms with the complexity of relationships to the university because it was forged and supported through university structures beyond our own individual affiliations. For instance, Brice and Ahmed were introduced through a creative nonfiction reading series sponsored by Brice's home department; Ahmed was introduced to the Center through Brice's existing programs there. When they began to conceive of a fellowship program that involved youth at the Center, Brice secured funding for the program through the university. From its inception, the program was a collaboration among the Center, the university, and Narratio itself, which disrupted the typical university/community dyad of collaborative work. In this way, the university was able to claim investment in the work of the program from the beginning. Brice reflects that,

> in some ways this claiming was and still is extractive, but it's also a way of valuing a particular type of community-engaged work as scholarship, as research and creative work, and this valuation opens up possibilities for reimagining – not just separating our academic work – in ways that not only benefit us and the program's participants and collaborators but also can fundamentally change the work and nature of the university.
> (B. Nordquist, personal communication, August 26, 2021)

Unlike our previous literacy and arts-based programs at the Center, the Narratio Fellowship was designed to move fluidly across university and community spaces, drawing on and intertwining the resources of both more directly. Program participants frequently move between activities and workshops at the Center and the university, using spaces in the Center and its surrounding neighborhood for composing, practicing with equipment, photographing, and shooting video and moving to university spaces to access library resources, computer labs, and studios. This movement across university and community spaces is made possible by Brice's position on the faculty and both Brice's and Gemma's knowledge and familiarity with the resources of the Center and its surrounding communities.

When discussing the way he connects his position at the university and his work at the Center, Brice says,

> If I'm feeling like I want to come across as being magnanimous, I make sense of [the connection] by saying that my goal is to redirect resources from a powerful, prestigious institution to a smaller organization . . . that needs those resources, but also . . . to help mediate and make relationships between collaborators and organizations reciprocal as possible.
>
> (B. Nordquist, personal communication, August 30, 2019)

Consider the different relationships of theory and practice involved in this statement. Brice must acknowledge his connection to the university in order to take advantage of his ability to use it as a resource. He cannot mask his university affiliation or attempt to declare independence from or of it; instead, he can offer concrete resources and connections that satisfy his needs and benefit his work while supporting an organization and a group of people with whom he has come to feel a powerful connection. Brice needs to understand his own positionality in relationship to the university – and the dialogues it creates – in order to enact this connection.

Over time and through our collaboration on this program, we've come to understand that this process of redirecting or circulating resources can and should be multidirectional. The university gains a great deal from sharing resources, from public appropriation to opportunities for credentialing university representatives (students, faculty, and staff) and conversions of "experiential learning" and engaged research and creative work to academic and occupational capital. Perhaps more fundamentally and transformatively, the university gains relationships that can potentially reshape its structures and functions to its benefit. Recognizing that we are not only redirecting resources from the university and benefitting individually from the work and relationships formed through the fellowship program but also that the program redirects resources from the Center – primarily in the form of talented, insightful, critically engaged youth – to actively transform university spaces brings us closer to authentic understandings of ourselves and our roles in this collaboration and authentic relationships with students in the program.

Building authentic relationships with the students in the program means that we can build critical connections with them. Knowing who you are across spaces of collaboration gives room to introduce the students with whom we work to the university not only as an educational goal but as a site for critical engagement. Bringing the students to a place where they have some agency in a university environment – where they are creating work in university spaces – gives the opportunity for them and for us to engage critically with that environment, à la Paulo Freire (1973).

In many cases, given our own complex histories with the university and with the Center, relationships forged through the fellowship program have led us to more multifaceted understandings of the fellows, of our own positionalities, and of the university as a complex system always constituted, to some degree, by people, things, ideas, and practices coded as *of* or *from* "the community." Gemma, for instance, notes that, when she learned that several of the former fellows were central to a prominent undergraduate social justice organizing project that aimed to change racist university policy, the fellows "became my people everywhere. They weren't limited to that space or that summer or that moment, they became people . . . I wanted to support and be invested in and care about everywhere" (G. Cooper-Novack, personal interview, August 26, 2021). The boundary between academy and community has grown fluid in our three years with the fellowship, enabling us to better recognize and make use of entanglements of ourselves and relationships across contexts of ongoing and integrated work.

Many community literacy projects that become the subjects of academic studies are short-term and designed to be so. Similarly, in many university courses that both of us have taught or the teaching artist work that constituted Gemma's early career, we pass in and out of the lives of students, they in and out of ours. As we develop longer-term relationships with current and former participants in the Narratio Fellowship, we are pushed to consider Fabian's (2002) idea of the *denial of coevalness*, the notion that anthropological (and other academic) studies often place research participants, explicitly or implicitly, in a different time, as if the researcher's understanding as a nominal observer is more temporally advanced (thus more sophisticated) than that of the participants. Considering this in our own circumstances, we think there is a structural expectation that university-based affiliations and relationships be long-term while community-based relationships are short-term, often limited to the duration of data collection, creative projects, courses, or internships. Similarly, in the context of community-engaged projects, it is the university-affiliated researchers, teachers, students, and staff who are expected to have fluidity of movement through one space or time and another, which defaults to a notion of the community and its members as fixed in both space and time. The program design of the fellowship, however, means that not only we but also the fellows move with some fluidity between spaces labelled "community" and "university." Per Fabian (2002), "for human communication to occur, coevalness has to be *created*. Communication is, ultimately, about creating shared time" (p. 30–31). The shared time of the Narratio Fellowship has become longitudinal and thus shared in a way that we couldn't imagine when we construed "community" connections as an escape from our "university" lives or when we were constructing short-term projects with the Center's students.

Conclusion

Cocreation – of a program, an event, an experience – *is* shared Time. The ideals of "community literacy" strive toward this shared Time but are frequently hampered by the essentializing of "the community" as inherently separate from "the academy" and the hegemonic obfuscation of the academy's multiple potential meanings. You cannot share Time with another without reckoning with where you are and where you believe yourself to be, particularly as part of a powerful institution; for us, a wealthy university in an impoverished city. The "positionality statement" so touted in research with a justice orientation is not simply a checklist – I'm white, I'm queer, I'm abled – but an opportunity to understand and *use* the ways we are situated in the communities of writing practice we wish to form, join, and support in university and community contexts. As we've discovered through this co/autoethnographic exercise, ongoing reflexion on positionality also attunes participants in community literacy projects to all the ways in which universities and communities are co- and continually reconstituted through movements of people, texts, ideas, and relationships across shared space and Time.

References

Badr, A. (2020). *While the earth sleeps we travel*. Andrews McMeel.

Coia, L., & Taylor, M. (2009). Co/autoethnography: Exploring our teaching selves collaboratively. In L. Fitzgerald, M. Heston, & D. Tidwell (Eds.), *Research methods for the self-study of practice*. (Vol. 9). Springer, Springer Science & Business Media.

Community Literacy Journal. (n.d.). *Journal home page*. Digital Commons. https://digitalcommons.fiu.edu/communityliteracy/; https://doi.org/10.1007/978-1-4020-9514-6_1

Cooper-Novack, G. (2019, August 26). Personal communication.

Cooper-Novack, G. (2019, August 27). Personal communication.

Doggart, J., Tedrowe, M., & Vieira, K. (2007). Minding the gap: Realizing our ideal community writing center. *Community Literacy Journal, 1*(2), 71–80. https://doi.org/10.25148/CLJ.1.2.009519

Duncan, M. (2004). Autoethnography: Critical appreciation of an emerging art. *International Journal of Qualitative Methods, 3*(4), 28–39.

Fabian, J. (2002). *Time and the other: How anthropology makes its object.* Columbia University Press.

Flower, L. (2008). *Community literacy and the rhetoric of public engagement.* Southern Illinois University Press.

Freire, P. (1973). *Pedagogy of the oppressed.* Seabury Press.

Hansen, F. B. (2009). Building the bridge between home and school: One rural school's steps to interrogate and celebrate multiple literacies. *Community Literacy Journal, 4*(2), 33–45. https://doi.org/10.25148/CLJ.4.2.009440

Holman Jones, S. (2016). Living bodies of thought: The "critical" in critical autoethnography. *Qualitative Inquiry, 22*(4), 228–237. https://doi.org/10.1177/1077800415622509

Martinez, A. (2014). A plea for critical race theory counterstory: Stock story versus counterstory dialogues concerning Alejandra's "fit" in the academy. *Composition Studies, 42*(2), 33–55.

Mutnick, D. (2018). Pathways to freedom: From the Archives to the street. *College Composition and Communication, 69*(3), 374–401.

Nordquist, B. (2019, August 30). Personal Communication.

Nordquist, B. (2021, August 26). Personal Communication.

Parks, S. (2014). Sinners welcome: The limits of rhetorical agency. *College English, 76*(6), 506.

Peck, W. C., Flower, L., & Higgins, L. (1995). Community literacy. *College Composition and Communication, 46*(2), 199–222. https://doi.org/10.2307/358428

Taylor, M., Klein, E. J., & Abrams, L. (2014). Tensions of reimagining our roles as teacher educators in a third space: Revisiting a co/autoethnography through a faculty lens. *Studying Teacher Education, 10*(1), 3–19. https://doi.org/10.1080/17425964.2013.866549

Wall, S. (2006). An autoethnography on learning about autoethnography. *International Journal of Qualitative Methods, 5*(2), 146–160. https://doi.org/10.1177/160940690600500205

Part Two

Setting the Stage for Program Design

Chapter 5

The Community Literacy Audit

Evaluating Community Literacy Needs to
Ensure Equitable Literacy Education

Ann M. Bennett

Author Note

Ann M. Bennett: https://orcid.org/0000-0001-6637-9824

Introduction

Until the development of culturally relevant pedagogy (Ladson-Billings, 1995, 2006, 2014), the curriculum in American schooling largely followed a standardized approach (Au, 2007; Berliner, 2011). In response, economically, culturally, and linguistically (ECLM) marginalized communities developed literacy initiatives, programs, and, in some instances, alternative schools to confront the colonization of literacy in education (Bennett, 2015). In order to better address the specific needs within the community, a community literacy audit, formal or informal, usually took place prior to the development of the response. These audits informed the communities of what resources were available and what programs already existed. This allowed the communities to develop the response that worked best for their community needs without placing excessive constraints on the community itself. Using a community literacy audit allows communities to evaluate current and needed resources and programs to ensure the success of the community's children.

Community Literacy

Before conducting a community literacy audit, it is essential to understand how community literacy might be defined. For the purpose of this chapter, community and culture are strongly interrelated in that community represents a social group with shared experiences, meanings, and language, or culture (Barker, 2012; Hall, 1986). Literacy is understood to be a social practice under the socio-cultural approach to literacy. This approach seeks to understand literacy as embedded within social, cultural, political, economic, and historical practices (Bourdieu, 1977; Gee, 1996; Lankshear & Knobel, 2007). In other words, no text can exist outside of the context in which it was created, and an individual cannot ascribe meaning to a text without considering their own contexts. Sociocultural literacy is contrasted with cognitive literacy or the idea that reading is a psychological process wherein individuals use tools and skills to give meaning to an arrangement of letters and words on a page or screen. The process of decoding print does allow one to determine what are the symbols on the page or screen. However, socially constructed agreements give meaning to those symbols (Gee, 1996; Lankshear & Knobel, 2007). Thus, community literacy, then, can be defined as social, cultural, political, economic, and historical literacy practices that are specific to a particular social group (Cairney & Ruge, 1998) with shared experiences, meanings, and language.

The Community Literacy Audit

A community literacy audit could be defined as a focused needs assessment within the field of program evaluation. Program evaluation is a form of applied research that "using valid and reliable research methods . . . examines the processes or outcomes of an organization that exists to fulfill some social purpose" (Grinnell & Unrau, 2010, p. 571). More specifically, a needs assessment seeks to identify "unmet needs, gaps in services, or problems that have not been previously recognized" (Royse et al., 2010, p. 55). In turn, a community literacy audit might best be defined as an assessment of unmet needs regarding literacy and an examination of the processes and programs available within the community to fulfill these unmet needs.

Step 1. Clearly understand:
  1) The purpose of the needs assessment
  2) The level of assessment: Statewide, community, neighborhood
  3) What stakeholders to include: Clients or potential clients, program staff, key community leaders, state officials, etc.
  4) Budget and available resources
  5) Time allotted for the project
Step 2. Identify the specific information you need to acquire.
Step 3. Determine whether the information already exists or can be obtained with your resources.
Step 4. Design the methodology and instrumentation (if necessary).
Step 5. Collect and analyze the data.
Step 6. Prepare the report.
Step 7. Disseminate preliminary results to key stakeholders to obtain their feedback.
Step 8. Formally disseminate results.

Figure 5.1 **Steps in Needs Assessment**

Royse et al. (2010) outline eight steps that they believe are required to conduct a needs assessment (See Figure 5.1).

As a community literacy audit should be able to be conducted by trained evaluators, educators, or community members, some modification to the steps proposed by Royse et al. (2010) are needed. First, the purpose of a community literacy audit is already understood to be clearly defined based on the previously stated definition as an assessment of unmet needs regarding literacy and an examination of the processes and programs available within the community to fulfill these unmet needs. Within this purpose statement, we are also given the level of assessment (community) and potential stakeholders (those engaged in literacy). Furthermore, in order to ensure equitable access, we also want to ensure that a community literacy audit can be undertaken at little to no cost. Similarly, steps four through eight are directly related to the fact that a needs assessment exists within the field of program evaluation as a form of applied research. Although we seek to have a rigorous methodology within a community literacy audit, we should also aim for applied research that is able to be conducted by any community member. With this in mind, Figure 5.2 shows the steps of a community literacy audit.

Step 1. Identify:
  1) The community with whom the audit will be conducted
  2) The members of the community engaged in literacy on which the audit will focus,
  3) Budget and resources (if available), and
  4) Time allotted for the project
Step 2. Identify the specific information you need to determine the unmet literacy needs of the community.
Step 3. Determine whether the information already exists or can be obtained with your resources.
Step 4. Determine existing processes and programs available within the community that may already be attempting to or would like to address unmet literacy needs.
Step 5. If available, design data collection methods that will contribute to information gathering and analyze the data.
Step 6. Disseminate preliminary results to community to obtain their feedback.
Step 7. Disseminate final results to the community.

Figure 5.2 Steps in a Community Literacy Audit

The Community Literacy Audit in Practice

As stated previously, in practice, a community literacy audit should be able to be conducted by trained evaluators, educators, or community members with little to no budget available. To illustrate this, a community literacy audit utilizing the steps outlined in this chapter is discussed. This community literacy audit was conducted with Dove Community Center[1] (DCC), a not-for-profit center located in an impoverished, urban, and predominantly Black community in a midsized city in the Southeastern United States. The center's primary goal is to provide for the educational needs of the community's children. Moreover, the center also has a secondary goal of providing for the emotional, spiritual, and social needs of both the children and their families. The DCC achieves its educational goals through tutoring and supplemental instruction in reading and mathematics for students in grades K-8. During the school year, children in the community spend approximately two hours weekly at the center as part of an afterschool program. Additionally, the DCC has a summer program that serves as an academic and summer day camp that provides all the components of the afterschool program plus field trips and other enrichment activities. The primary goals of the summer program are to ensure the children return to school in the fall having retained academic knowledge from the previous school year, as well as expanding the children's respect and knowledge of the community outside of their own everyday lived experiences (Bennett, 2015).

Step 1. Identify.

A community literacy audit of the DCC began in the summer of 2014. The audit was conducted with assistance from the children who attended the center, their parents, the staff of the center, and the community in which the center was located. The audit focused specifically on the literacy needs of the K-8 students who attended the center for both the afterschool program and the summer program. Outside of office-related materials and equipment provided to me by the center, the budget for this audit was zero. I conducted this audit as a volunteer within my community. It should be noted, however, that the center later became the focus of a research project. The timeline for the audit was the nine weeks over which the summer program took place.

Step 2. Identify the Specific Information You Need to Determine the Unmet Literacy Needs of the Community.

In order to determine the literacy needs of the children at the DCC, I needed to know four things. First, I needed to confirm the children's baseline level of literacy as established by "traditional" schooling standards. Although the center knew that the children were not receiving the literacy education that they needed within their local schools, gathering data on the perceived literacy knowledge of the children was a starting point on which the center could build. Second, I needed to evaluate the literacy education that was currently being provided to the children through the afterschool and summer program. This would allow me to conclude how the children's literacy needs were currently being supplemented by the DCC and if an expanded or redesigned program was necessary. Third, I had to conduct a search of existing programs and resources that could partner or collaborate with the DCC in order to expand program offerings and meet identified needs. Finally, I had to talk with children, parents, and staff to understand their perspectives on the literacy needs of the children.

Step 3. Determine Whether the Information Already Exists or Can Be Obtained with Your Resources.

As part of enrollment at the DCC, the children and parents were required to submit the progress reports and report cards given to them by their schools.

Progress reports were provided every 9 weeks, and report cards were released every 18 weeks. These progress reports and report cards assisted in establishing a baseline level of literacy for each child in both the afterschool and summer programs. The documents revealed that many of the children were below grade level in reading. The local school system used Lexile levels to evaluate reading ability. For many of the children in the program, their current Lexile level was developmentally inappropriate. Thus, this data source revealed that, based on schooled definitions of reading, the children in the program required supplemental instruction to meet school standards.

At the time of this audit, the DCC did not possess a way to measure the literacy levels of the children before and after receiving instruction in its supplemental programs. In turn, I needed to find a reliable and valid method to assess the reading levels of the children. This assessment also needed to be open access or freely available to ensure that a new budget would not be needed. After an exhaustive search, it was decided that the Qualitative Reading Inventory-5 (QRI-5; Leslie & Caldwell, 2010) would be used to assess reading for the first through seventh graders. Only one eighth grader attended the DCC that particular summer, and he moved into a counselor position later in the program, so eighth grade was not included. Moreover, although there is an assessment that is cheaply available for kindergartners, one of the limitations of this audit was that there was only one individual (myself) available to conduct the audit. Hence, administering a kindergarten literacy assessment in addition to the QRI exceeded the time available.

The QRI revealed that many of the children were close to the reading level of their grade, which contrasted with some of the Lexile level data from their schools. Using Harris-Jacobson Readability Levels found in the QRI, which indicate both grade level and month in school (e.g., 4.5), the children were entering their new grade levels slightly behind. For example, children who would be entering fourth grade at the end of the summer had reading levels ranging from 2.7 to 3.4 at the beginning of the summer program. At the end of the summer program, the entering fourth graders experienced tremendous improvement in their reading levels, which ranged from 3.9 to 4.6. This data demonstrated that the summer program was meeting the needs of the children.

Additional resources available for this audit were the parents of the children and the staff at the center. Both of these groups possessed intimate knowledge regarding the education that the children were receiving in both in- and out-of-school contexts. Furthermore, the parents and staff could speak to any linguistic or cultural concerns they had regarding the program and school's curriculum. More information is provided on this resource in Step 5.

Step 4. Determine Existing Processes and Programs Available Within the Community That May Already Be Attempting to or Would Like to Address Unmet Literacy Needs.

Outside of the programming provided by the DCC, I investigated other literacy programs in the area that might be interested in collaborating. This required a simple internet search and visiting with directors of other programs. Ultimately, this search led to the local library. Each summer, the library had a summer reading challenge wherein children documented all the books that they read over the summer and received prizes from the library at the end of July. The intent of this program was to stem summer reading loss (Allington & McGill-Franzen, 2003), which was in alignment with the goals of the DCC's summer program. One of the hurdles to participation in the library's program was that the program required parents to document their child's reading and submit a signed form by a specific deadline. Many of the parents were unaware of this program's existence and, due to family and work situations, were unable to document their child's reading. After speaking with the director of the library's program, the DCC was able to serve as the "individual" responsible for documenting the children's reading and as the signatory. All children in the DCC's summer program participated in the library's reading program, and all children met the summer reading goals established by the library and received rewards at the end of the summer. This program ensured that the children had access to books and a purpose for reading during the summer months (Allington & McGill-Franzen, 2003), which was an activity not undertaken by the local schools.

An additional resource was also found through an existing Children's Defense Fund Freedom Schools (CDFFS) program. One of the staff members of the DCC, as well as myself, had prior experience with a CDFFS program in the area. Given that the community with whom the center worked reflected the same communities with whom the CDFFS works, an examination of the CDFFS processes and curriculum occurred in order to make the programming of the DCC more culturally relevant to the children (Children's Defense Fund, 2021). Afro-centric and young adult books were incorporated into the DCC's programming to provide the children with authors and protagonists who looked like them and possessed similar life experiences (Children's Defense Fund, 2021; Jackson & Boutte, 2009). This also contributed to the children learning about the history of their ancestors that was not commonly taught in schools (Children's Defense Fund, 2021; Jackson & Boutte, 2009). For example, *Copper Sun*, a Coretta Scott King Award-winning historical fiction novel that tells the story of Amari, a young African girl who was taken from her village and sold into slavery (Draper, 2008), became a favorite book of many of the middle school girls in the program.

Step 5. If Available, Design Data Collection Methods That Will Contribute to Information Gathering and Analyze the Data.

In this audit, informal data collection did occur. I met with children, parents, and staff members separately for a conversational interview regarding the DCC and its supplemental programs. Through these conversations, I was able to determine that the parents were disappointed in the literacy education that was being provided to their children in local schools. Some of the books that the children read at home were not considered to be reading in school (for the in/out-of-school reading disconnect, see Groenke et al., 2012a, 2012b). Although there were some books in their schools that the children enjoyed reading, the books provided at home, from the library, and at the DCC were the source of the children's pleasure reading.

Though I could not change the local schools' opinions on the books, I could learn from the children exactly what kinds of books they liked to read. From the conversations with the children, funny books, mysteries, and books related to pop culture were added to the DCC library. This ensured that there was always a book available that the children would enjoy. For instance, the *Hank Zipzer* series (Winkler, 2003) was a humorous series that the elementary school boys enjoyed.

In conversations with the staff members, they revealed that they were unsure of whether they were providing proper literacy instruction to the children. In response to this concern, I, with the help of a few colleagues, located or created reading guides for many of the books found in the DCC's library in order to help the staff members navigate discussions around the books to improve the children's reading comprehension. Training sessions were held that helped the staff navigate reading instruction, including sessions on phonemic awareness, building fluency, and comprehension. For situations in which the staff member did not feel comfortable working with a child due to a diagnosed learning or reading disability, I gathered volunteers from the local university to come to the center weekly to work one-on-one with the children throughout the summer.

Step 6. Disseminate Preliminary Results to Community to Obtain Their Feedback.

The in-progress results of this audit were shared with the director and staff members of the DCC. This allowed for immediate additions or changes to the

DCC's programs that could result in better meeting the literacy needs of the children. This also meant that the director and staff could directly report when something was not working, such as the requests for additional training and assistance in working with specific children. In-progress results of the audit were shared with parents when possible. It did become difficult to meet with all the parents as the summer progressed due to work schedules. However, I made time to meet with parents when they picked up their children at the end of the day. These often two-minute conversations let the parents know that the DCC tried one of their suggestions or that their child experienced a reading success that day due to changes being implemented based on the audit. Maintaining communication with the parents was one of the most important aspects of this audit. It was the parents who let us know what was not working, what was needed, and what their children did or did not like. They knew what their children's needs were and how *they* would like to see those needs fulfilled.

Step 7. Disseminate Final Results to the Community.

The results were first shared with the Board of Directors of the DCC. This decision was made due to their many connections and networks both inside and outside of the community. Utilizing the results of this audit, board members were able to seek out additional funding and donations to support the work of the DCC. Additionally, the executive director eventually included the audit as part of a United Way grant application, which provided the center with over $400,000 in funding for three years. Finally, the data was also shared with the children and parents, but, as the parents received in-progress reports, the focus of this sharing was on the children. As every child who participated in the QRI-5 administration experienced reading gains, it was important to share this information with them to motivate them to continue the work that they had been doing at the DCC both in and outside of school.

Conclusion

The DCC, like many ECLM communities, undertook the community literacy audit as a response to the unmet needs of the community's children. Educators should consider honoring the work of these communities and employing their own formalized community literacy audit. An important note to make here is that educators should be conducting these audits *with* the community. Similar to the concerns of Ladson-Billings (2006) regarding culturally relevant teaching, the goal of the community literacy audit is not to see the "teacher as savior and charismatic maverick without exploring the complexities of teaching and nuanced intellectual work that undergirds pedagogical practices" (p. 29). Educators should not conduct a community literacy audit with the intent of "reaching out" to a community about which they may know nothing or with whom they have never previously interacted. The community literacy audit must start with the community (Step 1. Identify: The community with whom the audit will be conducted). Educators should also not be the leading voice of the community literacy audit. Although an educator can speak to the formal literacy needs of the children in the community, they might not be able to speak to the children's linguistic and cultural needs that are connected to literacy.

These caveats are not intended to deter educators from employing a community literacy audit. However, they are intended to ensure that ECLM communities are brought into the discussion around the curriculum within "traditional" schooling in the United States. ECLM communities should not be subjected to the curriculum. Instead, they should be the co-authors and co-designers of the curriculum.

Note

1. Pseudonym.

References

Allington, R. L., & McGill-Franzen, A. (2003). The impact of summer setback on the reading achievement gap. *Phi Delta Kappan, 85*(1), 68–75. https://doi.org/10.1177/003172170308500119

Au, W. (2007). High-stakes testing and curricular control: A qualitative metasynthesis. *Educational Researcher, 36*(5), 258–267. https://doi.org/10.3102/0013189X07306523

Barker, C. (2012). *Cultural studies: Theory and practice* (4th ed.). Sage.

Bennett, A. M. (2015). *Deficit discourse, literate lives: Success narratives of Black youth* (Publication No. 3493) [Doctoral dissertation, The University of Tennessee Knoxville]. Tennessee Research and Creative Exchange.

Berliner, D. (2011). Rational responses to high stakes testing: The case of curriculum narrowing and the harm that follows. *Cambridge Journal of Education, 41*(3), 287–302. https://doi.org/10.1080/0305764X.2011.607151

Bourdieu, P. (1977). Cultural reproduction and social reproduction. In J. Karabel & A. H. Halsey (Eds.), *Power and ideology in education* (pp. 487–511). Oxford University Press.

Cairney, T., & Ruge, J. (1998). *Community literacy practices and schooling: Towards effective support for students.* Canberra Department of Employment, Education, Training and Youth Affairs.

Children's Defense Fund. (2021). CDF freedom schools. Children's Defense Fund. www.childrensdefense.org/programs/cdf-freedom-schools/.

Draper, S. M. (2008). *Copper sun.* Simon and Schuster.

Gee, J. P. (1996). *Social linguistics and literacies: Ideology in discourses* (2nd ed.). Routledge.

Grinnell, Jr., R.M., & Unrau, Y.A. (2010). *Social work research and evaluation: Foundations of evidence-based practice* (9th ed.). Oxford University Press.

Groenke, S. L., Bennett, A., & Hill, S. (2012a). Not 'if,' but 'why' and 'how': What already-motivated black female readers can teach us about adolescent literacy instruction. In E. Ortlieb & R. Bowden (Eds.), *Educational research & innovations: 2012 Consortium for Educational Development, Evaluation and Research (CEDER) yearbook* (pp. 77–100). CEDER, Texas A&M University.

Groenke, S. L., Bennett, A., & Hill, S. (2012b). Reading contradictions: An exploration of reader self-concept, value, and the voluntary, out-of-school reading experiences of black middle school adolescents. In P. Dunston & S. Fullerton (Eds.), *61st yearbook of the Literacy Research Association* (pp. 257–269). Literacy Research Association, Inc.

Hall, S. (1986). Gramsci's relevance for the study of race and ethnicity. *Journal of Communication Inquiry, 10*(5), 5–27. https://doi.org/10.1177/019685998601000202

Jackson, T. O., & Boutte, G. S. (2009). Liberation literature: Positive cultural messages in children's and young adult literature at Freedom Schools. *Language Arts, 87,* 108–116.

Ladson-Billings, G. (1995). Toward a theory of culturally relevant pedagogy. *American Educational Research Journal, 32*(3), 465–491. https://doi.org/10.3102/00028312032003465

Ladson-Billings, G. (2006). "Yes, but how do we do it?": Practicing culturally relevant pedagogy. In J. Landsman & C. W. Lewis (Eds.), *White teachers/diverse classrooms: A guide to building inclusive schools, promoting high expectations, and eliminating racism* (pp. 29–42). Stylus. https://doi.org/10.1080/00131940701634718

Ladson-Billings, G. (2014). Culturally relevant pedagogy 2.0: Aka the remix. *Harvard Educational Review, 84*(1), 74–84. https://doi.org/10.17763/haer.84.1.p2rj131485484751

Lankshear, C., & Knobel, M. (2007). Sampling "the new" in new literacies. In M. Knobel & C. Lankshear (Eds.), *A new literacies sampler* (pp. 1–24). Peter Lang.

Leslie, L., & Caldwell, J. S. (2010). *Qualitative reading inventory-5*. Allyn and Bacon.

Royse, D. D., Thyer, B. A., & Padgett, D. (2010). *Program evaluation: An introduction*. Wadsworth Cengage Learning.

Winkler, H. (2003). *Hank Zipzer*. Grosset and Dunlap.

Chapter 6

Conducting a Community Literacy Audit

Tara Wilson

Author Note

Tara Wilson: https://orcid.org/0000-0002-5463-8478

Community Literacy

The terms *family*, *emergent*, and *digital* are common in the world of literacy education, but what about community literacy? Community literacy, a complex undertaking, is based on an understanding that improving literacy is everyone's responsibility. Often overlooked, community literacy deserves attention. Community literacy encompasses the growth of literacy for a group of people or any individual separate from the formal education system. Community literacy is a collective approach where learning transpires in the context of home and community (Decoda Literacy Solutions, 2019). Literacy skills of an entire family strengthen when involved in community-based literacy programs (Kim & Byington, 2016).

Every aspect of a community plays an important role in literacy, from businesses to service providers and municipal governments to stay at home parents.

All these entities can come together to address literacy concerns, establish priorities, and set plans in motion to generate positive change. Part of these plans includes creating programs. The programs can consist of one-time events, ongoing classes, workshops, and seminars that disseminate information and increase awareness on the importance of literacy.

In a study conducted by Kim and Byington (2016), little to no correlation was found between the duration of program exposure and differences in program effects. However, the researchers do believe that longer-running programs offer individuals more chances to engage in various types of literacy activities, whereas shorter programs can encourage more regular participation. These programs can vary based on who they serve (i.e., early childhood, adults, English Language Learners) and the theoretical framework that serves as the foundation for practice.

Theoretical Framework

Social learning theories create a framework for supporting community literacy. Several different social learning theories exist, but they all focus on the important role of social interaction in learning. When considering literacy, social learning theories emphasize the importance of social influences and social interaction. For the purposes of this chapter, three social learning theories will briefly be discussed: sociolinguistic theory (Bernstein, 1972), socio-cultural theory (Bronfenbrenner, 1979), and social constructivism (Vygotsky, 1978, 1986).

Sociolinguistic Theory

Bernstein's (1972) theory focuses on the language aspect of social interactions. Tracey and Morrow (2017) break down sociolinguistics into two palpable, distinctive parts, social and linguistic. Socially, reading establishes, creates structure, and maintains relationships among people. Linguistically, reading allows intentions and meanings to be communicated between people involved in a reading event (author and reader, any pairing of people involved in text). In a seminal study, Halliday (1973) posited that people learn to read in order to reach their goals associated with basic life functioning. To sum up sociolinguistic theory, Tracey and Morrow (2017) state:

> Sociolinguistics emphasizes that language is learned as a result of people's social interactions with each other and, therefore, varying language patterns are perpetuated with educational and social class differences. These

varying patterns of social and language interactions subsequently lead to differences in literacy abilities.

(p. 161–162)

Socio-Cultural Theory

Similar to Sociolinguistics, socio-cultural theory highlights learning's social aspect. However, socio-cultural theory focuses more on the broader aspect of culture. Three key researchers, Bronfenbrenner (1979), Au (1997), and Moll (1994) elaborate on this theory. Bronfenbrenner was one of the first to suggest that "concentric levels of influence affect children's development" (Tracey & Morrow, 2017, p. 163). Au (1997) studied the relationship between reading and the socio-cultural theory. Her research dissected the links among historical conditions, current contexts, and psychological functioning (both inter and intra). Moll's (1994) seminal research coined the term *funds of knowledge*. His studies centered on the application of socio-cultural theory to reading. Moll discovered that a child's funds of knowledge – sources of knowledge central to a child's home and community – influence one's reading. The previously mentioned researchers are considered socio-cultural because they stress the role of social and cultural influence on reading (Tracey & Morrow, 2017).

Social Constructivism

Lev Vygotsky (1978), probably the most famous learning theorist, created the social constructivism theory. This theory is comprised of two major ideas. First, children learn from social interactions. Second, a child's development relies on his or her interactions with a sign system. Sign systems include listening, speaking, the alphabet, words, and writing, and these are dependent on a culture's oral and printed language. Vygotsky claimed that the mastery of language, as evidenced by mastery of sign systems, affects a child's learning the most. He contemplated that the manipulation and use of these signs provide children with the proverbial tools necessary to think about and respond to their world. Further, Vygotsky believed that, by interacting with others, learning occurs.

Types of Programs

A community literacy program may have a specific mission or may have more than one service function. Three primary orientations include: Early childhood programs, adult programs, and English Language Learner programs.

Early Childhood Programs

Child development researchers all agree that early childhood lays the foundation of education. Children who develop well learn well. Therefore, supporting a child's development and learning is essential. A great need exists for several contexts supporting a child's development. Community, one of those contexts, is connected to early literacy and family literacy achievement. Community literacy programs can strengthen early literacy and language development through family participation in literacy activities (Comer & Ben-Avie, 2010). As theorized by Vygotsky and his social constructivism theory, children learn best through interactions. Early childhood-based community programs allow for children to interact with others and opportunities to enhance their receptive, oral, reading, and writing vocabularies. Thus, community-based literacy programs serve as a crucial jump-start for family engagement with early literacy and language at home.

Adult Programs

Kim and Byington (2016) posit that "community-based literacy programs have been shown to improve the basic skills of participating adults" (p. 2). In these programs, adults communicate with others similar to themselves. This coincides with Bernstein's sociolinguistic theory, that language is enhanced by people's social interactions with one another. The National Council for Adult Learning (2015) estimates that low literacy rates cost the United States of America at least $225 billion each year in nonproductivity in the workforce, crime, and loss of tax revenue (due to unemployment). Obstacles faced by adults with low literacy skills often create barriers to traditional educational settings, i.e., the inability to read, limited English proficiency, and difficulty with technology.

Parents with low literacy skills can hinder their child's literacy skills. According to ProLiteracy (n.d.), children of parents with limited literacy have a 72% chance of reading below grade level. As parents build their own skills, they lead the way for their children. When adults are provided literacy skills, they are able to contribute even more to their community.

English Language Learner (ELL) Programs

ELL community programs exist in different forms, i.e., English classes, English tutoring, and English conversation circles. According to Harrington (2012),

ELL programs offer non-native speakers opportunities to successfully assimilate into their community. Community ELL programs serve as a guiding light toward democracy, access, and citizenship.

When planning to establish a community ELL program, Harrington (2012) makes two recommendations: Study the demographics of the community and involve nonnative speakers. By knowing the demographics of the community (specifically information on nonnative English speakers), the right populations can better be served. Furthermore, including nonnative English speakers in the program's planning and evaluation processes allow for better insight into the needs of the population and more support.

Community Audit Procedure

How do people know what literacy programs, if any, exist in their community? Doing a Google search is a popular method, but to get a true feel of the community one should do a community audit. By conducting a community audit, one can discover what is available in the community as well as the design and practice lessons respective programs have developed over the years of existence. A community audit, as defined by McGuirt et al. (2011), is "a qualitative and quantitative research technique in which researchers drive through a community to observe its physical and social attributes, primarily through windshield tours and ground truthing" (p. 1). McGuirt et al. (2011) explain that ground truthing is a type of verification process in which data are gathered via direct observation to corroborate what has been gleaned from secondary sources. The author of this chapter drove around her community, with the guidance of Google, to pinpoint literacy programs. At each location, she was able to speak with the director of the program. Using a social learning lens, she investigated each program.

Following are descriptions of each program identified in this community audit. It should be noted that some of the program types in McGuirt's particular community were excluded. The programs described in this chapter were included because they were aligned with a social learning theory and fell into one of the following types: Early childhood, adult, or ELL. The town, type, and theory are listed along with the name of each program. Each description also presents the program's historical context as it is covered through the classifications of past, present, and future.

An Example of a Community Focused on Literacy

When people think of west Texas, the first thought that often comes to mind is liquid gold, oil. West Texas is often considered the Saudi Arabia of North America. In April 2018, west Texas became the largest oil field in the world, producing 4.2 million barrels per day (U.S. Energy Information Administration, 2018). What most people do not know is that west Texas is also home to a number of noteworthy community literacy programs. These programs serve various groups of people ranging from early childhood to the elderly or, in west Texas terms, "The cradle to grave pipeline."

Programs

Laura Bush Literacy Program (Midland; Early Childhood; Social Constructivism)

Past

The Laura Bush Literacy Program began in 2010. This program was developed as a way to honor both Bush first ladies, Barbara and Laura, and their promotion of literacy. In the beginning, the Laura Bush Literacy Program consisted of a few bookshelves housed across the street from George W. Bush's childhood home in Midland, Texas. Members of the community donated various levels of books. Parents or guardians stopped by the bookshelves to choose a free book to take home. One year later, in the fall of 2011, the Laura Bush Literacy Program expanded to include the Third Thursday Reading Program.

The third Thursday of every month, for an hour, children enjoy listening to books being read aloud by the staff of the George W. Bush Childhood home. Often, a special guest will read. This free event reaches capacity every month (30 children). The children also receive a snack and go home with a free copy of the month's featured book.

Present

In the Spring of 2019, the Laura Bush Literacy Program expanded to include a daytime reading program. Older students in the West Texas Homeschool Co-Op read to the younger children in the Co-Op. This program runs through the months when public schools are in session.

Future

Since inception, the staff at the George W. Bush childhood home have given away over 10,000 books to children of all ages, incomes, and demographics. The staff's goal is to expand the program through the use of larger facilities. Their current space only accommodates 30 children including their parents or guardians. The staff must turn families away each month due to the size limitation. They actively seek the use of a nearby facility, which will allow for the use of larger spaces so that more children can attend. Long term plans include a possible expansion of the current facility.

Bookworms (Odessa; Early Childhood; Social Constructivism)

Past

The Bookworms Literacy Program started in a single kindergarten classroom. The teacher purchased books for her students to address a serious need she discovered – the students did not have books at home to read. The teacher approached the Education Foundation for help with funding when other grade level teachers on her campus expressed interest in growing the program to their classrooms.

Present

What started in one classroom with 20 students is now in place at every Ector County Independent School District elementary campus, impacting thousands of students. During the 2019–2020 school year, the program impacted approximately 7,000 students monthly in grades pre-kindergarten, kindergarten, and first grade. Each month, students listen to a story read aloud by a community member and receive a copy of the book to take home. They keep the book in an effort to promote at-home family reading. Members of the community volunteer their time at an assigned campus to read once a month.

Future

Bookworms plans to continue for as long as funds allow. Gracious community partners support this program through monetary donations. Bookworm's dream is that this program will not only inspire their youngest students to read but also assist the district's teachers in providing a quality education to their students.

Club Read (United Way; Early Childhood; Social Constructivism)

Past

Since 2013, United Way of Midland has conducted Club Read. This program's main goal is to prevent students from decreasing their reading abilities over the summer months. Some call this phenomenon "the summer slide." The United Way of Midland had been partnering with one other organization to offer Club Read. In the beginning, this program served 72 students from low socio-economic homes. In the inaugural summer of Club Read, participants read for a total of 65,522 minutes, 912 minutes per student. The United Way utilizes the system Track-It to monitor the progress of each participant. In addition to reading, students also participated in creative activities and exercises to keep them engaged and make reading come alive. At the beginning and end of the first summer, celebrations occurred to help kickoff and conclude the program. All students who completed the program received five books and a medal for completing the program.

Present

The United Way of Midland collaborates with multiple partners for their Club Read program. These partners include Case de Amigos, Boys and Girls Club of the Permian Basin, Midland Fair Havens, and Unlock Ministries Fun Academy. Club Read is a specialized reading program where students not only read numerous books but also participate in group discussions, hands-on activities, and daily writing in reading journals. Club Read, along with other programs, has found these types of activities to greatly increase students' reading comprehension abilities. Over 2,000 books are ordered before the start of every summer and then delivered to each of the programs' 346 participants. The participants read for an average of 11.4 hours, with a total read time of 3,706 hours.

Future

The United Way of Midland plans to strengthen their fundraising efforts to support Club Read. The program costs $8,717 to run effectively. That amount breaks down to $25.19 per student. With successful fundraising efforts, the United Way of Midland will be able to continue the Club Read program for summers to come. They also plan on collaborating with more agencies.

Dog Tales (Midland; Early Childhood; Social Constructivism)

Past

In 2017, the Midland County library introduced dogs to library patrons. The therapy dog along with its handler visited the library on a weekly basis. The dog is specially trained and certified for working with individuals who need a little extra support. The public's interest in reading to the therapy dog quickly grew.

Present

The library offers four one-hour long sessions a week. During these sessions, children and adults read to a therapy dog. Reading to a dog increases a person's confidence in one's reading ability. Shy individuals are able to open up and enjoy reading to the dog. The handler of the dog is a retired schoolteacher and is also able to give support to the reader.

Future

The library plans on continuing the Dog Tales program. This program does not need any financial support; so as long as the therapy dog and handler keep coming for sessions, then the program will continue. The library would like to have more Dog Tale sessions, so they are looking for more therapy dogs and handlers.

Project Literacy (Midland and Odessa; Early Childhood; Sociolinguistic)

Past

The Project Literacy program is a community partnership that has existed since 2009. The program occurs once a year over a span of a few days. During that time, authors speak to the community and participants receive books, at no charge, to take home. Some notable authors that have participated in the program are Kate DiCamillo, Katherine Applegate, Nathan Hale, and Mac Barnett. The local paper is the sponsor of the program and helps to spread the word by distributing brochures on the Sunday before the program starts.

Present

The Project Literacy Program promotes literacy by delivering the gift of reading with free books and introducing the community to award-winning authors and illustrators. The event begins with a memorable moment. For example, in 2018, a stagecoach procession (sponsored by Wells Fargo Bank) went from a nearby elementary school to the library. During the event, authors visited local schools and autographed books at the library.

Future

Due to the history of Project Literacy, the library expects the program will continue for years to come. However, Project Literacy would like to obtain more sponsors in order to add to the program.

Permian Basin Adult Literacy Center (Midland; Adult; Socio-Cultural)

Past

The Permian Basin Adult Literacy Center (PBALC) received a one-year grant in 1984 from the Texas Education Agency. Since 1985, PBALC has been an independent organization funded by various grants, donations, and fundraising efforts. Following a capital campaign in 2000, PBALC moved from a donated office space at a local community college to their own facility, "Literacy House." Up until the spring of 2019, the program was called "Midland Need to Read"; it changed its name to better encompass the intent to expand the services into the surrounding counties.

Present

PBALC's mission is to develop the literacy skills of adults so they can achieve their goals, improve their lives, and influence their community. PBALC provides programs that address the foundational literacy skills adults need to fully participate in everyday life. The program's vision is that all adults will be able to accomplish their learning goals, regardless of language or literacy barriers. The three main services PBALC provides are English Language Learning (ELL) classes, adult basic reading and writing classes or one-to-one tutoring, and digital literacy classes. Computer classes at PBALC start with the basics of computer usage and build up to necessary 21st-century skills. They also offer citizenship, financial literacy, medical literacy, and workplace literacy instruction on an as-needed basis. PBALC's Café, an ELL conversation group, meets daily to provide ELLs opportunities to practice real-world interactions, such as talking to doctors or pharmacists, in a comfortable and informal environment.

Each student enrolled in PBALC works with a program director to create an individualized achievement plan, which includes leveled assessments, goal setting, and program placement. Students then participate in services through one-to-one tutoring, small group tutoring, small class instruction, and/or staff monitored educational software usage.

All PBALC instructors are volunteers trained in adult education techniques. These volunteer tutors are trained to come alongside developing adult readers and work with them toward functional literacy. The volunteers and staff witness their students who enter the program without the ability to read, write, or speak fluent English and then go on to pursue a GED, a college education, or a certification and then start a career.

Future

In order to expand their services, PBALC will continually seek funding. In 2018, PBALC served 191 students, and it has plans to increase that number each year. Due to the planned increase of students, PBALC needs a larger facility. This program is also working to expand services to satellite locations in Odessa, Andrews, Big Spring, and Monahans.

Casa de Amigos (Midland; Early Childhood, Adult, and ELL; Social Learning)

Past

A group of individuals at St. Mark's Methodist Church, who were concerned about the inequity in education, founded Casa de Amigos in 1964. Beginning with classes for preschool, kindergarten, general education development (GED), driver education, and tutoring, Casa de Amigos played a leading role in an effort to fill in the community's education gaps. Celebrating 55 years, Casa de Amigos' history of activities consists of providing comprehensive services in different program areas designed to empower people in the community to meet their individual and family's needs.

Present

Casa de Amigos is a multicultural neighborhood center located in southeast Midland, Texas. Their mission is "to improve the quality of life throughout the community by helping people help themselves." Its vision expresses "our clients will achieve their highest level of self-sufficiency in the community." Four main program areas make up Casa de Amigos' outreach: youth and adult education, senior services, social services, and health and wellness services.

Specific to literacy, Casa de Amigos offers after-school tutoring for children in second grade to eighth grade during the school year. It also holds a literacy camp with a focus on building leadership and character skills, content area literacy (math and science), and reading across four two-week sessions during the summer. Reading is the focus throughout. For adults, Casa de Amigos offers several programs: high school equivalency certificate (GED), English as a Second Language (ESL), financial literacy, volunteer income tax assistance (VITA), citizenship classes, and Take 2 Job Skills training. Casa de Amigo's main goal for the education programs is that all individuals in the community should reach their highest level of self-sufficiency and feel confident concerning their education.

Future

Casa de Amigos plans to continue evaluating their adult education programs. During evaluations, they hone in on individualized plans regarding clients' educational needs to make sure Casa de Amigos is assisting individuals and families with removing barriers to achieving goals. They also plan to strengthen collaborative efforts to address literacy with other programs (i.e. United Way, Boys and Girls Club, community colleges, and universities). Collaborative partnerships will help to ensure the community's literacy needs are being met. Casa de Amigos consistently seeks out dedicated people to volunteer to help their neighbors achieve educational goals.

Starting Programs in Your Community

Anyone can establish a community literacy program if there is determination and support. Through the conduct of a community audit, one learns much about the need for a program in a community and the processes for starting and maintaining a community literacy program. A review of the literature along with the knowledge gained in undertaking this audit provides a listing of key steps to be undertaken in developing a program.

Most individuals understand that support consists of financial means and dedicated volunteers. Still, before looking for monetary support and volunteers, some important steps need to be followed.

1. Know the community. Study the demographics. Find out what particular areas in literacy need to be addressed. Contact other non-profit organizations, talk to neighbors and city officials, post on community discussion

boards (for example nextdoor.com). Research other programs to find out about their history and what worked or did not work for them.

2. Develop a plan and create a budget. Write down what you are wanting to accomplish. It may be helpful to start with the big picture and work backwards. Make a list of smaller but specific tasks that need to be accomplished to reach the main goal. Go into the practicalities, such as equipment needed; number of employees; organization of volunteers, time, and space. Part of the plan should be to investigate liabilities and possible complications. When creating a budget, be practical, specific, and detailed.

3. Write a mission statement, including goals. The mission statement should include who (the organization/program), what (it intends to do), for whom (it intends to do it), and how (it intends to do it). Stay realistic and honest with expectations. See the resources section at the end of this text for more information on writing mission statements (p. 313).

4. Find people who believe in the mission of the program. If they believe, then they will be more likely to want to work with your program. These people might be paid or volunteers. Either way, they need to be like-minded, dedicated individuals. Schedule a convenient time to meet as often as necessary. Discuss time commitments.

5. Spread the news. Inform others of what you are doing. Social media is a popular way to get the word out about the program. Also promote the mission through press releases and flyers, and meet, again, with community members. This step can easily lead to grant opportunities, donation collection, and fundraising events.

6. Establish a bank account and meet with a tax accountant. The bank account is for receiving monies and paying debts. The tax accountant needs experience with filing IRS non-profit applications, in particular 501c3.

Now it is time to consider finances from grants, donations, and fundraising. A plethora of ways exist to raise money. Some of those ways include street collection (not advised though due to safety concerns); organized events (raffles, auctions, car wash); direct mail donations and crowdfunding websites (Kickstarter, DonorsChoose). Contacting local businesses is also an option but may need to offer some sort of incentive (advertising, tax write-off). Remember to not solely depend on one source for funding. Try a variety of sources and, have backup plans.

Developing a strategy will be an important part of collecting funds. Think about how money will be raised and the amount needed for any special event or project that is part of the literacy program. Share financial information with donors and the community. They should know exactly how their money is being spent. Apply for grants. Several organizations will award money to projects that they feel align with their beliefs. If a grant proposal goes unfunded, do not give up! Try submitting the proposal to a different agency.

Conclusion

In this chapter, you learned what community literacy is, theories in support of community literacy, an example of a community embracing literacy through various programs, and how to establish a literacy program. Community literacy, a collective approach, is an important aspect in increasing our society's literacy abilities. Every part of a community can become involved. Involvement can mean sponsoring a program, volunteering, promoting events, and donating money. The future depends on what we do now.

References

Au, K. H. (1997). A sociocultural model of reading instruction: The Kamehameha elementary education program. In S. A. Stahl & D. A. Hayes (Eds.), *Instructional models in reading* (pp. 181–202). Erlbaum.

Bernstein, B. (1972). Social class, language, and socialization. In P. Giglioli (Ed.), *Language and social context* (pp. 157–178). Penguin Books.

Bronfenbrenner, U. (1979). *The ecology of human development: Experiments by nature and design.* Harvard University Press.

Comer, J. A., & Ben-Avie, M. (2010). Promoting community on early childhood programs: A comparison of two programs. *Early Childhood Education Journal, 38,* 87–94. https://doi.org/10.1007/s10643-010-0391-3.

Decoda Literacy Solutions. (2019). *Community literacy planning guide: Working together for literacy.* British Columbia. https://decoda.ca

Halliday, M. K. (1973). *Learning how to mean: Explorations in the development of language.* Arnold.

Harrington, L. (2012). ELL programs in public libraries. *Public Libraries, 51*(5), 10–11.

Kim, Y., & Byington, T. (2016). Community based family literacy program: Comparing different durations and family characteristics. *Child Development Research,* 1–10. https://doi.org/10.1155/2016/4593167

McGuirt, J. T., Jilcott, S. B., Vu, M. B., & Keyserling, T. C. (2011). Conducting community audits to evaluate community resources for healthful lifestyle behaviors: An illustration from rural eastern North Carolina. *Preventing Chronic Disease, 8*(6), A149.

Moll, L. C. (1994). Literacy research in community and classrooms: A socio-cultural approach. In R. B. Ruddell, M. R. Ruddell, & H. Singer (Eds.), *Theoretical models and processes of reading* (4th ed., pp. 179–207). International Reading Association.

National Council for Adult Learning. (2015). *Adult education facts that demand priority attention.* National Council for Adult Learning. http://www.ncalamerica.org/AdultEDFacts&Figures1215.pdf

ProLiteracy. (n.d.). *U.S. adult literacy facts.* ProLiteracy. https://www.proliteracy.org/Portals/0/pdf/PL_AdultLitFacts_US_flyer.pdf

Tracey, D. H., & Morrow, L. M. (2017). *Lenses on reading: An introduction to theories and models* (3rd ed.). Guilford Press.

United States Energy Information Administration. (2018). *Permian basin oil production and resource assessments continue to increase.* USEIA. https://www.eia.gov/todayinenergy/detail.php?id=30952

Vygotsky, L. S. (1978). *Mind in society: The development of higher psychological processes.* MIT Press.

Vygotsky, L. S. (1986). *Thought and language.* MIT Press.

Chapter 7

Urban Literacy Education as a Vehicle for Social Change

A Community Audit of Charlotte, North Carolina

Candace Chambers and Annette Teasdell

Author Note

Candace Chambers: https://orcid.org/0000-0002-2436-9895

Annette Teasdell: https://orcid.org/0000-0001-5478-6692

Early examples of post-Civil War community literacy efforts can be traced to a key moment in American history. During the 19th century, former enslaved Africans risked their lives to educate and liberate themselves from the constraints of bondage to which they were subjugated physically and mentally for over 300 years (Anderson, 1988). Communal education was key to their mental and physical survival as they would educate themselves often in secrecy to learn fundamental literacy skills with a goal of universal education (Anderson, 1988). In a forward progression, this effort of education extended into the 20th century in one form as Freedom Schools, which were

DOI: 10.4324/9781003228042-10

established to assist disenfranchised African Americans in the South with the tools to become active citizens in their neighborhoods, cities, states, and in the country (Perlstein, 1990). These harbors of educational advancement would populate the state of Mississippi during the summer of 1964 as advocates within the Student Nonviolent Coordinating Committee (SNCC) worked to educate children and adults (Perlstein, 1990).

SNCC and other organizations identified a need to implement literacy initiatives in minority and often low-income areas of the deep South as they recognized that poverty and race are often indicators of limited access to quality educational resources. To further progress this construct, efforts such as the Freedom Schools of 1964 are still being made to address literacy discrepancies based on socio-economic status and race within the 21st century. The purpose of this chapter is to provide examples of literacy efforts within the 16th largest city in America – Charlotte, North Carolina (Chemtob & Off, 2019) – and demonstrate how these organizations are combating potential hindrances for adults and children who are experiencing poverty, for whom English is their second language, and/or who are in need of supplemental literacy enrichment for basic life skills.

Mission and Purpose

Central Connecticut State University in a 2017 study gathered data to determine the United States' most literate cities (Bell & Harrison, 2017). Indicators of literacy included the following factors: "number of bookstores; educational attainment; internet resources; library resources; periodical publishing resources; and newspaper circulation" (Bell & Harrison, 2017, para. 2). Among the top cities were the nation's capital, Washington D.C., and San Francisco, California, but notably, in the state of North Carolina, Charlotte, which compares in population to the aforementioned cities, ranked 44th out of the 82 cities featured. As of 2019, Charlotte (the Queen City) was the 16th largest city in the country (Chemtob & Off, 2019), but the city is home to residents with low percentage literacy rates for children and adults. In the Queen City, only 40% of third grade students were reading at grade level according to the National Assessment of Educational Progress (NAEP) in 2016; the third grade is a critical indicator for chances of high school graduation (Hallmark, 2016). In order to provide supplemental instruction for these students, attention must be placed on filling the gaps in literacy.

As a result of a growing population, many community organizations have focused on an increase of community literacy initiatives throughout the city to meet the population demand along with providing educational resources for the city's diverse urban population. This form of urban literacy aligns with the function of literacy to transform social practices to construct identities and relationships among members of communities (Kirkland, 2014). By viewing community literacy as socially constructed learning (Kirkland, 2014), this chapter examines urban literacy as a vehicle for social change by featuring community literacy offerings for adults and youth in Charlotte, North Carolina. Using a transformative education perspective (Mezirow, 1997), available literacy programs are featured that serve Charlotteans outside of the K–12 setting. The audit is grounded in this transformative theory with the goal of featuring youth and adult literacy programs that provide sustainable practices and equip participants to create, change, and challenge within their worlds (Bell, 2016).

Literature Review

Parents, students, and community organizations seeking to supplement current offerings in public and private charter schools and home schools and in the Charlotte-Mecklenburg School District can find multiple literacy programs to meet the learning needs of youth and adults. This literacy audit of Charlotte examines programs that are culturally affirming and transformative for communities and students. The specific models of instruction and their benefits are described to provide examples for anyone interested in community uplift through an investment in cultural and social capital. Also, the focus on literacy in urban communities demonstrates how these learning environments provide intellectual benefits and social development for participants (Cochran et al., 2017).

Academic Ruin Amid Urban Renewal: What Happens When Kids Can't Read

Charlotte is booming. New home construction and a steady influx of high paying jobs and industry, along with increasing numbers of diverse families moving to the area, are all indicators that Charlotte is a thriving urban city center (Delmelle et al., 2014). Nonetheless, a review of its success in promoting literacy development finds the city lacking. According to the National Assessment of Educational Progress (NAEP), only 40% of Charlotte's third graders are reading at grade level, and these numbers become more extreme when income is a variable (NCES, 2017). Among low-income readers, 78% are below third-grade reading levels. This forebodes serious consequences, as students who are not reading at grade level by third grade are four times more likely to drop out of school (National Center for Educational Statistics, 2017).

According to The Nation's Report Card, in 2017, only 29% of North Carolina readers are at proficient or advanced reading levels. Thus, 62% fall below basic reading levels. This translates to a high need for reading support outside of what is being offered in Charlotte-Mecklenburg schools. The effects of poverty and urbanization present unique challenges for literacy skills acquisition (Kirkland, 2014; Milner, 2012; Milner & Lomotey, 2014).

Literacy Skills Development as a Vehicle for Social Change

Anderson's *Education of Blacks in the South, 1860–1935* poignantly explained the theme of universal education as a necessary basis for freedom and citizenship, which is also foundational to the quest for literacy education today (Anderson, 1988). Literacy skills development can serve as a vehicle for social change because a firm foundation in reading and writing skills leads to limitless possibilities. Furthermore, efforts to improve literacy skills before critical fourth-grade benchmark testing can improve outcomes for communities. Those who test below third-grade reading levels are more likely to end up in the criminal justice system (Wiggan, 2011). Also, research confirms that reading above grade level at third grade is a strong predictor of high school graduation and college enrollment (Tuck, 2012). According to the National Assessment of Adult Literacy, in the United States, approximately 42 million adults aged 16 or older function at very low literacy rates. Over 25% of adult North Carolinians are negatively affected by reading and writing deficits to the extent that it limits the economic and physical well-being of the family (Taylor et al., 2010).

Youth Literacy Programs

Modeled after the pioneering work of Civil Rights activist Ella Baker and the Student Nonviolent Coordinating Committee, Freedom Schools began during the 1964 Mississippi Freedom Summer during the height of the Civil Rights Movement (Grant, 1999). From its onset in 1964, Freedom Schools were based on Baker's democratic education model. They were designed to "train and educate people to be active agents in bringing about social change" (Hale, 2011, p. 330). Since 1995, Marion Wright Edelman and the Children's Defense Fund (CDF, 2011) have operated Freedom Schools throughout the

United States. Today, they continue their efforts to educate and uplift young scholars through transformative education programs with a social action and critical education agenda (Jackson & Boutte, 2009).

In Charlotte, Freedom School Partners (FSP), a 501(c)(3) organization established in 2004, is committed to promoting "the long-term success of children by preventing summer learning loss through igniting a passion for reading and inspiring a love of learning" (Freedom School Partners, n.d.). Serving over 1,100 scholars in grades K–8, they are actively involved in advancing literacy skills development through a six-week summer program at over 18 sites in the Charlotte community (Freedom School Partners, n.d.). Freedom Schools use an Integrated Reading Curriculum (Jackson & Boutte, 2009), which includes two and a half hours per day of literacy instruction through the use of culturally relevant stories and novels (Bethea, 2012). Harambee, a Kiswahili word meaning "Let's pull together," is a signature element of Freedom Schools. This culturally rich opening forum energizes scholars, recognizes their accomplishments, and focuses on reading. Research confirms that cultural relevance is a means to improve learning and achievement among historically underrepresented students (Ladson-Billings, 1994, 1995). Servant Leader Interns (college students), parents, and community volunteers affirm scholars and introduce them to engaging literature while also supporting their academic, social, and emotional needs. Additionally, FSP benefits college student interns who use their expertise to improve outcomes for students while also serving as positive role models. Typically, scholars who participate in Freedom School have limited access to quality summer enrichment opportunities, so this free program provides needed support. FSP's collaboration with diverse community stakeholders also holds promise for the following:

- We promise to turn books into building blocks.
- We promise to create personal libraries of knowledge where children can immerse themselves. Find themselves. Fuel the imagination and possibility they never knew they had.
- We promise to keep learning from slipping.
- We promise to keep confidence from falling.
- We promise to increase opportunities, expand horizons, and ignite a passion for life-long learning.
- And most importantly, we promise to always carry the torch for children who need a chance to succeed (Freedom School Partners, n.d.).

In Charlotte, Freedom Schools avert summer reading loss by actively engaging scholars in a rich and rewarding literacy initiative. According to the University of North Carolina at Charlotte's College of Education (a partner of FSP), "Freedom School Partners' CDF Freedom Schools programs benefit the majority of participants by helping them maintain or improve in their ability to read" (Taylor et al., 2010, p. 24).

Though perhaps not so widely known as Freedom Schools, other programs help to promote literacy development. Founded in 1994, the Augustine Literacy Project (ALP) is a 501(c)(3) organization that serves struggling readers in first through third grade through a one-on-one tutoring program employing the Orton-Gillingham literacy model (Ring et al., 2017). With 11 chapters across the state, ALP enjoys data-driven success. The Charlotte ALP chapter has been serving the community since 2005. They aim to improve the reading, spelling, and writing skills of low-income children at Title I schools who have experienced literacy deficits. Tutors work one-on-one with students twice a week for 45 minutes. To qualify for the program, students must be economically disadvantaged as determined by free or reduced lunch eligibility. They must also be performing below grade level in reading, writing, or spelling. According to ALP, 90% of poor readers who participate in early intensive tutorial intervention through ALP improve their reading ability to age-appropriate average skill levels (Augustine Literacy Project, n.d.). ALP serves approximately 200 students in Charlotte Mecklenburg Title I schools. While tutors pay for a rigorous seven-day training, ALP services are provided free of charge to participants.

For both ALP and Freedom Schools, the common denominators are a commitment to transformative education alongside the teachers' belief in and their love for the scholars who, because of them, believe in the power of education. Christopher Emdin's thoughts on transformative education in *For White Folks Who Teach in the Hood . . . and the Rest of Y'all Too* (2016) are instructive:

> The effectiveness of the teacher can be traced directly back to what that teacher thinks of the student. If the teacher does not value the student, there is no motivation to take risks to engage with the student . . . How successful the teacher is in the classroom is directly related to how successful the teacher thinks the students can be. Teachers limit themselves and their students when they put caps on what their students can achieve.
>
> (Emdin, 2016, p. 207)

Whether it is a Freedom School college student Servant-Leader Intern or an ALP trained tutor, the emphasis on believing students can achieve and helping them succeed is evident in both training and results. A UNC Charlotte study of Freedom Schools reveals that 90% of scholars grew or maintained their ability to read as measured on the Basic Reading Inventory (Taylor et al., 2010). According to the 2018 Freedom School Partners Annual Report, 85% of parents surveyed reported an increase in their child's love of reading after participating in Freedom School (Freedom School Partners, n.d.). ALP boasts that tutees' spelling scores and word attack skills increased by a grade level, and fluency and comprehension increased by almost two grade levels (Augustine Literacy Project, n.d.). Both programs show an investment in the students they serve that results in literacy they can use to transform themselves and their communities. When these scholars become adults, they can contribute by supporting adult members of the community who need literacy skills development.

Adult Education Programs

Adult literacy programs operate similarly to youth education programs but cater to an older audience of approximately 16 years of age and older. These programs often extend into correctional facilities, libraries, community colleges, churches, and within the scope of the goals of community organizations (Armstrong, 2015; Miller et al., 2016; Moss, 2003; Taliaferro & Pham, 2018). According to McCaffery et al. (2007), learners are most effective when they consider the local context, resources, purposes of the learners, and their community in the context of learning. By acknowledging these factors, organizations can choose to approach literacy from various vantage points of literacy as skills, as tasks, as a social practice, and as critical reflection (McCaffery et al., 2007). Additionally, for the success of programs, the authors advocate for flexibility in the learning approach and encouragement for learners to be independent in their literacy development (McCaffery et al., 2007). Various adult education programs in the city of Charlotte will be featured based on the pillars of adult literacy as suggested by researchers within the field of community literacy.

Founded in 2002, Fill My Cup! is a 501(c)(3) non-profit organization that provides free one-on-one individual and small group tutoring for adult literacy, adult basic education, and life skills for residents in the Charlotte area (Fill My Cup!, n.d.). Students are required to be 16 years of age and older, not to have a high school diploma, and to be interested in learning how to read or improve their reading with the goal of functional literacy (Fill My Cup!, n.d.). Additionally, curricula for the program are based in pre-GED skills in the areas of reading, writing, spelling, and math. For continued support, the organization partners with organizations such as the North Carolina Literacy Association, Proliteracy of America, the North Carolina Community College System, and the United Way, along with individual support from the community.

Another example of an adult education literacy initiative occurring within the city of Charlotte is hosted at the International House, where the motto of the organization is "Where Charlotte Welcomes the World" (International House, 2017). The International House has been a pillar in Charlotte for over 30 years as they work to assist the city's foreign-born residents and immigrants to integrate themselves within communities through low-cost English courses, tutoring, legal assistance, and summer learning opportunities for young English Language Learners (International House, 2017). Over the past six years, the organization has assisted over 1,300 people with becoming U.S. citizens or permanent residents. Community members are able to sign-up for courses offered at the International House with a rate of $80 for a ten-week Citizenship Preparation Program and at no cost for the Multi-Level Adult English Classes (ESL) and an English Conversation Hour, which connects new and native English speakers in an informal setting (International House, 2017).

Funding

Since literary education is so important to the development of social capital, program funding is essential. Many literacy programs rely on community support, grants, and donors to remain operational. While Child Defense Fund (CDF) Freedom Schools programs are free for participating families, each site (serving 50 Scholars) costs approximately $59,000 to operate (Taylor et al., 2010). Local houses of worship, schools, colleges and universities, and community organizations known as community partners are responsible for raising operating funds for each Freedom School. In Charlotte, CDF Freedom Schools are hosted by Freedom School Partners, a 501(c)(3) organization founded in 1999 to serve historically underrepresented scholars and families living in poverty (Freedom School Partners, n.d.). Freedom School Partners' mission is to engage, educate, and empower children to succeed in school and in life through quality, year-round educational enrichment programs. Freedom School Partners (FSP) began hosting CDF Freedom Schools programs in 2004, and they have continued to expand their offerings in Charlotte since then. According to their 2018 annual report, Freedom School Partners has an operating budget of $2.5 million from various entities in the Charlotte community, and as Mary Nell McPherson, executive director, reports, it would not be possible without volunteer and financial support of the Charlotte community (Augustine Literacy Project, n.d.).

The Augustine Literacy Project (ALP) serves first and second graders through a one-on-one tutoring program modeled after the Orton-Gillingham literacy model. ALP receives support from partners such as the Belk Foundation, Merancas Foundation, OrthoCarolina Foundation, Parsec Financial Wealth Management, the Dowd Foundation, the Women's Impact Fund: Together, We Do, the James Family Foundation, and Make an Impact Foundation. Additionally, tutors pay $250 for training, which is used for operations.

In regard to adult literacy programs, Fill My Cup! relies on community contributions for operating expenses (Fill My Cup!, n.d.). As reported in 2017, the non-profit totaled $1,738 for net assets. In the same year, the operating balance for the International House was $431,892 (International House, 2017). The balance was reported as a combination of contributions, grants, and program service revenue.

Future Predictions Within Community Literacy in Charlotte

As the population continues to grow in Charlotte, North Carolina, an increase of literacy programs will be needed to accommodate the varying cultural inclusions within the city. Specific examples of growth would have to be in the areas of language acquisition for English Language Learners of all ages as well as more organizations that provide supplemental instruction for academic enhancement. Additionally, we predict that more nontraditional forms of instruction that are culturally based within communities will have to be established to maintain cultural traditions while filing potential cultural gaps within traditional schooling. Last, we predict that more programs will be needed to promote social uplift to bridge the literacy gap for adults and youth.

References

Anderson, J. (1988). *The education of Blacks in the south.* The University of North Carolina Press.

Armstrong, E. (2015). ESL and low income computer literacy learners: A microcosm for adult learning in libraries. *Public Services Quarterly*, *11*(2), 135–143. https://doi.org/10.1080/15228959.2015.1039748

Augustine Literacy Project (n.d.). Home page. https://alpcharlotte.org/

Bell, A., & Harrison, S. (2017). A national literacy ranking just came out. Charlotte didn't fare too well. *The Charlotte Observer*. www.charlotte observer.com/news/local/article143308769.html

Bell, D. V. (2016). Twenty-first century education: Transformative education for sustainability and responsible citizenship. *Journal of Teacher Education and Sustainability, 18*(1), 48–56. https://doi.org/10.1515/jtes-2016-0004

Bethea, S. L. (2012). The impact of Oakland Freedom School's summer youth program on the psychological development of African American youth. *Journal of Black Psychology, 38*(4), 442–454. https://doi.org/10.1177/0095798411431982

Chemtob, D., & Off, G. (2019). Charlotte jumps in rankings of largest U.S. cities, surpassing Indianapolis. *The Charlotte Observer*. www.charlotteobserver.com/news/business/biz-columns-blogs/development/article230790609.html

Children's Defense Fund. (2011). *Children's defense fund freedom schools, program operating principles*. www.childrensdefense.org/programs/cdf-freedom-schools/

Cochran, J. A., Gardner-Andrews, A., Benson, P. W., Durbin, T., & Peeler, M. (2017). What's RITE in St. Louis? Empowering urban youth through a community tutoring collaborative. *Education and Urban Society, 49*(8), 711–730. https://doi.org/10.1177/0013124516658521

Delmelle, E., Zhou, Y., & Thill, J. C. (2014). Densification without growth management? Evidence from local land development and housing trends in Charlotte, North Carolina, U.S.A. *Sustainability, 6*(6), 3975–3990. https://doi.org/10.3390/su6063975

Emdin, C. (2016). *For White folks who teach in the hood . . . and the rest of y'all too: Reality pedagogy and urban education*. Beacon Press.

Fill My Cup! Adult Literacy and Adult Basic Education Services. (n.d.). Home page. www.fillmycupliteracy.org/

Freedom School Partners. (n.d.). Home page. https://freedomschoolpartners.org/

Grant, J. (1999). *Ella Baker: Freedom bound*. Wiley.

Hale, J. (2011). The student as a force for social change: The Mississippi Freedom Schools and student engagement. *The Journal of African American History, 96*(3), 325–347. https://doi.org/10.5323/jafriamerhist.96.3.0325

Hallmark, G. (2016). Only 40% of Charlotte Mecklenburg third graders read at grade level, here's how to help. *The Charlotte Agenda*. www.charlotteagenda.com/37069/only-40-percent-of-charlotte-mecklenburg-third-graders-read-at-grade-level/

International House. (2017). Home. www.ihclt.org

Jackson, T. O., & Boutte, G. S. (2009). Liberation literature: Positive cultural messages in children's and young adult literature at freedom schools. *Language Arts, 87*(2), 108–116.

Kirkland, D. (2014). Urban literacy learning. In H. R. Milner IV & K. Lomotey (Eds.), Handbook of urban education (pp. 394–412). Routledge.

Ladson-Billings, G. (1994). *The dreamkeepers: Successful teachers of African American children.* Jossey-Bass.

Ladson-Billings, G. (1995). But that's just good teaching! The case for culturally relevant pedagogy. *Theory into Practice, 34*(3), 159–165. https://doi. org/10.1080/00405849509543675

McCaffery, J., Merrifield, J., & Millican, J. (2007). *Developing adult learning: Approaches to planning, implementing, delivering, literacy initiatives.* Oxfam GB.

Mezirow, J. (1997). Transformative learning: Theory to practice. *New Directions for Adult & Continuing Education, 74,* 5–12. https://doi.org/10.1002/ ace.7401

Miller, M., Grover, K. S., Deggs, D. M., D'Amico, M., Katsinas, S. G., & Adair, L. (2016). Adult education in community colleges: New challenges to old problems. *Journal of Adult Education, 45*(2), 17–23.

Milner, H. (2012). But what is urban education? *Urban Education, 47*(3), 556–561. https://doi.org/10.1177/0042085912447516

Milner, H., & Lomotey, K. (2014). *Handbook of urban education.* Routledge, Taylor & Francis Group.

Moss, B. J. (2003). *A community text arises: A literate text and a literacy tradition in African-American churches.* Hampton Press.

National Center for Educational Statistics. (2017). National Assessment of Educational Progress (NAEP): Reading assessment. Institute of Education Sciences, United States Department of Education. https://nces.ed.gov/ pubsearch/pubsinfo.asp?pubid=2018041

Perlstein, D. (1990). Teaching freedom: SNCC and the creation of the Mississippi freedom schools. *History of Education Society, 30*(3). 297–324. https://doi.org/10.2307/368691

Ring, J. J., Avrit, K. J., & Black, J. L. (2017). Take flight: The evolution of an Orton Gillingham-based curriculum. *Annals of Dyslexia, 67*(3), 383–400. https://doi.org/10.1007/s11881-017-0151-9

Taliaferro, W., & Pham, D. (2018). Incarceration to reentry: Education & training pathways in Ohio. *Reconnecting justice in the states* (pp. 1–15). Center for Law and Social Policy, Inc. https://eric.ed.gov/?id=ED586093

Taylor, D. B., Medina, A. L., & Lara-Cinisomo, S. (2010). *Freedom school partners children's defense fund freedom schools® program evaluation report.* Center for Adolescent Literacies at UNC Charlotte. https://literacy.charlotte.edu/sites/literacy.charlotte.edu/files/media/2011%20FSP%20eval%20report-final.pdf

Tuck, E. (2012). *Urban youth and school pushout: Gateways, get-aways, and the GED.* Routledge.

Wiggan, G. A. (2011). *Power, privilege, and education: Pedagogy, curriculum, and student outcomes.* Nova Science Publishers.

Chapter 8

From Idea to Reality

Developing an Early Literacy Action Plan with Community Partners

Terry S. Atkinson, Kimberly L. Anderson, Elizabeth A. Swaggerty, and Marjorie W. Rowe

Author Note

Terry S. Atkinson: https://orcid.org/0000-0002-2166-9139
Kimberly L. Anderson: https://orcid.org/0000-0002-3944-9919
Elizabeth A. Swaggerty: https://orcid.org/0000-0002-0901-5204
Marjorie W. Rowe: https://orcid.org/0000-0002-3562-5567

Introduction

Seeking to bring about change in a community often begins with an idea or an observation leading to action. However, if such change is meant to improve long-term social problems such as low literacy, poverty, or education inequality, solutions call for far more than mere individual champions or quick fixes (Bradley & Katz, 2013). Literacy coalitions serve as one example of collective impact organizations that seek to identify and implement solutions for complex social problems by moving beyond the siloed efforts of individual groups or programs, gaining momentum and impact from collaborative cross-sector

DOI: 10.4324/9781003228042-11

enthusiasm, effort, and investment. Kania and Kramer (2011) identify five conditions that contribute to the success of collective impact initiatives. These include: (a) sharing a common agenda; (b) employing measurable outcomes; (c) initiating mutually reinforcing activities; (d) ensuring ongoing communication; and (e) engaging the support of backbone organizations.

Acknowledging the role of literacy in many societal problems, the United States experienced a civic engagement movement beginning in the 1980s that resulted in the establishment of more than 300 literacy coalitions (Ridzi & Doughty, 2017). While many initial literacy coalition efforts concentrated on supporting adult learners, community-wide efforts to improve early childhood literacy have become more common during the past decade, owing in part to the influence of the national Campaign for Grade Level Reading (CGLR, 2019a). Established in 2010 through the sponsorship of the well-regarded Annie E. Casey Foundation, the CGLR offers support and resources to both public and private groups seeking to organize collective impact efforts aimed at increasing grade-level reading proficiency by the end of grade three. Convincing research documents third-grade reading proficiency as a key predictor of school and later career success (Hernandez, 2012), offering a rationale for community investment in early childhood. Championing this idea are notables such as Nobel Laureate economist James Heckman (2008), whose life work has promoted the argument that maximum return on financial investment and success in addressing social change can be gained through efforts focused on the earliest years of childhood (see Figure 8.1).

The efforts of one rural Eastern North Carolina community to organize and launch a collective impact literacy coalition initiative are described in the sections that follow. The impetus for the coalition was a local speech and language pathologist's observation that many of her young clients who demonstrated significant lags in language development shared a common factor: their homes contained few, if any, children's picture books. Knowing that such books served as key tools for shared reading and language-rich discussions within families, she connected community members with individuals and organizations at the local, state, and national level who might offer insight about early literacy coalition development. Her vision ignited cross-sector interest in improving early literacy opportunities for all the community's children.

Across three planning years, stakeholders examined a wide array of ideas, resources, and possibilities for moving this effort forward. Substantive progress took place once the coalition's Steering Committee partnered with a state-level early childhood foundation and developed a Community Solutions Action Plan (CSAP) to formalize the coalition and guide its work five years

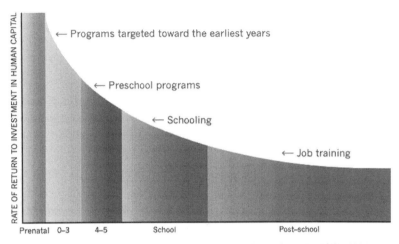

Heckman, James J. (2008). "Schools, Skills and Synapses," *Economic Inquiry*, 46(3): 289-324

Figure 8.1 Return to a Unit Dollar Invested at Different Ages from the Perspective of the Beginning of Life, Assuming One Dollar Initially Invested at Each Age

hence. The context and background framing this endeavor are described, as well as the process and outcome of CSAP development. Finally, lessons learned and conclusions are offered to support others who are interested or engaged in similar work.

Context and Background

Pitt County is a diverse and growing region of Eastern North Carolina. The county's long-term general and child poverty rates have exceeded 20% for more than 30 years (USDA, 2015), and, according to state assessments, about half of each year's kindergarten class is considered ready for school learning. These statistics fueled community stakeholders' engagement in meetings and discussions about improving young children's readiness for school that took place during the summer of 2015.

A large contingency of early participants in this work were reading specialists, early childhood professionals, or other educators who understood that early literacy skills and school readiness are key indicators of third grade-reading proficiency, high school graduation, and the achievement of promising jobs leading to middle-class citizenry (The Annie E. Casey Foundation, 2013).

Stakeholder interest grew as the coalition's potential impact became understood. What began as a commitment to increasing access to early childhood literacy resources became recognized as an important opportunity to invest in the future potential and prosperity of Pitt County and its citizens.

As diverse groups and voices joined the community conversations, the United Way of Pitt County, an early and enthusiastic coalition partner and advocate, committed to seeking funds to launch Dolly Parton's Imagination Library (DPIL, 2019) book distribution program across the county. Multiple census tracts in Pitt County are designated as book deserts (Unite for Literacy, n.d.) where a scarcity of books can seriously limit children's learning opportunities prior to school entry (Neuman & Moland, 2019) and consequently constrain later reading achievement (Mol & Bus, 2011). The DPIL program mails high-quality picture books monthly to the homes of all enrolled children aged 0–5 in participating areas. Initiating this program in March 2016 was viewed as an important first step in addressing one of the proposed coalition's agreed-upon goals: Improved early literacy development and kindergarten readiness. In support of this effort, faculty from East Carolina University (ECU), another early partner in coalition discussions, agreed to conduct a five-year study to examine DPIL's impact on children's reading-related skills at kindergarten entry (Imagination Library Kindergarten Impact Study, n.d).

Public community meetings and small group meetings continued throughout 2016 and early 2017, exploring ideas about which strategies might best support young children and prepare them for school success. During this same time, a coalition Steering Committee comprised of community leaders representing public schools, public libraries, local non-profits, higher education, local economic development, and business/industry began meeting to explore how to formalize, lead, and fund the coalition. As the United Way launched and led a community-wide campaign to register children in DPIL, literacy coalition interest and momentum increased, and the Steering Committee connected with the North Carolina Early Childhood Foundation (NCECF, 2018), the state's lead organization for the national Campaign for Grade Level Reading (2019c). NCECF's Community Engagement Leader facilitated two local sessions in fall 2017, bringing together the Steering Committee and all community individuals and groups who were involved in the ongoing literacy coalition conversations. Thus, affiliation with NCECF served as the catalyst that transformed community discussions about myriad ideas into the reality of a jointly constructed strategic plan.

Community Solutions Action Plan Development

NCECF's well-established process for developing a community literacy action plan proved an important asset; the two public sessions resulted in the formation of four action teams of community volunteers who soon began work on key areas of what CGLR terms a Community Solutions Action Plan (CSAP). With agreement that the overall CGLR objective of increasing the number of third graders reading at grade level would serve the community's coalition well as its overarching goal, action plan work commenced in August 2017. Action teams focused on one of the following research-based factors impacting school success and third-grade reading (Campaign for Grade Level Reading, 2019b): (a) readiness for school learning at kindergarten entry; (b) access to and participation in summer learning opportunities; (c) regular attendance while reducing chronic absenteeism; and (d) literacy engagement across the community.

Action teams were led by co-chairs with specific interest in or expertise related to their focus area. Information shared during the NCECF sessions provided teams with examples of how other communities had built community action plans. Thus, each team left the second session with the task of: (a) crafting a measurable area goal for the upcoming five years (and identifying related existing data in the community to document such measurement); (b) creating prioritized targets or strategies that would enable the area goal to be reached; (c) creating timebound milestones for each target; and (d) identifying coordinated activities that would facilitate goal achievement. Prior to beginning CSAP development work, action teams engaged and sought input from current or potential community partners and identified existing activities, initiatives, and services in each of their areas. As work progressed, teams were encouraged to involve parents in their work whenever possible and seek ongoing feedback or guidance from the coalition's Steering Committee and NCECF. Examples (see Table 8.1) were offered to refine terminology understandings and jump start each action team's work.

As action team work began, the Steering Committee guided the teams' work, building public and community support for the coalition's mission, mobilizing resources, and identifying backbone organizations to provide ongoing support and guidance. As per CGLR process, the Steering Committee Chair submitted a Letter of Intent indicating that a Pitt County Early Literacy Coalition CSAP was currently under development and would ultimately be submitted for review. Additionally, the chair continued to meet with action teams and their co-chairs to provide support and set completion goals.

Table 8.1 Terminology for the Campaign for Grade Level Reading's Community Solutions Action Plan (CSAP) Development

Term	Example
Overarching CSAP Vision (No numbers, aspirational)	All students have the resources and support needed to read on grade level by the end of grade 3.
Action Team Goal (Timebound, measurable with numbers)	By the year XXXX, 75% of children will score at benchmark on the state kindergarten entrance assessment.
Targets/Strategies	Increase access to the Raising a Reader program in area childcare centers to more children who do not currently have access.
Timebound Milestones	By the year XXXX, XX% of children in area childcare centers will have access to the Raising a Reader program.
Coordinated Activities/ Partners	Martin-Pitt Partnership for Children, Community Literacy Coalition, and United Way.

Across the next six months, action team productivity varied. One team sought feedback from NCECF's Community Engagement Leader and drafted a goal and corresponding targets, milestones, and activities that the Steering Committee Chair used as a template to help other teams move forward. Ultimately, the Steering Committee Chair compiled the work of the action teams into a draft and added background information, a vision statement, and a community overview, all components suggested in the CGLR's Community Solutions Action Plan Framework (CGLR, 2019c).

While this action team work was in progress, the Steering Committee interacted with multiple committee partners, including the local public library system, the United Way of Pitt County, and ECU to craft a collaborative commitment to the Early Literacy Coalition. By the summer of 2018, it became apparent that the cadre of volunteers, as committed and talented as they were, was not sufficient for coordinating all aspects of the coalition's work and carrying out its ever-growing agenda for meeting the community's needs. Thus, in addition to formalizing the coalition, the Steering Committee sought to designate an individual to lead the Early Literacy Coalition's work building on the existing multisector investment of a local family foundation, the United Way, and Vidant Health (the local health care system and hospital), all of whom served as initial and ongoing funders of the coalition's early DPIL implementation. At that point, ECU deepened its commitment, and Dr. Terry S. Atkinson (first author), an ECU faculty member, accepted a part-time assignment as the coalition's executive director. With an executive director on board to finalize the coalition's CSAP and launch implementation, work began in earnest on completing it. Working closely with NCECF and surrounding communities who had crafted similar plans, essential supporting trend data was acquired from the local public school system, and the CSAP measurable outcomes and goals were revisited and realigned. Next, input and feedback from the Steering Committee and action team members were sought and considered. Last, a final version of the CSAP was submitted to the CGLR in late October 2018. At the same time, the Pitt County Early Literacy Coalition (now formally named READ ENC Community Literacy Coalition) commenced strategy implementation related to kindergarten readiness, summer learning, school attendance, and literacy engagement across the community. A favorable review of READ ENC's CSAP (2018) was received in early November, which formalized affiliation with CGLR and granted access to all of their resources and support. Key excerpts of the plan are provided in Appendix L, including details offering access to the full CSAP document.

Lessons Learned

Much has been learned throughout the experience of bringing together community members with a shared vision of improving early literacy opportunities for all the community's young citizens. In the paragraphs that follow, the authors share suggestions for community coalition planning based on their perspective as long-term stakeholders and participants in coalition work and CSAP development. Suggestions include: (a) identifying key resources, (b) embracing a collective impact model, and (c) balancing the time necessary to include multiple voices while keeping the final goal in mind.

Identifying Key Resources

Early discussions among those interested in establishing a community-wide early literacy coalition were rich with idea exchange, revealing myriad viewpoints and priorities about the work of such a group. Ongoing efforts were made to ensure input from diverse groups and voices, but, with limited early progress toward the final goal of establishing a coalition, the number of invested volunteers waxed and waned across time. Identifying outside resources and expertise to support the community's work shifted long-term conversations toward significant progress. The guidance and support of the NCECF was invaluable in helping community members transfer caring intentions into action. Of particular importance were the free research-based resources provided on the NCECF (2018) website (buildthefoundation.org), which offered substance for public meeting discussions and presentations to community leaders, and the assistance of NCECF's Community Outreach Leader in facilitating the sessions that jump-started action team work and led to eventual CSAP completion. It was also through the NCECF that the community learned about the national Campaign for Grade Level Reading's mission and accompanying resources and support that are offered at no cost to affiliating communities. This information led to networking with many communities that had already engaged in organizing literacy coalitions or writing community literacy action plans.

Additional key organizations that provided valuable guidance in the community literacy plan development included: the Literacy Coalition of Onondaga County (Onondaga County, NY), Raising Moore Readers (Moore County, NC), READ Charlotte (Mecklenburg County, NC), Twin Cities Rise to Read (Nash-Rocky Mount, NC), and Read by 4th (Philadelphia, PA). Lastly, one suggested key resource for others interested in this work is Ridzi and Doughty's book, *Does Collective Impact Work? What Literacy Coalitions Tell Us* (2017), which provides a deep examination of literacy coalition development across the past 30 years. The many insights and resources included in this book would serve as invaluable assets in any early community literacy plan development.

Embracing a Collective Impact Model

Those engaged in the earliest work and conversation about forming an early literacy coalition capitalized on the energy, enthusiasm and interest of many caring community members and organizations to move beyond the siloed efforts of individual programs and groups. These cross-sector conversations engaged multiple partners to develop a plan for improving kindergarten readiness and school success. Such agreement about a common agenda for this work mirrors one key condition of success for collective impact organizations identified by Kania and Kramer (2011). The fact that collective impact coalitions are typically championed by community leaders, however, differentiates collective impact efforts from grassroots or social movements. Comprised of a group of local community leaders, the literacy coalition's Steering Committee built on the direction and guidance of NCECF and was ultimately responsible for the decisions that led to CSAP completion and the commitment of community resources to lead coalition work beyond the implementation of DPIL (Kania & Kramer, 2011).

The engagement and support of community leaders set the stage for achieving additional conditions important for the coalition's future and ongoing success, including (a) the establishment of committed staffing, (b) the implementation of goal-aligned activities and strategies that are shared regularly within the community, and (c) the establishment of a system of shared measurement (Kania & Kramer, 2011). While early talk and discussions about the coalition's vision and future agenda served an important purpose, had the commitment of these key community leaders and decision-makers not been in place, interest in coalition organization might have languished.

Balancing Time

Identifying and implementing solutions to a long-term, complex social problem such as low literacy requires patience and diligence to avoid embracing seductive messiahs, quick fixes, or silver bullets that offer little promise of substantive change (Bradley & Katz, 2013). However, discussions that focused on ideas, resources, and possibilities were long, repetitive, and exhausting at times, and volunteer commitment to coalition planning diminished and varied over time. In retrospect, the four years that led to the finalization and implementation of READ ENC Community Literacy Coalition's CSAP (2018) would likely have benefitted from more deliberate planning to balance investment in idea generation, discussion, stakeholder inclusion, and input with synthesis, decision-making, and concrete actions.

Epilogue

While this chapter has focused on literacy coalition building and the writing of a CSAP with realistic and attainable goals to formalize its work, a brief overview of how that plan played out in the months that followed attests to the power of strategic planning as a firm foundation for substantive outcomes. Collaboration with multiple community groups and organizations has led to strategy execution in all four CSAP goal areas. Noting resulting early accomplishments and fully crediting the contributing community partners involved would demand far more detail than this epilogue allows. However, with implementation of a system to enroll newborns in DPIL at Vidant Health's Birthing Center, the Kids Read Now (2019) K–3 summer reading program, a year-long school attendance campaign with Pitt County Schools, a community-wide Book Nook initiative, and increased early literacy public library programming, much progress was made prior to the impact of the COVID-19 pandemic.

Due to the pandemic, most coalition work shifted to a virtual format in March 2020, resulting in the following changes:

- As a result of COVID restrictions, the DPIL enrollment program at Vidant Birthing Center was suspended, and online enrollment was encouraged. The in-person enrollment program was reinstated in late 2020 with the addition of COVID modifications for hospital volunteers. Throughout the pandemic, Pitt County DPIL enrollment held at ~64% of the 0–5-year-olds eligible.
- READ ENC published and regularly updated an at-home learning webpage featuring links to >50 free resources for families and educators.
- READ ENC Facebook posts increased to three per day featuring additional shared reading tips and encouragement, as well as updates about local virtual offerings for children and families.
- A READ ENC initiated K-3 summer reading program, Kids Read Now, delivered more than 7,000 self-selected books to the homes of ~1,400 of Pitt County's most economically disadvantaged students during summer 2020 and 15,000 books to ~1700 children in summer 2021.
- Activity at Pitt County's 30 Little Free Libraries accelerated after repeated promotion of locations on READ ENC's website map. The executive director and community members became involved in regularly refreshing collections.
- Public library story time offerings increased to daily virtual programming for babies, toddlers, preschoolers, and school-aged children. Virtual programming continued due to overwhelmingly positive community feedback, supplementing face-to-face story time events as COVID restrictions eased.

READ ENC is on firm footing for long-term progress and continues to adapt with input from the community. The role and value of a Community Solutions Action Plan to guide these efforts during the coming years cannot be overstated. Follow the progress of this community literacy initiative by visiting READENC.org.

References

Bradley, J., & Katz, B. (2013). *The metropolitan revolution: How cities and metros are fixing our broken politics and fragile economy*. Brookings Institution Press.

Campaign for Grade-Level Reading (2019a). *Joining the grade level reading communities network*. https://gradelevelreading.net/our-network/joining-the-grade-level-reading-communities-network

Campaign for Grade-Level Reading (2019b). Our work. https://gradelevel-reading.net/our-work

Campaign for Grade-Level Reading (2019c). Homepage. http://gradelevel-reading.net/

Dolly Parton's Imagination Library (2019, February 14). Homepage. https://imaginationlibrary.com/

Heckman, J. J. (2008). Schools, skills, and synapses. *Economic Inquiry, 46*(3), 289–324. https://doi.org/10.1111/j.1465-7295.2008.00163.x

Hernandez, D. J. (2012). *Double jeopardy: How third-grade reading skills and poverty influence high school graduation.* The Annie E. Casey Foundation. www.aecf.org/resources/double-jeopardy/

Imagination Library Kindergarten Impact Study (ILKIS) (n.d.). https://sites.ecu.edu/ilkis/

Kania, J., & Kramer, M. (2011). Collective impact. *Stanford Social Innovation Review, 9*(1), 36–41.

Kids Read Now (2019). *About kids read now.* https://kidsreadnow.org/

Mol, S. E., & Bus, A. G. (2011). To read or not to read: A meta-analysis of print exposure from infancy to early adulthood. *Psychological Bulletin, 137*, 267–296. https://doi.org/:10.1037/a0021890

Neuman, S. B., & Moland, N. M. (2019). Book deserts: The consequences of income segregation on children's access to print. *Urban Education, 54*(1), 126–147. https://doi.org/10.1177/0042085916654525

North Carolina Early Childhood Foundation (2018). https://buildthefoundation.org

READ ENC Community Literacy Coalition (2018). *Community solutions action plan.* https://readenc.org/csap.

Ridzi, F., & Doughty, M. (2017). *Does collective impact work? What literacy coalitions tell us.* Lexington Books.

The Annie E. Casey Foundation. (2013). *Early warning confirmed: A research update on third-grade reading.* The Annie E. Casey Foundation. www.aecf.org/m/resourcedoc/AECF-EarlyWarningConfirmed-2013.pdf.

Unite for Literacy. (n.d.). *Global book desert map.* www.uniteforliteracy.com/corp/esri.

U.S. Department of Agriculture (2015). *Persistent poverty by county in North Carolina.* Economic Research Service. www.ers.usda.gov/data-products/county-typology-codes/descriptions-and-maps/ – pcpov

Chapter 9

Understanding the Psychology of Getting Funded

Beverly Browning

Author Note

Beverly Browning: https://orcid.org/0000-0001-8789-5510

Introduction

When you think of psychology, your mind quickly remembers this definition: The science of mind and behavior (Merriam-Webster, n.d.). Another meaning is the mental or behavioral characteristics of an individual or group. After 43 years in the grant professionals' industry, I can attest that there is, in fact, a psychology of getting funded. Over the years, I have sat in the chair of a grant writer, internal and external peer reviewer, and grant maker. Along the way, I have observed the thought process that goes into each of these roles.

What does it take to get funded in a climate of cautious decision-makers scrutinizing your grant proposals and applications? It takes putting yourself in each of the funding decision maker's chairs wearing the *how we think* and *how we fund* hat. Yes, as grant writers (anyone tasked with writing a grant request), we write in a way that encourages the minds of funding decision-makers to recommend our requests for funding. We write as if we know what they want, what they're thinking, and what will touch their hearts. There are multiple ways to research potential funders before you jump into writing a grant request.

Deep Dive into Researching Potential Corporate and Foundation Funders

Here are some questions that must be answered from your due diligence in researching potential funders:

- What targeted geographic areas does the funder specify in its online profile or on its website (geographic matching is critical)?
- What grants have been awarded in my state or region (once money crosses your state line from potential funders, it will come back over and over when you submit a well-written, highly competitive grant request)?
- What are the priority areas that the funder specifies (the funder's priority grant-making areas must match your project or program 100%; there are no exceptions)?
- How much do we need, and what is the range of grants awarded by the funder (if you're a new grant applicant, always request a low amount in your first request)?
- When is the funder's application submission deadline (rushing and working on a short deadline can be fatal and result in rejections)?
- Who do our governing board members and top-level administrators know on the funder's staff or board (having an established connection is a bonus)?

Corporate and Foundation Subscription-Based Grant Research Databases

The Foundation Center's Directory Online

The Foundation Center (https://fconline.foundationcenter.org/welcome/quick-start) has been around for decades and is a non-profit organization with Funder Information Networks (free-access locations) worldwide. With a subscription (varying levels), you can find the corporation or foundation you're looking for by name, employer identification number, location, assets, or range of grant awards. Subscribers can also view IRS Form 990s for the funders in this database of 100,000 private sector funders.

Tip: Often, when there is no direct contact information in the funder's profile or on their website, you can use their IRS Form 990 to find names and contact information for governing board members. This directory also has the option to search for federal grant funding.

Instrumentl

The Instrumentl worldwide grant database (www.instrumentl.com?grsf= t2nrr3) is all-encompassing with profiles, weblinks, and Form 990s for corporate and foundation funders. Also, Instrumentl includes state and federal agency funding research options. Created by fundraisers and academicians, this grant database is a one-stop, all-in-one subscription-based source for grant-seekers.

Tip: This grant database allows you to create project profiles with up to ten keywords. Instrumentl does the work for you and searches for every possible funder based on your keywords, geographic location, grant amount range, and more. It even allows you to break your project's location down to the county/ city levels.

Funder Relationship Building Processes

If you have diligently researched each potential private-sector funder, you are building your insight into what they do, why they do it, when they do it, and how much they do it. What's "it"? The published facts about their grant-making processes. How does having this information help you understand the psychology of the funder? When you have the funder's grant database information and scrutinize their website, you should be able to answer all the questions posed earlier in this chapter. In other words, your due diligence has resulted in your profiling the funder by learning every nuance about their grant-making behaviors.

What's Next?

Your next step is to prepare for making the initial contact with a foundation administrator or program officer. How do you know who to call or e-mail? All the information you need can be found on the funder's website as well as in their database profile. Think of the database as the crib sheet (a depository that contains notes of information about the funder to help you read and remember the most important points). The funder's website fills in the blanks (scan annual reports, mission, philosophy of giving, senior staff members (names and titles), and governing board members (names and positions). Why do you need so much information about every private-sector funder your organization intends to approach for a grant? Because you must be able to reach out and introduce yourself and your organization. You must be literate about every aspect of what the funder funds and who to reach out to in your first telephone call or e-mail. Make notes and keep them in front of you during any calls. Use your notes to compile a short introductory e-mail message.

Tip: The individual reaching out from your organization to build relationships with potential funders should be of similar title and authority as the person they will be building relationships with at the funder's office. For example, your development director should reach out to a high-level program officer. Someone with the title of grant writer should not be the introductory staff member reaching out to a potential funder.

Keys to Communicating with Potential Funders

E-Mail Protocol

Today, many funders prefer that grant applicants contact them via e-mail. While it may sound easy and quick, it's not as easy as you think. Remember, sending a cold e-mail to a potential funder is your first attempt to connect and start two-way communications. Your message must be orderly, clear, and succinct. There are several important steps to creating your initial contact email.

First, introduce yourself (name, organization, job title). Write a short paragraph about the grant applicant organization, including the year it was founded and the year that the Internal Revenue Service approved the tax-exempt status. Write about the location (state, county, city, town, township, or village), and tell the funder if there are multiple locations and where they are located.

Second, tell the potential funder why you are contacting them (shared mission, previous funding from them, board member connection, attendance at one of their technical assistance meetings or webinars, or some attention-grabbing connection).

Third, state your need of why the organization is in need of funding support.

Fourth, convey the solution that will eliminate or reduce the need.

Fifth, include the amount of funding needed to solve the problem.

Sixth, ask the potential funder for permission to submit a full funding request based on their published guidelines.

Seventh, thank the potential funder for their time. Wait, don't hit send yet! Always proofread any email communications at least three times before you hit send. Once you hit send, follow-up with a telephone call to the potential funder's office in five to seven days.

Telephone Contact Protocol

Here are some tips to help you prepare for a telephone call with a potential funder. It's important to be prepared to speak with knowledge about your non-profit organization. Please don't assign this task to a new employee or a new board member. Also, this is not a job for a volunteer. Remember, stored knowledge about the organization, its finances, and service population is gained from day-to-day work experiences of employees and board members with long-term commitment and a vested interest in getting additional revenue streams for the organization. It's best to assemble experienced board members and administrative staff to craft a script for telephone calls with potential funders. Practice the script by doing role plays. Have a timer and keep any initial dialogue to three minutes or less. Please keep it simple and be ready to answer questions asked by the potential funder. Speak with a smile and take lots of notes.

Face-to-Face Meeting Protocol

Most often, a grant seeker will only get one chance to meet with a potential funder face-to-face, either in person or via a video call. Do not leave your office without having a well-prepared folder with relevant information about your organization (mission, year formed, tax-exempt status, year founded, who founded it and why, a list of your programs, and a fact sheet about the organization's target population). Tuck in a copy of your Internal Revenue Service Form 990 (annual federal tax return for non-profit organizations) and a copy of your tax-exempt letter. Include your business card in the folder. It's a good idea to spend a few more dollars for a glossy, sturdy, two-pocket folder versus a 20-cent flimsy paper folder. You've heard the saying, dress to impress. Well, prepare the informational packet to impress too! Follow the same protocol as the telephone contact protocol by keeping your own personal introduction less than three minutes. Listen intently to the potential funder's staff and take notes, if needed. Whatever you do, do not act desperate or disappointed if the staff appears uninterested in funding your organization. Remember to thank everyone for their time.

Before you schedule telephone calls or face-to-face meetings with potential funders, remember to come with memorized answers in your head, because there will be several queries about the project in need of grant funding and how you plan to validate the need for funding and the impact that any grant funding will make. In addition, you may be asked about the grant applicant organization's ability to keep rigorous financial records and submit grant reports in a timely manner. Most importantly, always be prepared to talk about the sustainability plan for ongoing funding to keep the proposed grant-funded project operating beyond the initial grant award.

Point of Entry Protocol for Private Sector Funders

Most private sector funders (foundations and corporations) require a Letter of Inquiry (LOI) as the first entry point to begin a dialogue about your organization, what it does, where it's located, and its funding needs. The following components are important to include in your letter of inquiry. First, write a one-paragraph introduction (to the organization and the board; you are writing the potential funder on behalf of your board of directors . . . always!). Next, write a one-paragraph overview of your non-profit organization. Include a one-paragraph statement of the problem or need (remember to cite sources for any demographics and never write with assumptions or in generalities). The next paragraph should be a description of the project (short-term) or program (long-term) in need of funding. Remember to add information about other funding sources for the project or program. Tell the funder how your organization fits with their mission, focus, geographic location, target population, and current funding priorities. Write your closing (Tip: Avoid "sincerely" or "with regards"). Here are some examples of really impactful LOI closings: "With hope," "With the belief that you will understand our dire need," "Believing in miracles," and "Awaiting a sign that you'll partner with our organization."

Remember to write your LOI using the non-profit's letterhead for the first page of the letter. The letter should not exceed two pages. It is advisable to attach your IRS tax-exempt letter and a list of your board members (names, positions on the board, length of appointment, role in the community, and contact information). You will find a full example in *Grant Writing for Dummies* (Browning, 2016).

Invitation to Submit a Grant Proposal

When you are invited to apply for a grant, this is no time to hurriedly throw something together under the false perception that your organization is going to get a grant. This is the time to know how to craft a highly competitive, well-written grant application, whether you're allowed to upload a word processing document, or you end up copying and pasting your edited text into an online template. The invitation to submit a grant request means that all your relationship building efforts were successful. Celebrate briefly!

Required Corporate and Foundation Grant Proposal Components

1) Organization History and Capability[1]
2) Statement of Need or Statement of the Problem[2]
3) Program Design,[3][4]
   a) Purpose of the request
   b) Goals
   c) SMART Objectives
   d) Implementation Strategies
   e) Workplan[5]
4) Management Plan[6]
5) Evaluation Plan[7]
6) Sustainability Plan[8]
7) Budget Summary and Detailed Budget Narrative[9]
8) Mandatory Attachments

Researching Government Grants

Grants.gov (n.d.) is the free-access depository for 26 federal government grant-making agencies. The database is updated seven days a week. You can search online at the website (www.grants.gov/web/grants) or subscribe to a daily e-newsletter. In addition, Grants.gov also has a downloadable mobile phone application for quick searches. This online system makes it faster, easier, and more cost effective for grant applicants to electronically interact with federal grant-making agencies. It also provides the following key benefits, among many others, to the grant community by helping grant seekers learn more about available government funding opportunities.

The Grants.gov system centralizes more than 1,000 different grant programs across federal grant-making agencies awarding more than $500 billion annually. It also standardizes grant information, application packages, and processes for finding and applying for federal grants. The Help Desk system facilitates interaction with the federal government. Grant writers have a love-hate relationship with Grants.gov because the online system has multiple maintenance timeouts and can be a bit intimidating to use for those planning to submit grant applications via the workspace feature. However, Grants.gov does streamline the federal grants process by eliminating the need to navigate complex processes to find and apply for federal grants. Once you register your organization in the Grants.gov system, you can easily request updates on any active grant funding that may have changes in the application guidelines.

The intent of Grants.gov is to simplify the grant application process to save applicant's costs, time, and hassle. The system also eliminates the need to expend resources, time, postage, and reproduction costs associated with traditional paper-based grant applications. Most importantly, Grants.gov reduces training costs related to learning several different grant application systems and processes. The federal government designed a free-access web portal, making it easier to research and find federal grant opportunities. New users will quickly catch on to conducting grant opportunity research due to the improved search capabilities that begin with a simple key word search and can be expanded to advanced searches over numerous grant opportunity categories, including agency and grant category.

For grant researchers, having federal grant funding opportunities sent directly to our desks is timesaving. Potential applicants can be notified via email or RSS feeds of future grant opportunities as they are posted by federal agencies. Grant.gov simplifies the grant application process and reduces paperwork by increasing the ease-of-use through enhanced features common to the Web, such as downloadable and fillable forms, auto populated data, error checks, and e-mail notifications. The system also facilitates applicant use of electronic grant applications by providing built-in data quality checks, online support functionality, and a dedicated customer support team to help complete and submit applications.

For federal grant funding seekers, the Grants.gov system provides a secure and reliable source to apply for federal grants by validating grant applicants via a five-step registration process (www.grants.gov/web/grants/applicants/organization-registration.html). The system also allows completion and uploading of grant applications by authenticated and authorized users. Most importantly, Grants.gov ensures website stability and security through Secure Socket Layer (SSL) technology to encrypt transactional data and communications over the internet. The entire system monitors network traffic to identify unauthorized usage.

Focusing on a Federal Grant Funding Opportunity

When you click on a Grants.gov application notification link, the first web-page you see is the Synopsis (overview) of the grant funding opportunity. The webpage has tabs for the Synopsis, Version History, Related Documents, and the Package (federal grant application forms).

The synopsis contains this information about the funding available:

- Funding Opportunity Number (this is the tracking number for all queries regarding the grant funding program and your submitted grant application).
- Funding Opportunity Title (this is the title of the grant program).
- Opportunity Category (this tells you the type of funding – cooperative agreement or discretionary).
- Category of Funding Activity (this tells you the focus of the funding, for example, education or health).
- Expected Number of Awards (this tells you how many grants will be awarded).
- Cost Sharing or Matching Requirement (this tells you if a cash or in-kind match is required).
- Version (this tells you how many times the synopsis has been modified or changed; remember to read all of the versions).
- Posted Date (this tells you the date the synopsis was posted).
- Closing Date for Applications (this tells you when the grant application is due).
- Estimated Total Program Funding (this tells you the total dollars allocated to the grant program).
- Award Ceiling (this tells you the maximum amount of funding that you can request).
- Award Floor (this tells you the minimum amount of the funding that you can request).
- Eligible Applicants (this is where you check to see if a non-profit organization is eligible to apply).
- Additional Information (this is a brief description of the grant program that will be funded).
- Grantor Contact Information (this tells you who to contact for questions and their position title and provides a clickable link to their e-mail address).

Politics Matter

Do not apply for a federal grant without contacting your elected Congressional team members' offices in Washington, D.C. Finding a synopsis, starting to write your grant application, and submitting it for federal funding consideration is not the way to win a highly coveted federal grant award. What's missing? Your connectivity to your state's Congressional team members. What is their role? To provide advocacy between their grant-seeking constituents and federal grant-making agency program staff. Will your Congressional officials lobby on your behalf? No! However, they will track your grant application from submission to peer review to the final decision-making process (program staff recommendations for who will be awarded grants). Your chances of winning a federal grant award are higher with Congressional team member advocacy.

Government Grant Writing Expectations[10]

Include a DUNS Number

A DUNS Number must be included in order for an application to be reviewed. DUNS numbers can be obtained by accessing the Dun and Bradstreet website (www.dnb.com/duns-number/get-a-duns.html)[11] or by calling 1-866-705-5711.

Keep the Audience in Mind

Peer reviewers will use only the information contained in the application to assess the application. Therefore, the applicant should be sure the application and responses to the program requirements and expectations are complete and clearly written. Do not assume that peer reviewers are familiar with the applicant organization. Keep the review criteria in mind when writing the application.

Start Preparing the Application Early

If applying electronically through Grants.gov please ensure that adequate time is allotted to register and download applicable software and forms. Grants.gov offers a "Webcast" (registration required) entitled "Get Started with Grants.gov" (www.grants. gov/applicants/applicant-training.html) that provides startup requirements and tips.

Follow the Instructions and Application Guidance Carefully

The instructions call for a particular organization of the materials, and peer reviewers are accustomed to finding information in specific places. Present information according to the prescribed format.

- Be brief, concise, and clear. Make each point understandable. Provide accurate and honest information, including candid accounts of problems and realistic plans to address them. If any required information or data is omitted, explain why. Make sure the information provided in each table, chart, attachment, etc. is consistent with the proposal narrative and information in other tables.
- Be organized and logical. Many applications fail because the peer reviewers cannot follow the thought process of the applicant or because parts of the application do not fit together.
- Be careful in the use of appendices. Do not use the appendices for information that is required in the body of the application. Be sure to cross-reference all tables and attachments located in the appendices to the appropriate text in the application.
- Carefully proofread the application multiple times. Misspellings and grammatical errors will impede the peer reviewers in understanding the application. Be sure pages are numbered (including appendices) and that page limits are followed. Limit the use of abbreviations and acronyms and define each one at its first use and periodically throughout the application.

The Not Funded Follow-Up Process

If your grant application was rejected by a state or federal funding agency, you're entitled to review the grant reviewer's comments under the Freedom of Information Act (FOIA). Unfortunately, if you're rejected by a foundation or corporate giving entity, you probably won't receive any reviewer's comments, and you can't use the FOIA to get them.

Government agencies, especially federal ones, typically send a summary sheet with the section scores and an overview of strengths and weaknesses for each application section. If you receive a rejection notice from a state or federal funding agency that doesn't include such a summary or if the summary doesn't give you enough information, write a letter requesting the peer reviewers' comments. Each federal grant application usually has three peer reviewers (see www.dummies.com/business/nonprofits/grants/how-to-request-peer-review-comments-when-your-government-grant-application-is-rejected/).

When you use the FOIA, you receive the federal peer reviewers' actual written comments and scores (the points they bestowed on each narrative section in your grant application). If you plan to apply for this funding in the next grant cycle, you'll need to fix all the weaknesses noted in your grant application by the peer reviewers.

Myths About Federal Grant Funding

If your organization wins a federal grant award, it will take care of all your project or program costs. Fact: A federal government grant can be a great way to fund a promising project that otherwise might never get off the ground. But you can't believe everything you've heard. To receive a federal government grant, you must be eligible. For most federal grant programs, that means you must be a non-profit community-based organization, a college or university, or a state or local government agency. You must have your own funding, too. Most grants don't cover all costs. A federal grant is not "free money." Getting a grant requires serious effort, and it doesn't end when the check hits your account. You must report back regularly, show you're meeting all terms and conditions of the award, and do all the things you promise in your application, which is like the business plan for your project (see www.hrsa.gov/grant-myths/index.html).

It's easy to get a grant – it's free money! Fact: Applying for a grant requires a serious time-commitment (40 to 60 hours) to fully understand the grant application guidelines, its requirements, and your organization's capacity, structure, and resources essential to fulfill the purpose of the grant. Responsiveness to review criteria (published in every federal grant funding opportunity announcement) is essential, as well as other requirements of the grant, to be considered favorably for funding. You will need time to research and develop your proposal, write the application, and meet the submission requirements specified in the grant application guidelines.

Most government grant applications get approved if they are done right. Fact: Actually, you can submit a well-designed grant proposal and still not get funded. Writing the proposal well is, of course, important, but grants are given, except in rare cases, on a competitive basis. This means that the applications that are scored highest by a peer review committee are funded. Unfortunately, there is only so much money to go around, and because numerous organizations apply for the same money, most proposals are not funded. An organization, in fact, may send out dozens of proposals before one is funded. Additionally, even when a grant is received in one year, there is no guarantee that it will be funded again the next year. That is why funding agencies warn organizations not to depend on grants alone for their financial survival.

Reducing Your Chances of Getting a Rejection Notice

Our team designed an assessment tool to help you make decisions about applying or not applying for grant funding. This assessment should be used on every private and public sector grant funding opportunity. The author of this chapter has created a Grant Readiness Assessment (see Appendix F) that can be employed as you answer the following fundamental questions, and you also consider the targeted recommendations for governmental grant-seeking activities.

Fundamental Questions for Funding Opportunities

Is your organization an eligible grant applicant? Is the project in need of grant funding listed as a funding priority with your targeted potential funders? For example, if your project is about improving adult literacy and your targeted funder has published a list of grant funding areas of interest that includes reducing illiteracy, then your project is a match for this specific funder. Is there alignment between the grant applicant organization's mission and focus with the potential funder's mission and grantmaking focus?

Is the grant funding range high enough to support your grant application's request? Does the potential funder require successful grant applicants to collaborate with other community organizations (aka partners)? Does your management team have the capacity and experience to implement a grant-funded project? Does the grant applicant even have a chance of winning a competitive grant award? If awarded a grant, how will the grant applicant sustain the project when all the award monies have been spent? Does the potential funder require special data management systems or multiple collaborations that will slow down the grant-funded project's successful implementation?

Federal Grant Funding Opportunities

It's important to conduct due diligence in all these areas:

- Pay attention to the number of grants that will be awarded (low numbers below 20 are a red flag; do not apply!).
- Federal grants are not continually awarded in the same Congressional districts. Do your homework by researching where the grant has been awarded in the past three to five years. If there are no grantees in your

Congressional district, then your organization has a chance of applying and getting awarded a large federal grant award.

- Read all the application's guidelines and highlight any mandatory requirements. What should you look for? Some grant funding opportunities require sending your grant application information to a local and/or state government agency (Single Point of Contact approval) prior to submission.
- Reach out to your Congressional team's state and federal office staff. Ask for advocacy in tracking your submitted grant application. You will need all the help you can get to win a federal grant.

These are all very important questions to ask of your management and service delivery staff members for all grant seeking activities as well as equally important points to be considered in seeking government grants. Pushing forward when many of the required internal assets are weak or missing is not a good idea.

Conclusion

Throughout this chapter there has been coverage of the basics of the grant-making process with coverage of a dozen key topics. Appendix G provides a summary document containing the points covered in this chapter that can be used when discussing the grant seeking process and opportunities with the stakeholders in your community literacy program.

It is recommended that each of the individuals involved in the grant seeking and proposal writing processes in the community literacy program be thoroughly aware and comfortable with the processes covered in this chapter (see Appendix G). For a deeper read the reader should consider reviewing the practical and friendly guide *Grant Writing for Dummies* now in its sixth edition (Browning, 2016).

Notes

1. www.dummies.com/business/nonprofits/grants/how-to-present-your-organizations-capabilities-in-a-grant-application/
2. www.dummies.com/business/nonprofits/grants/how-to-construct-your-grant-applications-statement-of-need/
3. www.dummies.com/business/nonprofits/grants/how-to-write-your-grant-applications-program-design-section/
4. www.slideshare.net/NonprofitWebinars/writing-effective-program-designs

5 www.dummies.com/business/nonprofits/grants/how-to-prepare-a-grant-funding-timeline/

6 www.dummies.com/book-extras/grant-writing-for-dummies-6th-edition-resource-center/

7 www.dummies.com/business/nonprofits/grants/writing-evaluation-plan-grant-application/

8 www.thebalancesmb.com/how-to-write-sustainability-section-of-grant-proposal-2501955

9 www.thebalancesmb.com/the-basics-of-preparing-a-budget-for-a-grant-proposal-2501952

10 www.hhs.gov/grants/grants/get-ready-for-grants-management/tips-for-preparing-grant-proposals/index.html

11 www.dnb.com/duns-number/get-a-duns.html

References

Browning, B. A. (2016). *Grant writing for dummies* (6th ed.). Wiley.

Foundation Center. (n.d.). Foundation directory online. Candid. https://fconline.foundationcenter.org/

Grants.gov (n.d.). Office of Management and Budget. www.grants.gov/web/grants

Instrumentl. (n.d.). The institutional fundraising platform. https://www.instrumentl.com/

Merriam-Webster. (n.d.). *Merriam-Webster.com dictionary*. www.merriam-webster.com/dictionary/science.

Part Three

Case Studies from the Field

Chapter 10

More Than Contaminated Water

Flint, Michigan's Community-Wide
Efforts for Literacy

Chad H. Waldron

Author Note

Chad H. Waldron: https://orcid.org/0000-0002-9234-7655

Introduction

Flint, Michigan is not unlike most cities in the United States. It has faced significant economic and societal challenges like many other industrial urban centers. It has faced these challenges over years of economic decline as manufacturing jobs disappeared from the region (Highsmith, 2015). The Water Crisis, while making international headlines, was not unique to Flint either. There are studies showing the harm of lead entering drinking water supplies, both in Flint and beyond (e.g., Hanna-Attisha et al., 2016; Triantafyllidou & Edwards, 2012; Evans, 2004). Sadly, thousands of communities across the United States – rural, suburban, and urban – are facing challenges with their drinking water supplies – from lead to fluorinated pollutants (PFAS) to other chemical exposures (e.g., Enking, 2019; Hersher, 2019).

What is unique about Flint, Michigan is the way the community has responded to these crises with resilience and action. Even before the Water Crisis, Flint was on a mission to change the literacy trajectories of the region through the Flint and Genesee Literacy Network. This shared, collaborative work is under the banner of the *Flint Kids Read* campaign – a multi-partner strategy from various assets and leaders within the community. This chapter will zoom in on the collaborative work lead by the county-wide school district and its local educational partners to promote early literacy success. This chapter will take a community audit approach in sharing how community-driven resources and programming in one key initiative are being coordinated for children's learning and success in their community.

Background and Brief Review of Literature

Background

The Flint Water Crisis, beginning in 2014 and continuing to the present day, occurred in large part because of a failure to treat the water sources properly. This occurred after switching from treated lake and river water sources to solely rely on the Flint River without proper corrosion inhibitors (Pieper et al., 2017). While the Water Crisis's line replacement program is nearing completion, there are still tap sources that are unsafe to drink from or bathe in as the water lines, damaged by the previously corrosive water, have yet to be replaced (Fonger, 2021; Carmody, 2019). Community distrust in water quality as well as civil and federal lawsuits resulting from harm and failure to act linger on, seven years since its discovery. Out of the Flint Water Crisis came increased funding sources and opportunities to improve young children's access and quality of early childhood experiences. High-quality early childhood experiences have been proven to be effective in supporting young children after exposure to lead (Centers for Disease Control, 2015; Evans, 2004; Anderson et al., 2003). This need will continue as young children continue to develop and progress to school entry.

The Flint and Genesee Literacy Network, a community-based and action focused organization that has worked for many years to improve the literacy outcomes across generations, helped to organize efforts after the Flint Water Crisis (Flint & Genesee Literacy Network, 2021; Waldron & Jamerson, 2018). Its constellation of community partners includes but is not limited to university and college partners, the public library systems, health care providers and hospital systems, religious institutions, non-profit community support systems, the county-wide school district and its local educational partners, and community members. The partners come from across the community and diverse contexts with the shared goal of improving literacy access. What became apparent in this work was increased access to high-quality early childhood experiences and early literacy experiences for the Flint community.

With the support of the Community Foundation of Flint as well as other national and local donors, several initiatives were undertaken, including Dolly Parton's Imagination Library as part of the *Flint Kids Read* campaign. Dolly Parton's Imagination Library is an international book-giving program, providing a free book each month for a child from birth through their fifth birthday (Dolly Parton's Imagination Library, 2021). Previous research has proven this program to be beneficial for young children's exposure to texts, shared storybook reading experiences with adults, and the early literacy skills and strategies often assessed in preschool and kindergarten contexts (e.g., Szumlas et al., 2021; Skibbe & Foster, 2019; Waldron, 2018a; Samiei et al., 2016; Ridzi et al., 2014). Locally, this campaign would prove to be an instance of where community, educational, and health resources could be brought to bear to support children from birth through their school-age years. It has provided a unique opportunity to study the possibilities of supportive collaboration across multiple sectors to support young children's short- and long-term health and success in literacy.

Brief Review of Literature

The importance of children having high-quality early literacy experiences has been well established, across home and community to educational contexts. Within the home environment, research has proven the importance of talking to and reading with your child daily for the potential literacy skills acquired in those shared literacy experiences with an adult (Hart & Risley, 2003; Heath, 1982). A home with access to print has the potential to greatly benefit a child's language acquisition and literacy growth (Allington et al., 2010). High-quality early educational settings emphasizing literacy skills and strategies create opportunities for young children's literacy acquisition and success (Barnett & Frede, 2011; Anderson et al., 2003). Literacy skills and strategies, such as storybook reading, concepts about print (which are acquired in storybook reading), and alphabetic knowledge, are critical to children's short- and long-term successful progress in literacy (e.g., Lonigan & Shanahan, 2008). In supporting these young children, early childhood educators need professional development focused on knowledge and practice as well as on-site support in the form of instructional coaching to integrate these literacy skills and strategies (Zaslow et al., 2011; Neuman & Wright, 2010; Powell et al., 2010; Neuman & Cunningham, 2009). Beyond the home and educational sites, community programming around literacy, such as book-giving programs or educational programming for families, is often critical to creating a literate-rich environment where children and their families can thrive in literacy learning together (Purcell-Gates, 1996, 2007). This previous research has demonstrated the need to build supportive, collaborative systems for literacy in support of children, families, and communities.

As one considers the important work of community and family literacy efforts, the theoretical frameworks underlying such research are important to understand. Audits, the systematic review of a phenomenon, require one to look at the people, artifacts, systems, and structures at play in a community that can shape or detract from its desired outcomes. Much of the early literacy work in this community, like others, is centered upon the success of the child and its family unit. The ecological contexts and social interactions in which literacy occurs are important in shaping a young child's literacy success as well as translating the cultural importance of literacy (Bronfenbrenner, 1986; Cole, 1996). These contexts translate family, cultural, and situational norms to the child. Parental and other adult involvement in storybook reading provides expert scaffolding in shared reading with young children, who are acquiring early literacy strategies (Vygotsky, 1978; Wood et al., 1976). The potential to create multiple contexts – or ecosystems – that enhance a child's literacy success are necessary to study for the educational opportunities afforded to children, families, and communities. This chapter will zoom in to one key attribute of the *Flint Kids Read* campaign and how the local county-wide school district is supporting children and families across educational sites, in homes, and into the community.

Sharing Knowledge, Time, and Resources for Early Literacy Success

Flint's local county-wide school district serves multiple communities, including the city itself. The city was the hardest hit during the Water Crisis due to corrosion of the main water lines. The city's core zip codes were of the highest priority because of the known cognitive and physical effects to children who are exposed to lead. In the *Flint Kids Read* campaign, it was important to start the work there. The school district received funding, in part for this work, from the Flint Kids Fund of the Community Foundation of Flint. This funding would support the early literacy work of *Flint Kids Read* within

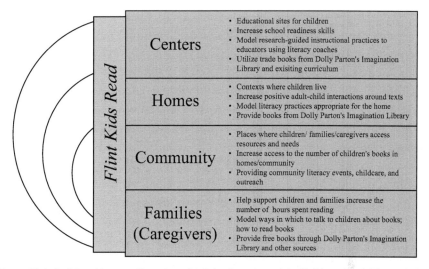

Figure 10.1 Building Literacy Capacity of Adults Engaging with Children, Birth Through Age Five, in *Flint Kids Read*.

educational sites, homes, and the community. This work has been in progress for the last two years. Out of this work, a model for building literacy capacity in adults interacting with children from birth to age five has been established across early childhood centers, at home, in the community, and with families and caregivers (see Figure 10.1). Knowledge, time, and resources were shared across these varying contexts to work toward an ecosystem that has the common goal of children's early literacy success.

The early childhood centers were the first component for this literacy capacity building. A key goal for this context was to increase school readiness skills in young children. The school district selected, trained, and implemented a core team of five early literacy coaches who have worked across 204 birth to age five classrooms across the last two years. These classrooms include private and publicly funded center-based sites. With these centers, the coaches modeled research-guided, developmentally appropriate instructional practices with the young children and their educators. The coaches also utilized trade books from Dolly Parton's Imagination Library to build shared home-to-center book experiences with the children. The modeled lessons and books were also connected to existing early childhood curriculum. The centers received sample lesson plans and resources to increase the likelihood that an educator would implement these instructional practices in their setting. This created opportunities to enhance the quality and experiences of the educational programs in early childhood for the community's children.

Considering that a center-based educational experience is only one part of a child's day and some children do not participate in such programming, it was important to be able to reach out and across to children and their families beyond the walls of an early childhood center. The next component in the model for building adult's literacy capacity with young children was the home environment (see Figure 10.1). The goal in this component was to increase positive adult and child interactions around texts. Some families and caregivers struggle greatly in making time to interact with their child around texts, and some may even be illiterate. Yet, interacting with a child around texts is more than just "reading the words." It can simply be a child and adult looking at the pictures and making up a story together from those pictures. As part of reaching out to home environments, the early literacy coaches modeled for families and caregivers how to interact around texts (books) with children. The coaches also helped families sign up for Dolly Parton's Imagination Library, provided tips and tricks when reading at home, and provided them with additional free books to use in the home.

It has been well established that access to texts in the home can be one of the biggest barriers to reading at home and children's literacy exposure (Allington et al., 2010). Being out and involved with the community was another key component of building literacy capacity (see Figure 10.1). The early literacy coaches needed to be present in places and spaces where children, families, and caregivers access daily needs and resources. In this component, it was important to increase everyone's access to the number of children's books in homes and within the community. This included providing books and literacy resources at community literacy events, childcare environments, and community outreach services. The coaches often modeled literacy activities that could be used at home with the children present. This included readily available resources to use at home, such as questions to ask your child while reading and how to read with a young child across the years. The literacy coaches would directly model and interact with the children for families and caregivers to observe and see examples of possible home interactions around literacy. This increased the level of experiences and opportunities provided at such events to the community and its children, families, and caregivers.

The last component – but critically important – was the support of families and caregivers around early literacy (see Figure 10.1). As the saying goes, "We don't know what we don't know." It can be assumed that most families and caregivers have some general ideas about reading to their child and about what their child needs for literacy success. They may be involved with their child's literacy in ways other than those believed to be "right" by traditional educational settings (Paratore et al., 2015). Yet, many others may have no idea where to start or what is appropriate for their child. The coaches worked with families and caregivers around the simple goal of increasing the number of hours spent reading with their child. This was done by modeling how to talk with their child in enrichment activities and how to read to their child through the use of interactive storybook reading. Increasing oral language and interactive storybook reading would in turn increase a child's exposure to literacy concepts, skills, and strategies. It was important to give families and caregivers explicit examples of working with their children around literacy. The coaches also provided copies of books from Dolly Parton's Imagination Library – purchased through book vendors – or other books that related to themes found in those monthly books. Additionally, a monthly newsletter full of literacy activities was shared via email with all families and caregivers participating in the Imagination Library. This created a network of collaborative literacy support for families and caregivers.

These four key components, as part of the larger *Flint Kids Read* campaign, focused on coordinated and systematic ways of building the early literacy capacity through people, systems, actions, and resources. The resources and support offered through each of the model's components could then be taken up by children, families, caregivers, early childhood education sites, and the community across settings. It is important to note how each of these components works in connection to one another. It would be impossible to build capacity in any one of these contexts without the others. This built toward the buy-in and importance of the common goal for all. The common goal of increasing early literacy experiences then became the norm, not the exception. It was also commonly shared across these participants and stakeholders in the community.

Solutions and Recommendations

Beyond establishing the four components of the literacy capacity model, the soft skills of communication, collaboration, and connection within and across the systems proved to be critical as well. This would be key for any community that would want to replicate the work completed in Flint. In communication, it is important for community partners, members, and stakeholders to make clear a common vision. In the case of Flint, it was to increase early literacy experiences through building adult and child interactions around literacy. This means sitting down at the same table and completing an analysis of your community: What's there, what's needed, and what could be. This work can be done initially using a SWOT (Strengths, Weaknesses, Opportunities, and Threats) analysis. Returning back to Bronfenbrenner's ecosystem, there are many micro-, macro-, and exo-systems at work across time in a community setting (Bronfenbrenner, 1986). It is critical to work within and across community stakeholders. This can help everyone to reach understandings of how these systems co-exist and support one another. It is important to audit the resources, opportunities, and needs of your community for this work. This requires months and years of shared, ongoing work in common spaces.

While not always perfect, this shared work often leads to common connections and collaboration opportunities. The traditional, often artificial, roadblocks or silos of all stakeholders are identified, acknowledged, and eliminated as much as possible. It is important to recognize where strengths and needs lie within each community stakeholder. In Flint, the Flint and Genesee Literacy Network's quarterly meetings were important gathering events for the community to meet as a whole and focus on common goals. In building connections, it is important to work together to reach out to the children, families, caregivers, stakeholders, and the community. These collaborations within Flint and Genesee County have uncovered new commonalities and avenues in which to work together toward the common goal of increasing literacy in our community.

The literacy capacity building model for Flint is yielding positive results in its first two years. Initial research completed on this work has demonstrated the following outcomes:

- Early childhood educators, who have participated in the center-based literacy coaching and professional development, have improved and strengthened their use of research-guided instructional practices for early literacy. This was based on observations of instructions, self-reported survey responses, and participation in interviews.
- Families and caregivers are utilizing the books of Dolly Parton's Imagination Library by reading with their child more often and value having these books for their children. They have also reported positive experiences in community-based activities around literacy.
- The books of the Imagination Library have become "shared stories" between a child's home, educational sites, and community settings. More homes in the Flint community have been or are participating in the Imagination Library. These books are now widely recognized and present across various settings in the community (Waldron, 2018b, 2019).

These initial findings are positive, yet there are many outcomes yet to be explored from this model and the research being conducted on this work. This model is not only responding to evident needs in the aftermath of the Flint Water Crisis for supporting young children but also is providing a common-sense model for literacy change that could be adapted to benefit many communities.

Conclusion

Flint, Michigan is so much more than contaminated water. It is a vibrant community working to build systematic change for its children and families in literacy and in life. The community is using activism through literacy to create positive opportunities and outcomes out of a tragic series of events. Using common goals and research-guided practices, the community of Flint is organizing for a better tomorrow as part of its road to recovery and renewal. The model for building literacy capacity across adults and children in birth to age five is scalable to other communities. It is also scalable for children and adults across the school-age years, leading to lifelong literacy success and improved community health through education. It takes time, investment, and strategy.

This chapter provided an analysis of a model of building capacity in adults interacting with children around literacy. It can provide other communities and their stakeholders in education, business, non-profit work, and beyond, with the necessary tools to begin their own work. The strategies found in this model can be used to enact community-guided literacy efforts. These efforts can further literacy equity, access, and capacity for this generation and generations to come.

References

Allington, R., McGill-Franzen, A., Camilli, G., Williams, L., Graff, J., Zeig, J., & Nowak, R. (2010). Addressing summer setback among economically disadvantaged elementary students. *Reading Psychology, 31*, 411–427.

Anderson, L. M., Shinn, C., Fullilove, M. T., Scrimshaw, S. C., Fielding, J. E., Normand, J., & Task Force on Community Preventive Services. (2003). The effectiveness of early childhood development programs: A systematic review. *American Journal of Preventive Medicine, 24*(3), 32–46.

Barnett, W. S., & Frede, E. C. (2011). Preschool education's effects on language and literacy. In S. B. Neuman & D. K. Dickinson (Eds.), *Handbook of early literacy research* (Vol. 3, pp. 435–450). The Guilford Press.

Bronfenbrenner, U. (1986). Ecology of the family as a context for human development: Research perspectives. *Developmental Psychology, 22*(6), 723.

Carmody, S. (2019, April 25). *Five years after Flint's water crisis began, is the water safe to drink?* NPR Michigan Radio. www.npr.org/2019/04/25/717104335/5-years-after-flints-crisis-began-is-the-water-safe

Centers for Disease Control. (2015). *Educational interventions for children affected by lead.* U.S. Department of Health and Human Services. www.cdc.gov/nceh/lead/publications/educational_interventions_children_affected_by_lead.pdf

Cole, M. (1996). *Cultural psychology: A once and future discipline.* Harvard University Press.

Dolly Parton's Imagination Library. (2021). About us. https://imaginationlibrary.com/about-us/

Enking, M. (2019, August 19). 'The next Flint,' and America's problem with lead in its water. *The Grist.* https://grist.org/article/the-next-flint-and-americas-problem-with-lead-in-its-water/

Evans, G. W. (2004). The environment of childhood poverty. *American Psychologist, 59*(2), 77–92.

Flint & Genesee Literacy Network. (2021). About us. http://flintliteracynetwork.org/our-community/

Fonger, R. (2021, January 21). *Judge gives preliminary OK to $641 million Flint water crisis settlement.* MLive. www.mlive.com/news/flint/2021/01/judge-gives-preliminary-ok-to-641-million-flint-water-crisis-settlement.html

Hanna-Attisha, M., LaChance, J., Sadler, R. C., & Champney Schnepp, A. (2016). Elevated blood lead levels in children associated with the Flint drinking water crisis: A spatial analysis of risk and public health response. *American Journal of Public Health, 106*(2), 283–290.

Hart, B., & Risley, T. R. (2003). The early catastrophe. *Education Review, 17*(1), 110–118.

Heath, S. B. (1982). What no bedtime story means: Narrative skills at home and school. *Language in Society, 11*(1), 49–76.

Hersher, R. (2019, April 22). *Scientists dig into hard questions about the fluorinated pollutants known as PFAS.* NPR Morning Edition. www.npr.org/sections/health-shots/2019/04/22/708863848/scientists-dig-into-hard-questions-about-the-fluorinated-pollutants-known-as-pfa

Highsmith, A. (2015). *Demolition means progress: Flint, Michigan and the fate of the American metropolis.* The University of Chicago Press.

Lonigan, C. J., & Shanahan, T. (2008). *The executive summary: Developing early literacy: Report of the national early literacy panel. Executive summary. A scientific* *synthesis of early literacy development and implications for intervention.*The National Institute for Literacy. http://files.eric.ed.gov/fulltext/ED508381.pdf

Neuman, S. B., & Cunningham, L. (2009). The impact of professional development and coaching on early language and literacy instructional practices. *American Educational Research Journal, 46*(2), 532–566.

Neuman, S. B., & Wright, T. S. (2010). Promoting language and literacy development for early childhood educators: A mixed-methods study of coursework and coaching. *The Elementary School Journal, 111*(1), 63–86.

Paratore, J. R., Edwards, P. A., & O'Brien, L. M. (2015). Helping parents help children achieve the Common Core State Standards: Reaching out in different ways. In L. B. Gambrell & L. Mandel Morrow (Eds.), *Best practices in literacy instruction* (5th ed., pp. 390–413). The Guilford Press.

Pieper, K. J., Tang, M., & Edwards, M. A. (2017). Flint water crisis caused by interrupted corrosion control: Investigating "ground zero" home. *Environmental Science & Technology, 51*(4), 2007–2014.

Powell, D. R., Diamond, K. E., Burchinal, M. R., & Koehler, M. J. (2010). Effects of an early literacy professional development intervention on head start teachers and children. *Journal of Educational Psychology, 102*(2), 299.

Purcell-Gates, V. (1996). Stories, coupons, and the TV guide: Relationships between home literacy experiences and emergent literacy knowledge. *Reading Research Quarterly, 31*, 406–428.

Purcell-Gates, V. (Ed.). (2007). *Cultural practices of literacy: Case studies of language, literacy, social practice, and power.* Lawrence Erlbaum Associates.

Ridzi, F., Sylvia, M. R., & Singh, S. (2014). The Imagination Library program: Increasing parental reading through book distribution. *Reading Psychology, 35*(6), 548–576.

Samiei, S., Bush, A. J., Sell, M., & Imig, D. (2016). Examining the association between the Imagination Library early childhood literacy program and kindergarten readiness. *Reading Psychology, 37*(4), 601–626. https://doi.org/10.1080/02702711.2015.1072610

Skibbe, L. E., & Foster, T. D. (2019). Participation in the Imagination Library book distribution program and its relations to children's language and literacy outcomes in kindergarten. *Reading Psychology, 40*(4), 350–370.

Szumlas, G. A., Petronio, P., Mitchell, M. J., Johnson, A. J., Henry, T. R., & DeWitt, T. G. (2021). A combined reach out and read and imagination library program on kindergarten readiness. *Pediatrics, 147*(6), e2020027581. https://doi.org/10.1542/peds.2020-027581

Triantafyllidou, S., & Edwards, M. (2012). Lead (Pb) in tap water and in blood: implications for lead exposure in the United States. *Critical Reviews in Environmental Science and Technology, 42*(13), 1297–1352.

Vygotsky, L. (1978). Interaction between learning and development. *Readings on the Development of Children, 23*(3), 34–41.

Waldron, C. H. (2018a). *Improving early literacy experiences through Flint Kids Read: Teachers' experiences in developing early literacy practices.* Unpublished internal document. Genesee Intermediate School District.

Waldron, C. H. (2018b). "Dream more, learn more, care more, and be more": The Imagination Library influencing storybook reading and early literacy. *Reading Psychology, 39*(7), 711–728.

Waldron, C. H. (2019). *Survey of family literacy practices in Flint: An executive summary.* Unpublished internal document. Genesee Intermediate School District.

Waldron, C. H., & Jamerson, J. (2018). After the water crisis: Flint's community-based initiative changing young children's lives. *Childhood Education, 94*(5), 58–63. https://doi.org/10.1080/00094056.2018.1516474

Wood, D., Bruner, J. S., & Ross, G. (1976). The role of tutoring in problem solving. *Journal of Child Psychology and Psychiatry, 17*(2), 89–100.

Zaslow, M., Tout, K., Halle, T., & Starr, R. (2011). Professional development for early childhood educators: Reviewing and revising conceptualizations. In S. B. Neuman & D. K. Dickinson (Eds.), *Handbook of early literacy research* (Vol. 3, pp. 425–434). The Guilford Press.

Chapter 11

Leveraging Tutoring Center Literacy

Katherine Marsh

Author Note

Katherine Marsh: https://0000-0002-7051-3819

This chapter presents a view of the Linton Foundation (LF, a pseudonym), a small, non-profit foundation with a mission to be a valuable education resource in its local community. LF teachers work with students to enhance the academic skills of students who learn differently and to accelerate the overall performance of students through one-to-one individualized instruction. LF professional educators offer educational testing and consultation to parents and deliver research-based professional development to teachers and administrators.

We provide a brief background of the history of tutoring and the pedagogical philosophy of LF's founders and highlight the impact of student experiences with research-based models of pre-K-through-adult literacy instruction. The chapter will provide education professionals with an understanding of and appreciation for the role such an organization can play in the broader school community in its efforts to positively impact the literacy of the students and families (and by extension the schools) it serves.

DOI: 10.4324/9781003228042-15

As an independent non-profit organization, LF views itself as a resource for parents and a partner to educators in public, private, and home schools. Although all public schools and many private schools support students with learning differences, at times specific expertise is not within the reach of students when needed. Services offered by LF such as one-to-one tutoring, educational assessments, professional development, funding for other non-profits focused on education, and community outreach to parents and the public can help to bridge that gap.

Historical Background

In the first two centuries of college in the United States, part of the routine of academic work was tutorial in nature, established to ensure the proper preparation of white male students for college-level work (Fraser, 2014). During that time, with primary schools mandated though not universally available and secondary schools just becoming established in cities and larger towns, students relied on local tutors for college preparation. As public secondary schools began to flourish by the late 1800s, tutoring became less common. Students attending secondary schools prepared for college work there before enrolling in college. In the 1970s colleges began recruiting a more diverse body of students and tutorial work became associated with the stigma of remediation for students who were not able to do college work upon enrollment (Arendale, 2010). Mori (2009) found that the remedial approach persists in many tutoring situations today. Yet, tutoring is also viewed as supplementary in nature, related to Lareau's (2011) concept of concerted cultivation, a style of parenting focused on adding extra-curricular activities and opportunities to children for the purpose of fostering potential talents. Parents may seek tutorial interventions such as the Wilson reading method (What Works, 2010) as an alternative to a failing educational system (Booth, 2004), or seek additional specific content area practice (e.g. algebra, literary essay writing) or test preparation to better prepare children for private high schools or college.

Some tutors work in conjunction with public and private school teachers such as in a writing lab (Tinberg & Cupples, 1996). More often tutors work apart from the classroom such as when students are pulled out of their classes to attend one-to-one or small group tutoring at school. Most tutors work far apart from the classroom, seeing students outside of school and having little to no interaction with their tutees' regular teachers. For these tutors, tutorial focus is driven by parents or by joint agreement between the parent and tutor. One-to-one support outside of school, including peer tutoring (Mastropieri et al., 2003), can be motivating for struggling students (Paquette & Laverick, 2017). Unfortunately, very little research in the United States has assessed the effectiveness of tutorial support outside of school. In Switzerland, Hof's (2014) study results suggested improved reading achievement for moderately struggling high school students. Other studies outside of the United States suggest that pressure to pass college entrance exams drives parents to pay for the extra costs associated with tutoring (Pallegedara & Mottaleb, 2018; Seo, 2018). Some researchers suggest the need for regulation of outside tutoring in some countries to prevent harm to the health of children under extreme pressures to succeed (Msiska, 2016).

LF and Its Mission

LF, a 501(c)(3) non-profit institution, was set up by the donor of an endowment in the latter part of the 20th century. The donor was inspired by his parents, the founders and administrators of a small junior college specializing in avant-garde computer courses during the mid-20th century. When that junior college was absorbed into another college, funds became available for the endowment of LF, which was organized to be free from the need to seek donations. Dedicated to teaching students with learning disabilities, LF makes educational grants in local communities and fully supports two tutoring centers in suburban locations in the northeastern United States. Some years after its founding, one of the tutoring center directors spearheaded the idea of training teachers as a way to reach more students, leading to the implementation of professional development for educators.

The two tutoring centers are each run by a separate director who oversees the staff and daily operations of the center including both full- and part-time teachers and an administrative assistant. Each center has a few full-time teachers and may have a dozen or more part-time teachers, depending on schedules and the needs of the current population of tutees. Each director reports to the president of LF, and the president reports to the board of directors. All teachers are certified, and many have specialized program credentials for reading, writing, or content areas. LF does not make use of volunteers or lay people as tutors.

The partnerships between the foundation's own entities are of primary importance. LF maintains a strong commitment to professional development for its in-house teachers. The teacher training offered by LF provides access to LF potential staff who are trained by the best practitioners, which in turn benefits all students. Equally, LF provides tutoring center teachers with opportunities for no cost teacher training within its professional development entity. For example, in-house LF teachers may be eligible to be trained as reading specialists or attend remote or in-person seminars and workshops.

LF partners with other non-profits to provide tutoring services using both financial aid and grant monies. The foundation provides grants to education-based non-profits. Sometimes that relationship is simply donor–recipient. LF also offers online reading instruction courses to volunteers who tutor homeless children. Many non-profits that use volunteers for tutoring express a need for training beyond their standard training in the areas of executive functioning (EF) and in reading and writing strategies. LF can help to fill those needs by providing targeted grant monies as well as free or low-cost direct training for the volunteers of those other non-profits. LF regularly partners with other non-profits to sponsor workshops, seminars, and webinars for parents and educators.

Literacy Perspectives

LF meets the individual needs of each student using evidence-based, multisensory methods. With increasing numbers of children diagnosed with a reading disability such as dyslexia or other disabilities that can impact reading, it is critical that LF provide remediation appropriate for each individual student. LF teachers are diagnostic and prescriptive in their approach to literacy remediation. Teachers continually observe, make notes, and analyze during each tutoring session and use that information to plan out the next lessons.

During intake of potential tutees, LF directors ensure that a basic literacy foundation (i.e., phonemic awareness) is in place before selecting a tutor to begin a phonics-based approach. Directors determine if a student needs intervention at the phonemic, decoding, fluency, comprehension or at all levels of literacy. Early grades curricula tend to focus on phonics and the alphabetic principle, which can leave students who are lagging in phonemic awareness confused and guessing, rather than strategizing when decoding. The growing awareness of brain-based differences in dyslexics (Shaywitz, 2020) highlights the need to strengthen and lengthen teaching that supports phonemic awareness.

LF's literacy philosophy stems from a goal to provide support for students with learning disabilities. Students with dyslexia and language-based learning disabilities (LBLDs) were the initial focus of LF's efforts when it opened its first tutoring center. Research-based reading programs such as Orton-Gillingham (OG) and Wilson, two programs developed specifically to teach struggling readers, form the basis of LF's offerings. Foundational work in reading diffi-culties done by Orton (Sayeski et al., 2019) in the early 1900s highlighted the complex characteristics of dyslexia. Orton worked with Gillingham, who pro-duced a multisensory, structured, sequential curriculum and provided teacher training in its use. OG focuses on the needs of individual students but has been adapted for use with small groups (see Ring et al., 2017, for example). It com-bines reading, spelling, and writing in a comprehensive, multisensory approach that is tailored for individual pacing and targeted repetition, introducing new material only when the student demonstrates mastery of previous material. The OG approach requires specialized training and as a result may not be implemented by a majority of school districts that have not experienced the pressures of a large population of students with LBLDs. The result is a majority of LBLD students, particularly those of lower socio-economic status, being left with meager support in reading (Sayeski et al., 2019).

Based on OG, the Wilson method (What Works, 2010) was developed by Wilson in 1988 to support students struggling to learn to read. The Wilson method is more structured than OG and involves a set of 12 definitive steps progressing from the alphabetic principle through fluency and comprehen-sion. The Wilson method has been shown to improve reading for struggling readers (Duff et al., 2016) but has not yet been designated by the United States Department of Education as effective due to a lack of comparative studies (What Works, 2010).

These programs were chosen by LF because research indicated that students who struggle with reading respond best to multisensory, structured, phonics-based instruction. LF actively recruits teachers trained in both the OG and Wilson methods and selects a method based on individual student need. LF not only provides the one-on-one tutoring schools may need for indi-vidual students (i.e., on site at a school, at one of its centers, or remotely via the internet), but it can also provides direct professional development to schools or groups of teachers via literacy workshops and OG trainings held throughout the year and overseen by Academy of Orton-Gillingham Practitioners and Educators (AOGPE) fellows.

Services to Students and Schools

Parents concerned with their child's academic progress may turn to LF in lieu of or in addition to support received at their child's school. Parents may be reluctant to approach their child's school due to discomfort with the idea that their child may need extra help. They may feel that their child's struggle with reading is a manifestation of their lack of parenting skills. They may also be unfamiliar with how to approach their child's school, particularly if their child's teachers have not raised any concerns. Some parents wish to avoid the stigma associated with special education at their child's school and the potential negative effects of labeling their child within the school community. For other parents, cultural and linguistic differences between their home life and their child's school may lead them to LF as a first option or as a source of oversight or second opinion if they are confused about or unsatisfied with services offered by their child's school. Students who might otherwise have to wait while their school conducts assessments and arranges services can be served in a timelier fashion through LF since assessments through LF can often be scheduled immediately. Some parents seek tutoring as an aspect of concerted cultivation (Lareau, 2011), providing tutoring irrespective of any academic concerns.

Schools may turn to LF when one or more students require specialized education services but a specialist with the specific training is not currently available. LF teachers can provide services temporarily while the district hires or trains staff, or they can provide ongoing services for districts as needed. Some schools arrange for tutoring with LF for students who would benefit from summer tutoring to prevent regression or to catch up with peers. Recently, LF has also been called upon to provide COVID-19 compensatory services to students either to prevent regression or as a supplement to remote or hybrid school services.

LF's tutoring centers provide instruction to public, private, and home-schooled students ranging in age from kindergarten through adult. Many LF students have been identified with a learning disability, and a majority benefit from tutoring in reading. LF teachers have experience in supporting children with specific disabilities (e.g., dyslexia, dysgraphia, dyscalculia, LBLD, and non-verbal learning disability) as well as attention deficit hyperactivity disorder (ADD/ADHD), and weaknesses in EF. Some LF students are general education students who enroll to receive general or content area academic support to increase their achievement level. Based on demand and the availability of trained staff, LF's tutoring centers offer test preparation for many standardized tests (e.g., independent high school, state-mandated, high school equivalency, college entrance).

One limitation to LF's services is the location of the tutoring centers in suburban areas. Parents must be able to arrange transportation, limiting the number of students of lower socio-economic status who can be served directly by LF. The COVID-19 pandemic has altered this limitation somewhat. Since most students attended school remotely during the height of the pandemic, access to devices for remote tutoring increased among the population LF serves. Although some parents prefer in-person tutoring, opportunities for remote and hybrid tutoring situations have increased access to LF teachers and provided parents with additional flexibility with scheduling and transportation.

The expanded LF mission includes teacher training and workshops in research-based reading, including offering online teaching certificate courses in partnership with a local college that offers graduate level credit for the work. The teacher training entities stay on the forefront of current education topics as well as ongoing research for updated practices. LF has a robust commitment to providing professional development, and staff are encouraged to read current research, attend conferences, and participate in professional development workshops or courses to translate that research into practice for the students they serve.

The foundation conducts parent and community outreach for local, public school special education parent advisory groups (SEPACs) for parents and educators of children with special needs. It sponsors or arranges parent evenings geared toward bringing parents up to date on current research and introducing parents to related professionals in the special education field. LF fields regular requests from SEPACs for no-fee, remote or in-person presentations and fulfills these requests using LF staff. Recent presentations include how to motivate children who are doing distance learning, how to prevent regression over the summer months, and an in-depth look at dyslexia remediation. LF conducts community outreach to parents with an informal speaker series on topics such as attention deficit disorder (ADD), EF, and navigating the Individual Education Plan (IEP) process.

The frequency and duration of tutoring can be an obstacle for some parents. Children with dyslexia may need many months of tutorial support to make gains in reading and a minimum of two or three tutorial sessions per week. To support these students, LF sets its own affordable rates for direct student services. Families who qualify are supported by income-based sliding scale scholarships. The percentage of eligible families varies from year to year but on average is greater than 20% of students served. Enrollment for the academic year (September to June) or the summer (June through August) is handled on a first come, first served basis. Some students attend just for the summer and some just for the academic period, while others attend year-round.

LF is committed to open communications among parents, teachers, and tutorial staff and encourages tutors to act as a resource to parents and teachers. LF teachers do not engage directly in student advocacy such as attending an

IEP meeting to specifically advocate for school-provided services on behalf of students. Parents may pay for their child's tutor to attend an IEP meeting to explain their work with the student. LF teachers are encouraged to coordinate with their tutee's teachers via email or phone conversations as appropriate and at no charge to parents. LF teachers provide periodic written reports to parents detailing the nature of tutorial instruction, status of progress, and proposed future work if needed.

The majority of LF students benefit from individualized tutoring with some students demonstrating dramatic gains. For example, an LF high school tutee received three hours per week of additional instruction in reading and writing during the summer of 2020. His noteworthy progress prompted his IEP team to continue his services with LF through the summer of 2021 while staff adopted LF's strategies. In LF's experience, the one-to-one tutoring improves student self-esteem. Students may come to their first tutoring session with an attitude of discouragement. LF teachers encourage their tutees to develop strategies to manage their learning and increase their responsibility and independence while building academic skills and confidence. During tutoring sessions, the tutee is the only student in the class, providing the freedom to ask questions and expose confusions and other vulnerabilities in an atmosphere of care and support.

LF students can return to their regular classrooms armed with individualized strategies and increased confidence. Perhaps the greatest impact from such tutoring comes in the form of increased self-efficacy and self-advocacy. Students can begin to see themselves as successful, moving away from the edges of discouragement toward a more positive recognition of ways they can help themselves achieve academic goals. The success of one or two students may persuade administrators to consider professional development training through LF. Some private schools lacking staff with special education backgrounds rely on LF for special education consultation. One small private school retains an LF teacher as a special education liaison to parents and teachers to provide direct tutoring, to conduct informational meetings with parents about recommended services, and to support classroom teachers to accommodate or modify curricula.

Schedules at the tutoring centers are flexible; they are generally open Monday through Saturday, from 9:00 a.m. to 8:30 p.m. during the week and 8:00 a.m. to 2:00 p.m. on Saturdays. During the school day, services can be provided to public and private schools by an itinerant LF teacher. LF teachers do not travel to private homes for tutoring, but occasionally students are tutored in community spaces such as a public library. During the COVID-19 pandemic shutdown, LF tutors transitioned entirely to remote tutoring, seeking electronic resources and modes of delivery such as online whiteboards, as well as emailing or mailing materials directly to parents for use during a remote tutoring session. As COVID-19 restrictions were lifted, LF teachers returned to the centers and to schools while still offering remote or hybrid tutoring options. Except for test preparation packages, LF does not offer fixed tutoring packages because LF directors cannot predict a predetermined number of hours a student will need for instruction. LF also does not lock parents into a contract. If parents or LF teachers see a need for a change, then tutoring can end and no further fees are incurred.

LF has responded to a strong need in the community for educational evaluation services due to long wait times and exorbitant prices from competitors. Staff are trained in educational assessments for reading, writing, math, and vocabulary skills. Parents may opt for a full evaluation or for only reading or only math assessments. Partial assessments can be provided if a parent is looking for a specific, individual test. Based on background information provided by the parent, each tutoring center director determines the area of evaluation needed and which assessment tools to use for a particular student.

Future Trends in Tutoring

LF has begun to serve adult students lacking skills necessary to perform in the workplace (i.e., that prevent advancement within their company). Often these adults did not receive sufficient special education services while in K-12 schools, or they may have received a later-in-life learning disability diagnosis. Companies see the importance of skills such as basic writing and are willing to support their employees financially to retain valuable staff. These adults may not be able to take advantage of other avenues of advancing their academic skills due to learning differences that require specialized one-to-one intervention.

Similarly, pressures for college readiness will continue to increase as students from culturally and linguistically diverse (CLD) backgrounds and English Language Learners (ELLs) pursue post-secondary education. LF can continue to provide high-quality teachers trained in research-based reading programs, multisensory math, and study skills. A current trend in education is for greater family engagement that views students as individuals with specific CLD backgrounds, rather than as a member of a more generalized group with a specific disability. LF has experience working individually with students and their families, tailoring learning programs to suit specific needs, and is able to adapt and adjust curricula to honor and incorporate diverse funds of knowledge (Moll et al., 1992).

Another emerging trend in education is recognition of the importance of EFs in academic achievement. LF has designed its own curriculum materials to support students as they develop EFs. During workshops for groups of students and in individual tutoring, LF teachers help students develop study skills, note-taking, test preparation, attention, memory, and time-management skills. The intersection of language and literacy skills with study skills and self-efficacy highlights EFs as the "foundation for academic proficiency" (Newhall, 2014), because it is the underpinning of the skills and attitudes students need to succeed in school. Teaching skills is not enough for students to succeed even if learning differences are addressed. Students must gradually take over management of their learning including their time, materials, and information. These are the EF building blocks that make it possible for students to become engaged self-regulated, life-long learners.

Position in the Marketplace

Public or private schools often find out about LF by word of mouth. For many private schools, school staff may learn about LF because parents are willing to pay privately for LF teachers to see a child at their private school. The school reaps the benefits of the tutoring and may inquire further about LF services. In the past LF did not actively reach out to schools in an organized marketing effort. Beginning in 2019, LF sent letters to schools it had never had a contract with before as an introduction and to highlight its unique services.

LF faces competition from private tutors whose rates are often lower and from other local and national tutoring centers. Unlike private tutors, LF carries insurance and vets its teachers by conducting background checks in addition to ensuring that they have the proper licensure and training. LF considers itself an expert when it comes to instructing students with learning disabilities such as dyslexia and nonverbal learning disabilities.

LF differs from other center-based tutoring organizations in that it is a non-profit and therefore mission driven. As a non-profit, LF can provide a sliding scale for those students who ordinarily could not afford its services and thus reach a wider, more diverse population. Unlike other center-based tutoring organizations, all LF's instruction is one-to-one to meet the individual needs of the student. Parents do not sign contracts, and there is no penalty for terminating tutoring. Further, LF believes in continuity of instruction, so once a student is matched with a tutor, they remain with that tutor each week. Students do not shift from tutor to tutor as is the case with many other center-based tutoring organizations. When students remain with the same tutor, a strong, personalized bond is formed. The tutor comes to know each student and establishes a strong rapport with the student's family, which often spurs greater leaps in learning and overall academic confidence.

One measure of LF's effectiveness is that it does very little advertising. Until recently, LF has not reached out to schools but has developed new clients through word of mouth. Community outreach to SEPACs and informal presentations aimed at parents are supplementary as far as gaining new clients, compared with ongoing referrals from current and past students. LF helps students and their parents identify resources and develop strategies to succeed in academics, providing a perspective that is separate from a child's school, yet solidly established within the education community. LF students sometimes prefer this "outside of school" perspective since it removes the stigma of tutoring at school and fosters the perspective that the student chose tutoring. LF's main literacy focus is not only to help students become better at the skill of reading but also to help students become better at seeing themselves as readers.

References

Arendale, D. R. (2010). Access at the crossroads: History of learning assistance in U.S. postsecondary education. *ASHE Higher Education Report, 35*(6), 23–59. https://doi.org/10.1002/aehe.v35:6

Booth, S. (2004). "I can't read". *Teen People, 7*(2), 99.

Duff, D., Stebbins, M. S., Stormont, M., Lembke, E. S., & Wilson, D. J. (2016). Using curriculum-based measurement data to monitor the effectiveness of the Wilson Reading System for students with disabilities: An exploratory study. *International Journal on Disability and Human Development, 15*(1), 93–100. https://doi.org/10.1515/ijdhd-2015-0007

Fraser, J. W. (2014). *The school in the United States: A documentary history.* Routledge.

Hof, S. (2014). Does private tutoring work? The effectiveness of private tutoring: A nonparametric bounds analysis. *Education Economics, 22*(4), 347–366. https://doi.org/10.1080/09645292.2014.908165

Lareau, A. (2011). *Unequal childhoods: Class, race, and family life.* University of California. https://doi.org/10.1525/9780520949904

Mastropieri, M. A., Scruggs, T. E., Spencer, V., & Fontana, J. (2003). Promoting success in high school world history: Peer tutoring versus guided notes. *Learning Disabilities Research & Practice, 18*(1), 52–65. https://doi.org/10.1111/1540-5826.00057

Moll, L. C., Amanti, C., Neff, D., & Gonzalez, N. (1992). Funds of knowledge for teaching: Using a qualitative approach to connect homes and classrooms. Theory into Practice, 31(2), 132–141. https://doi.org/10.1111/1540-5826.00057

Mori, I. (2009). *Backgrounds of supplemental education in the United States.* Conference Papers – American Sociological Association, 1–11.

Msiska, F. G. W. (2016). Regulating private tutoring for public good: Policy options for supplementary education in Asia. *International Review of Education*, *62*, 239–241. https://doi.org/10.1007/s11159-016-9531-3

Newhall, P. W. (2014). *Executive function: Foundations for learning and teaching.* Landmark School Outreach Program.

Pallegedara, A., & Mottaleb, K. A. (2018). Patterns and determinants of private tutoring: The case of Bangladesh households. *International Journal of Educational Development, 59*(C), 43–50. https://doi.org/10.1016/j.ijedudev.2017.10.004

Paquette, K. R., & Laverick, D. M. (2017). Enhancing preservice teachers' skillsets and professionalism through literacy tutoring experiences. *Reading Improvement, 54*(2), 56–66.

Ring, J. J., Avrit, K. J., & Black, J. L. (2017). Take flight: The evolution of an Orton Gillingham- based curriculum. *Annals of Dyslexia, 67*(*3*), 383–400. https://doi.org/10.1007/s11881-017-0151-9

Sayeski, K. L., Earle, G. A., Davis, R., & Calamari, J. (2019). Orton Gillingham: Who, what, and how. *Teaching Exceptional Children, 51*(3), 240–249. https://doi.org/10.1177/0040059918816996

Seo, E. H. (2018). Private tutoring and academic achievement: Self-study as a mediator. *Social Behavior and Personality, 46*(5), 823–830. https://doi.org/10.2224/sbp.6689

Shaywitz, S. (2020). *Overcoming dyslexia* (2nd ed.). Penguin Random House.

Tinberg, H., & Cupples, G. (1996). Knowin' nothin' about history: The challenge of tutoring in a multi-disciplinary writing lab. *Writing Lab Newsletter, 21*(3), 12–14.

What Works Clearinghouse. (2010). *Wilson reading system.* https://ies.ed.gov/ncee/wwc/EvidenceSnapshot/547

Chapter 12

The Chinatown Youth Organizing Project
Community Literacies for Social Justice

Mary Yee

Author Note

Mary Yee: https://orcid.org/0000-0003-3840-2227

Introduction: Background and Context

This case study is about the Chinatown Youth Organizing Project (CYOP), a youth leadership development program for first-generation Asian immigrant high school students centered around community-based literacy practices. This program evolved uniquely out of a 2009 youth organizing campaign against school violence in Philadelphia (Yee, 2016). Veteran Asian American community activists developed CYOP after student leaders of the campaign who requested ongoing workshops to address the "why" of inter-racial school violence and the under-resourcing of public education. Subsequently, in 2010 CYOP was established at Asian Americans United (AAU), a long-time social justice organization in Philadelphia, to teach youth about the socio-political forces that affect their families and communities and to motivate them to take action against injustice. Centering youth voices and lived experiences, CYOP embraces participatory democratic process and collective decision-making, as well as learning about ethnic histories, systems of power and privilege, institutional racism, and hierarchies within public education. Its vision is to provide a place for youth to belong, to understand the conditions of their life in America, and to take action against societal injustices through community campaigns around education, health, or civic engagement.

Vision, Mission, and Primary Audience

AAU conceives of its vision for its youth programs as "education for liberation," founded on "the belief that re-envisioning the education of our youth can transform communities." Its curricula embrace "diverse experiences and cultures and counters the incessant materialistic and selfish culture permeating our world" (AAU website). For CYOP, in particular, the aim is to work with "underserved Chinese youth" around issues they confront as new immigrants (e.g., school violence, language barriers, little knowledge of college access resources, marginalization in schools and neighborhoods, and few artistic and recreational opportunities). Moreover, the program seeks to develop youth leaders, who are personally, socially, and politically aware and who will actively engage in social justice struggles on behalf of their community and society at large (AAU website). Ultimately, CYOP aims to instill an obligation to give back to the community locally and globally.

Conducted in Mandarin, CYOP specifically targets first-generation Chinese immigrant youth, who are low-income, high school age, and English Language Learners (ELLs). The following is an excerpt from the annual online application:

Qualifications 资格:

- You are a recent immigrant student who speaks Chinese 说中文的移民学生
- You are looking for a meaningful summer internship opportunity 你在寻找一份有意义的暑期实习机会
- You care about your community 你关心你的社区
- You are punctual, responsible, passionate, and hardworking 你是一个守时，负责任，充满热情，努力的人
- You have an open mind and are willing to learn and grow 你有一个开放的思想并愿意学习和成长
- You are a team player and want to be a better leader 你可以在一个团队里工作并想成为更好的领袖

WorkReady Eligibility Requirements/WorkReady申请要求

- Will be 14–18 years of age as of July 1, 20XX 在20XX年7月1日时的年纪在14–18岁之间
- Are a Philadelphia resident 是费城居民
- Meet specific Temporary Assistance for Needy Families (TANF) income guidelines as determined by annual income and family size (see TANF guidelines) 符合TANF收入要求 (看以下收入列表)
- Are eligible to work in the United States 可以合法在美国工作
- Are registered with the Selective Service, if male and 18 years of age on or before July 1, 20XX 男性如20XX年7月1日是18岁或18岁以上, 需要在Selective Service 报名

CYOP hires approximately 25 high school students annually for its six-week summer program.

Theoretical Frameworks

The AAU's concept of "education for liberation" harkens from its early modeling after Freedom Schools as well as the critical pedagogy of veteran Asian American community organizers influenced by tenets of community and youth organizing and Pablo Freire. The establishment of CYOP, following in the same philosophical and political vein, is unique in addressing the issues of newly arrived immigrant students and their experience of American urban schooling. Given AAU's social justice stance, the program, in bell hooks' (1994) words, "teaches to transgress" as a way to seeing education as "the practice of freedom" and develops "critical consciousness" and "praxis" in young people (Freire, 2000).

CYOP embodies the critical pedagogy of Pablo Freire and youth activism and, by extension, related critical literacy practices. Thus, the literacy practices are student-centered, facilitated, inquiry-based, and interactive. Rejecting the "banking model" of education, the youth organizers/facilitators practice a collaborative learning environment where lively dialog and analysis are encouraged as knowledge is co-constructed. Critical literacy, as defined by Luke (2012), is "an overtly political orientation to teaching and learning and to the cultural, ideological, and sociolinguistic content of the curriculum. It is focused on the uses of literacy for social justice in marginalized and disenfranchised communities." Furthermore, it has "an explicit aim of the critique and transformation of dominant ideologies, cultures and economies, and institutions and political systems" (2012, p. 5). CYOP does not shy away from talking about the "isms" (e.g., imperialism, colonialism, capitalism, or neoliberalism). The concept of multiple literacies aligns with the work of Brian Street (1984), which recognized literacy as social practice and ideological (i.e., related to power dynamics); the work of Barton et al. (2000) around situated literacies (i.e., socially contextualized literacies); and the work of the New London Group (1996) around multimodal literacies, (i.e., the combined use of many communicative modes).

In the youth activism literature, Fox and colleagues (2010) present critical youth engagement as a conceptual and political framework and discuss the importance of spaces for critical youth education, "to harvest what Freire calls critical consciousness (Horton and Freire, 1990) [b]y inviting young people to unpack the historic and current role of structural forces such as. . . [the − isms] and the history of social justice movements" (p. 633). Each summer CYOP incorporates a youth participatory action research project (YPAR), which many scholars regard as a democratic and liberatory practice for engaging young people in changing social institutions that negatively affect them and their communities (Cammarota & Fine, 2008a; Fox et al., 2010). Cammarota and Fine (2008b) have observed how emerging critical awareness of institutions and processes affects "one's life course" and capacity to act and "to provoke change" (p. 3). Ginwright and Cammarota (2002) position "youth as agents of change"; introduce an ecological approach incorporating social context; and draw attention to the need for healing from trauma and the effects of oppression, (i.e., "fostering the emotional, spiritual, and psychological, and physical wellness") of young people (pp. 86, 92). While Paris and Alim (2017) make a case for "culturally sustaining pedagogy" and the importance of understanding the history and culture of youth participants from marginalized and racialized groups. Lee and Walsh (2017) extend this to the issues of curricular content for immigrant youth in their explication of "social justice culturally sustaining pedagogy," which speaks to issues of language, citizenship, and transnational identities. By highlighting the contributions of selected scholars, I have provided an overview of the conceptual or theoretical frameworks that undergird the work of CYOP.

A Critical Literacies Model for Community Education

In this section, I share "A Day at CYOP" to describe the program model. As a way to further distinguish the program, I provide a perspective on how teacher characteristics, the setting, and the interactions between facilitators and students matter, and conclude by highlighting the program's critical pedagogy and critical literacies.

A Day at CYOP

On a day in July 2014, I arrived at 8:45 AM to shadow the lead youth organizer/facilitator "JT" who, having forgotten that he was supposed to supervise breakfast, arrived late and a bit harried. After reviewing the agenda, JT started the day's program. (See sample weekly schedules in Figure 12.1.)

In a large all-purpose room, JT led a morning chant in Chinese, welcoming each and every student by name. The group formed a large circle for a warm-up activity, which generated a lot of teasing, joking, and laughter among the youth – putting everyone in a good mood. After reminding the students about ground rules (see Figure 12.2), including mutual respect, good listening, confidentiality, and no pressure to reveal anything one did not want to, JT introduced the day's theme, identities.

Other staff had the youth participate in "Stepping In, Stepping Out," an exercise where individuals step into a large circle if a question applies to them (e.g., *Who is the eldest child?* or *Who is an ESOL student?*). The questions move from general, more innocuous ones to more serious ones such as, *Who has experienced racial harassment in school?* or *Who has undocumented family members?* The objective was to have youth see they are not alone in experiencing these situations. JT shared his own family's experience of family separation, migration, and hardship to which the youth responded with empathy and understanding. The students then worked in five small groups of five to discuss which of these questions they identified strongly with, which made them uncomfortable or challenged them. Each group negotiated a division of labor to include a scribe, recorder, and reporter and then worked on the questions. Meanwhile staff circulated and noted responses on chart paper when groups reported out.

In the next activity small groups developed courses of actions for hypothetical vignettes of immigrant young people in distressing situations (e.g., having experienced date rape; dropping out of high school because belittled for not knowing English; or being detained for deportation because of a juvenile crime). The youth discussed social context, probable causes and dominant attitudes related to the scenarios, and possible courses of action. Because the activities are conducted in Mandarin and the topics are relevant to their lives, the students are generally eager to learn, socially comfortable, and highly engaged in the sessions.

Week 2: 7/13–7/17	Monday	Tuesday	Wednesday	Thursday	Friday
9:30–10:00	Icebreaker: None	Icebreaker: Start Tour	Icebreaker: Dance	Icebreaker: None	Icebreaker: Fun Out
10:00–10:30	S. Philly tour and gentrification 1. Casino mural, notice the changes. 2. Cambodian Association to tour with us	Chinatown Tour and Debrief History of Chinatown	Small Circle/Big Circle: Individual/ small circle solutions are easy to think of but not big circle	Take Out Movie	Sexuality Workshop
10:30–11:30					
11:30–12:00 PM	Lunch	Lunch	Lunch	Lunch	Lunch
12:00–12:30	Gentrification and Housing Workshop; Tour of Southwest	AAU History or organizing YMCA development site?	Gender Workshop	4 1's; Apache	CAAAV Workshop or organizing for Black Lives Matter
12:30–1:00					
1:00–1:30					
1:30–2:00 PM	Closing: Icebreaker	Closing: Reflection Journal, Cuban Shuffle	Closing: Journal Reflection	Closing: Snake, Energizer	Closing: Dance or Unity Clap
Week 3: 7/20–7/24	Monday	Tuesday	Wednesday	Thursday	Friday
9:30–10:00	Icebreaker: None	Icebreaker: Trust chair circle/virus attach	OFF	Icebreaker: Go over ground rules	Icebreaker: Fun Out
10:00–10:30	Pyramid of Power	White Supremacy (3 pillars?)	OFF	Greet and help with set up: Know Your Rights, CLS Workshop	Patriarchy and Gender
10:30–11:00					
11:00–11:30					

11:30–12:00 PM	Lunch	Lunch	Lunch	Lunch	Lunch
12:00–12:30	Organizing 101: Wealth and Inequality	12:30 start time. Panel of Philly social movements now. Exploration of Black community struggles and Black Lives Matter and police state	OFF	Fred to come and speak: What is capitalism?	Introduce Interview Project: Brainstorming with youth about questions they want to ask community; come up with names of people to interview
12:30–1:30					
1:30–2:00 PM	Closing: Feedback Journal and share	Closing: Journal, What Did You Learn	OFF	Closing: Dance	Closing: Sheets!!! (Facilitator survey and workshop survey); HW: brainstorm list of questions to ask community members

Figure 12.1 CYOP Week 2 and 3 Schedule: Locating Ourselves and Understanding Power and Institutions

Note: Names of staff assigned to activities have been deleted.

Source: Asian Americans United

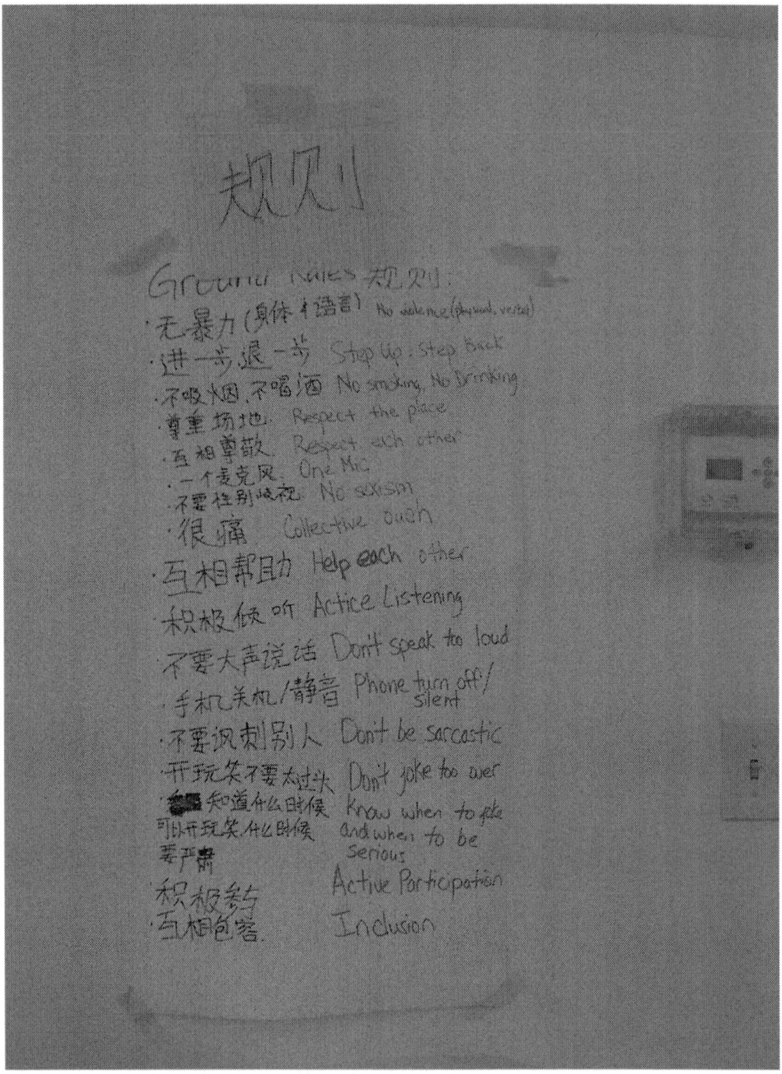

Figure 12.2 CYOP Ground Rules in Chinese and English

After lunch the youth blew off some steam with a physical activity, then the small groups reported out on the vignette task. Following this there was a "Small Circle, Big Circle" exercise focusing on homelessness. Groups were asked to list reasons why someone might be homeless and to write them in a small circle on chart paper. They provided answers such as disability, laziness, no family, or no education. The second part of the exercise was to think about what larger causes would have led to the reasons for homelessness. Their answers included lack of social supports, natural disaster, war, discrimination, unemployment, gambling, and so on; these were recorded in the larger concentric circle. Then the staff asked what possible solutions there were to deal with what they saw in each circle. Thus, the youth were exposed to discussions of how personal issues related to larger social issues and ideological, political, and economic factors. The last activity of the day was discussing how to focus the research project that the students were planning. The overarching questions were

- What is the experience of immigrant students in public schools?
- What can we do with this information?
- What can we do to make a change?

Students settled on examining the experience of immigrant students with the Pennsylvania Keystone Exams for graduation.[1]

Before dismissal, staff led a chant:

Wherever we go,
People want to know,
Who we are.
So we tell them,
We are AAU,
Mighty, mighty AAU!

They can't hear us.
Say it louder!
We are AAU!
Mighty, mighty AAU!

JT also wrote an affirmation in Chinese and English on the board: "I have voice. I choose to use it. I have things to say. I want to be heard!" Everyone put their right hands together to form a wheel with spokes as a gesture of unity. Then students filed papers in their portfolios and signed out. The youth group had been together from 9 a.m. to 2 p.m. During CYOP, JT presented certain activities, listened to and circulated among students, and mediated conflicts while simultaneously monitoring how the day was going.

After a short break, JT and college-aged staff convened to debrief on the day. This day people wondered about the appropriateness of some of the questions for stepping in and out of the circle. One concern was whether a question allowing a third category for gender identity might have caused young people to out themselves inadvertently, another was about whether being undocumented was right or wrong, good or bad. Citing laws enforcing slavery and Japanese American incarceration, JT pointed out that laws are not always just and being undocumented was not wrong or bad. Staff then raised any problematic social interactions among the staff or within the student groups. Each staff was assigned several students with whom they would meet individually in rotation to check-in, to receive or give feedback, or to help with any problems. That day JT met later with a male student who was having anger management issues and negative interactions with other students. JT told me he often had to deal with rivalries and resentments among students. From his own experience, he learned the importance of acknowledging mistakes, hearing people out, and resolving conflicts promptly. This required considerable emotional intelligence and emotional labor from JT and the staff of emerging adults.

Other features of the CYOP summer program were field trips to other activist organizations and guest speakers who presented on topics such as Islam, LGBTQIA issues, and the history of Chinatowns. To strengthen youth leadership, staff also recruited a small number of the youth to be in a leadership group that met weekly to help develop and critique the program and take on some program tasks such as organizing the culminating event at the end of the summer. Youth were also encouraged to participate in the AAU voting rights campaign and cultural activities such as the Mid-Autumn Festival. Later in the summer, I attended the culminating event, a showcase of small group projects to demonstrate their important learning over the course of the summer. These included skits, videos, musical pieces, and multimedia presentations, which revealed talents that the immigrant youth did not generally have the opportunity to display in their high schools.

Importance of Teacher, Setting, and Relationships

In traditional educational terms, pedagogy composed of the triad of curriculum, instruction, and assessment is used to explain and develop educational progress (Achtenhagen, 2012). This conceptualization neglects the importance of teacher identity, setting, and the interpersonal relationships important in fostering trust and learning. Burke (2004) paraphrases bell hook's belief:

Teachers must be aware of themselves as practitioners and as human beings if they wish to teach students in a non-threatening, anti-discriminatory way. Self-actualisation should be the goal of the teacher as well as the students.

(https://infed.org/mobi/bell-hooks-on-education/)

In the context of CYOP, AAU has realized that the most effective leaders/facilitators are former youth activists, who are first-generation working-class immigrants proficient in Mandarin. In other words, these leaders/facilitators have undergone the process of conscientization and engaged in social justice campaigns on behalf of the immigrant community. Having lived under the same marginalized circumstances as the youth, they understand and empathize with the youth they lead and mentor in the program. They are able to build trust.

The community setting at the Folk Arts-Cultural Treasurers (FACTS) Charter School is vastly different from the high schools that the CYOP students attend. There are no metal detectors and no school police. The school is the site of many Asian community activities and afterschool programs. Signs and posters are multilingual, and student work and artwork cheerfully fill the corridors.

Established as the result of grassroots advocacy, the school maintains a social justice and folk arts curriculum. This place is safe from the bullying and racial harassment that many immigrant students experience in public school. Translanguaging or multilingualism is the norm; the languages and cultural heritages of all who attend are respected and valued. CYOP operates here during out-of-school time under the auspices of AAU, which is housed at FACTS. As Shaun Ginwright (2016) asserts, community-based organizations are important sites for developing critical consciousness and caring relationships, which are important in healing.

Additionally, in contrast to public school settings and mentioned earlier, the CYOP program staff are extremely attentive to the relationships between staff and students and among students. CYOP embraces a caring ethic that nurtures youth and supports them in dealing with personal, family, and interpersonal issues.

The Practice of Critical Pedagogy and Critical Literacy/Literacies

The program description based on a site visit provides examples of progressive curriculum content, democratic processes, critical methodology, and authentic

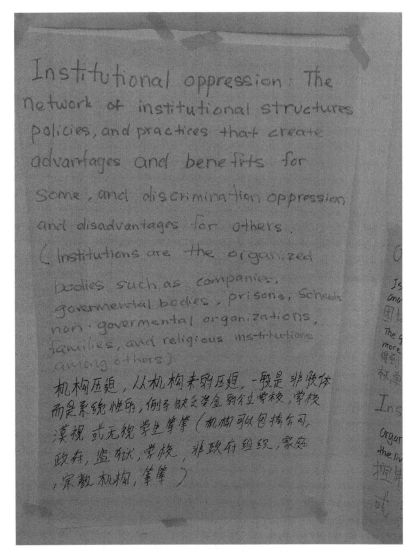

Figure 12.3 Bilingual Definition of Institutional Oppression

and multidisciplinary ways of assessing knowledge and skills. Clearly, the education that the CYOP youth receive is geared toward providing them with critical literacies, tools to challenge their racialization and marginalization (See Figure 12.3).

Aligning with Lee and Walsh's (2017) call for "social justice culturally sustaining pedagogy" (SJCSP) for immigrant youth, CYOP has developed in similar directions by "1) fostering a justice-centered citizenship that encourages youth to be active agents in the political process; 2) encouraging critical dialogues around race; 3) and recognizing the evolving and hybrid nature of immigrant youths' identities" (p. 197).

Moreover, Freirean and youth activist concepts referenced are practiced in many ways. Challenging the language ideology prevalent in their public high schools, the use of translanguaging is a critical literacy practice. The adult staff and students relate their own immigration narratives and counternarratives counteracting dominant discourses – also forms of critical literacy.

The value placed on socio-emotional literacies is reflected in the attention paid daily to evaluating group process as well as individual interactions among participants and between participants and staff. As an aspect of critical pedagogy, this attention to social emotional learning is significant in helping first generation youth find empathy, hope, inspiration, and understanding while "learning a new land." Moreover, students employ analyses of power and institutions to identify and analyze social issues within their own communities and their families as well as seek solutions to issues such as under-resourced schools, gentrification, or interracial conflict. Furthermore, students apply these critical literacies in the process of community research through which they contest institutional inequities and develop actionable findings (see Figure 12.4).

In this out-of-school time setting, freed from the constraints of traditional schooling, CYOP has no testing, no requirement to answer or participate against one's will, no disciplinary code, and no rigid hierarchy between staff and students. Thus, student participation is totally voluntary and motivated by what the program offers the student: camaraderie, validation of immigrant experience, valorization of first language and heritage culture, new knowledge about the socio-political context of their lives, a confidential space in which to explore identity, and empathy from staff and fellow students. Critical pedagogy and critical literacies have enabled this. What students demonstrate is the potential left untapped by conventional public schooling, traditional pedagogy, and demeaning attitudes toward ELLs. The youths' summer CYOP experience is evidence of their potential and counternarrative to deficit discourses.

Research, Evaluation, and Relation to Schools

Documenting the work of Asian youth organizers was part of a multi-case study examining how participating in political activism influenced

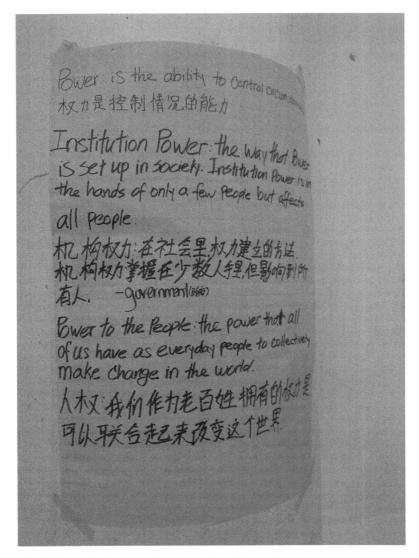

Figure 12.4 Bilingual Definitions of Institutional and People Power

post-secondary trajectories and aspirations for the future (Yee, 2018). What is presented in this chapter is a secondary analysis based primarily on my interaction with JT, a high school activist, who became a full-time bilingual youth organizer. As one of the original AAU founders, I have been a continuous ally and supporter of their social justice work. Consequently, I was not a total stranger and was easily accepted while shadowing JT and observing CYOP activities. In subsequent summers, I was asked to present on Asian American history and to conduct a workshop on interviewing and qualitative research in preparation for a youth research project on community needs. I also observed the youths' culminating presentations and multimodal projects in Mandarin and English. The data for this chapter was collected through these visits, interviews with JT and other adult organizers, and review of archival documents.

Given its small scale and shoe-string funding, AAU has not conducted formal program evaluations or research. Since CYOP is not a standardized program with a prescribed curriculum funded by any particular institution, there has not been a requirement for a formal evaluation. The usual metrics used for measuring success, such as the impact on grades, school attendance, or disciplinary actions, would not likely show the main benefits. More significant is the student growth seen in the discussions of sophisticated concepts and ideas, self-confidence, more grounded identities, and demonstration of talent in their multimodal final projects. Similar to other community youth leadership and development programs, it is likely that students improved their school literacies as well, given that they participated in authentic tasks in which they were interested and which were relevant to their lives (Yee, 2018; Cammarota & Fine, 2008b).

What might be regarded as formative assessment is done almost daily by staff during the program. As mentioned earlier, the debriefing after each day included staff reflection of the process and pedagogical content, students' intellectual and emotional states, personal reactions to activities of the day, and recommendations for improvement and concrete work with individual students. While not articulated as the cycle of "continuous quality improvement," it is indeed that.

CYOP recruits students from high schools across the city but has no formal relationship with the school district. Conducted in the spirit of Freedom Schools and bell hooks' "teaching to transgress," CYOP is an alternate model of education that challenges the usual pedagogical model in urban comprehensive high schools. Arising out of the student struggle against school violence, CYOP is thus radical counter-schooling in the sense that it is examining and questioning the roots or foundations of education. In resisting the hegemony of traditional public education, CYOP embraces CSP, antiracist and inquiry-based learning, ethnic studies, translanguaging, and a democratic process to amplify student voices and agency. CYOP operates in the out-of-school time space where community literacies for social justice can be freely practiced and transmitted to successive cohorts of young people.

The Outlook for the Future: Funding and Sustainability

AAU, CYOP's parent organization, is a community-based organization that has been in existence for over 30 years in Philadelphia's Asian community. Engaged in youth leadership development from an activist stance, it has received funding from various sources such as Bread and Roses, small local family foundations, various arts funders, youth-serving networks, and individual donations. Through the Philadelphia Youth Network, youth receive minimum wage pay for 20 hours/week for participating in CYOP. Without this money, many would be pressured to find work in restaurants or retail. The summer youth program also participates in the Department of Agriculture (USDA) Summer Food Service Program.

Given that funding is always precarious for non-profits, especially grassroots organizations that challenge the status quo, the future is never a sure thing. Working with children and youth who live in under-resourced and marginalized communities means long hours, stressful emotional labor in caring for and supporting students, and uncertainty about employment. While the goal of CYOP is to train youth who will someday become leaders and staff, there is no straight path to success. As the current cohort of youth organizers and CYOP facilitators develop from emerging adulthood to a stage where life goals are more firmly set, the issue of who will take their place is a crucial one as they start to set sights on other types of progressive work where their livelihood might be more stable. Undoubtedly, a more substantial level of philanthropic funding or the development of some income-generating enterprises would ease the pressures by enabling the hiring of more staff and higher salaries. Thus, the future of AAU and CYOP depends at least as much on the commitment of community allies and supporters as on funders to develop innovative and ingenious ways of funding community and youth activism in pursuit of social justice.

Note

1. See CYOP's 2014 publication on high school graduation testing presented to City Council, "Report and Findings: Chinese Immigrant Student Experiences with the Pennsylvania Keystone Exams." http://aaunited.org/wp-content/uploads/2010/04/KeystoneReport3_toCity-Council.pdf

References

Achtenhagen, F. (2012). The curriculum-instruction-assessment triad. *Empirical Research in Vocational Education and Training, 4*(1), 5–25. https://doi.org/10.1007/BF03546504

Asian Americans United. (n.d.). *Youth Programs.* http://aaunited.org/youth/

Barton, D., Hamilton, M., & Ivanic, R. (2000). *Situated literacies: Reading and writing in context.* Routledge.

Burke, B. (2004). *bell hooks on education.* The encyclopedia of informal education. https://infed.org/mobi/bell-hooks-on-education/

Cammarota, J., & Fine, M. (Eds.). (2008a). *Revolutionizing education: Youth participatory action research in motion.* Routledge.

Cammarota, J., & Fine, M. (2008b). Youth participatory action research: A pedagogy for transformational resistance. In J. Cammarota & M. Fine (Eds.), *Revolutionizing education: Youth participatory action research in motion* (pp. 1–11). Routledge.

Fox, M., Mediratta, K., Ruglis, J., Stoudt, B., Shah, S., & Fine, M. (2010). Critical youth engagement: Participatory action research and organizing. In L. Sherrodoo, J., Torney-Purta, & C. Flanagan (Eds.), *Handbook of research on civic engagement in youth* (pp. 621–649). John Wiley. https://doi.org/10.1002/9780470767603.ch23

Freire, P. (2000). *Pedagogy of the oppressed* (Revised 30th anniversary ed.) Continuum.

Ginwright, S.A. (2016). *Hope and healing: How urban activists and teachers are reclaiming matters of the heart.* Routledge. https://doi.org/10.4324/9781315757025

Ginwright, S.A., & Cammarota, J. (2002). New terrain in youth development: The promise of a social justice approach. *Social Justice, 29*(4), 82–95. www.jstor.org/stable/29768150

hooks, b. (1994). *Teaching to transgress: Education as the practice of freedom.* Routledge. https://doi.org/10.3366/para.1994.17.3.270

Horton, M., & Freire, P. (1990). *We make the road by walking: Conversations on education and social change.* Temple University Press.

Lee, S. J., & Walsh, D. (2017). Socially just, culturally sustaining pedagogy for youth: Possibilities, challenges, and directions. In D. Paris & S. H. Alim (Eds.), *Culturally sustaining pedagogies: Teaching and learning for justice in a changing world.* Teachers College Press.

Luke, A. (2012). Critical literacy: Foundational notes. *Theory into Practice, 51,* 4–11. https://doi.org/10.1080/00405841.2012.636324

New London Group. (1996). A pedagogy of multiliteracies: Designing social futures. *Harvard Educational Review, 66*(1), 60–93. https://doi.org/10.17763/haer.66.1.17370n67v22j160u

Paris, D., & Alim, S. H. (Eds.). (2017). *Culturally sustaining pedagogies: Teaching and learning for justice in a changing world.* Teachers College Press.

Street, B. (1984). *Literacy in theory and practice.* Cambridge University Press.

Yee, M. (2016). "We have the power to make change." The struggle of Asian immigrant youth against school violence. In J. Connor & S. M. Rosen (Eds.), *Contemporary youth activism: Advancing social justice in the United States* (pp. 289–310). ABC-CLIO, Greenwood.

Yee, M. (2018). *Transformative trajectories of first-generation immigrant youth activists* (Publication No. 10840716) [Doctoral dissertation, University of Pennsylvania Graduate School of Education]. ProQuest Dissertations and Theses Global.

Chapter 13

Health Literacy in a Diabetes Education Center

Megan Hughes

Author Note

Megan Hughes: https://orcid.org/0000-0001-7427-8337

Health Literacy in a Diabetes Education Center

How we understand health information is one of the most important things in our lives. What makes this area of literacy so important is we often don't need it until a crisis situation occurs, and we suddenly are required to become an expert. As Barton and Hamilton (2012) state, "This is an area where the knowledge seems very specific, is often technically complex. People investigate such areas only when a problem impinges on their lives and they move rapidly from a position of having very little knowledge or background to one where they become experts" (p. 232). We need to learn the complex activity of managing our health and the literacies associated with that process quickly.

Unfortunately, health literacy is often thought of by health literacy researchers as a deficit within the patient. The patient with low health literacy is imagined by those researchers as a person with low general literacy. As Pleasant and Kurkuvilla

DOI: 10.4324/9781003228042-17

(2008) wrote, "health literacy is seen as a problem patients have and physicians need to overcome" (p. 152). But when one imagines the well-educated individual who is unable to effectively navigate the system and the information presented to them by the health care professionals, it is reasonable to question whether the deficit lies in the patients and their families or in the communication practices within the health care professional community and the health care system in general.

Health Literacy

Health literacy is a "contested concept" (Black, 2012, p. 147) within the health literacy research community and among health professionals. There is no agreed upon definition of health literacy in the research or practitioner literatures (Sørensen et al., 2012). This lack of consensus on the definition of health literacy leads to a lack of consensus regarding how health literacy should be assessed and studied and how patients should be supported. While there is no consensus, existing definitions tend to fall into two categories: 1) focus on individual skills, or 2) focus on societal level issues. Clinical health researchers tend to focus on the skills of individual patients while public health researchers tend to include a societal perspective. Literacy researchers can offer an important perspective by bringing the lens of literacy as a social practice.

When we think of literacy as a social practice, we see that being health literate means more than being able to decode text. It's how we comprehend, use, and interpret health information in various contexts. As Knobel and Lankshear (2007) note, "Understanding literacies from a socio-cultural perspective means that reading and writing can only be understood in the contexts of social, cultural, political, economic, historical practices to which they are integral" (p. 1). Knobel and Lankshear go so far as to say it is "impossible" to "abstract or decontextualize 'literacy bits' from their larger embedded practices and for them to still mean what they do in fact mean experientially" (p. 2). In the same tradition, Barton and Hamilton (2012) define literacy practices as "what people do with literacy" (p. 6). These practices involve the values, beliefs, and social relationships integral to that practice. In order to study how patients use literacy in the management of their health, we must examine their experience in a real-world context.

Health Literacy in Context

Case study offers an opportunity to study health literacy in a contextualized, nuanced manner. Descriptive case study in particular is used to "describe a phenomenon (the 'case') in its real-world context" (Yin, 2014, p. 238). This case study is a study of a single case bounded by an individual site, the Diabetes Education Center (a pseudonym), in which I was able to directly observe the patients' interactions within the setting.

I used activity systems analysis methods (Yamagata-Lynch, 2010) to help bound and define the case. I also draw on third generation activity theory (Engeström, 2001), which encourages researchers to examine the intersections of bounded activity settings. In this study, I describe the health literacy practices of patients at the Diabetes Education Center and their health literacy practices related to diabetes management engaged in at home. The center and home are two intersecting activity systems bounded by place but also by shared goals, objectives, and subjects.

Activity systems analysis defines units of analysis, by drawing on the work of Engeström (1987) and Rogoff (1990), as the "human activity itself embedded within its social context" (Yamagata-Lynch, 2010, p. 6). When using this method of analysis, the human activity (i.e., their health literacy practices) are studied within the social context in which they take place. As part of the analysis, which I describe in detail later in this chapter, the raw data is parsed into "goal-directed action units" (Yamagata-Lynch, 2010, p. 26). In this case, those goal-directed action units are what Rogers (2003) calls literacy events. These events were identified and connected back to the larger system in order to determine literacy practices.

This case study describes the literacy practices of patients with Type 2 diabetes as they learn to manage this disease. The activity system of the center is preserved through observations, interviews with staff and the patients, and collection of various artifacts associated with the education process. These literacy practices are situated within the intersecting activity systems of the center through direct observation and the patients' homes through interviews and artifacts. Description of these two intersecting activity systems and the tensions within and between the systems is an attempt to capture the complex and social nature of health literacy practices.

Methods

Research Site

The Diabetes Education Center is housed in a hospital in the suburbs of a major American metropolitan area. The population of the suburb is diverse in race, ethnicity, and economic status.

The center is accredited through the American Diabetes Association. Center staff consists of two nurse practitioners who handle patient education about diabetes and a nutritionist who handles the meal planning and education about foods and nutrition. The center offers both individual education sessions and small-group education sessions. For this study, I interviewed patients who participated in either individual or small-group sessions.

Participants

There are three permanent staff members on the diabetes education side of the center, two nurse practitioners and one nutritionist. The patients I observed and interviewed were all diagnosed with Type 2 diabetes and were participating in either individual education sessions or small-group sessions. I interviewed eight patients from the center. Four of the patients I interviewed participated in the individual education sessions with either the nurse practitioner, nutritionist, or both. Four of the patients I interviewed participated in small-group education sessions at the center.

Patients Participating in Individual Education Sessions

Tasha. Tasha is a young woman who has struggled with pre-diabetes for years. When she became pregnant, she developed gestational diabetes, and her doctor referred her to the center for extra education. Sadly, she lost the baby. The diabetes didn't go away.

Sam. Sam is a 63-year-old man who has had diabetes for 30 years or so, by his estimation. He's been coming to the center for about five years. Sam works as a forklift driver and has a high school education. He hopes working with the nurse and the doctor will help him get his blood sugar under control.

Laura. Laura first developed diabetes when she was carrying her son, 25 years ago. After her son was born, the diabetes went away but doctors warned her it would probably be back, and they were right. Sixteen years later she developed Type 2 diabetes and has been living with the disease for nine years.

Sue. Sue is learning how to use a new blood sugar monitor and how to enter her blood sugars into a logbook. Sue has no time for an interview because her doctor's appointment is directly after her appointment with the nurse, so I observed her session but did not talk with her directly.

George. George grew up in rural Arkansas and, until last year, ran a farm back home while living up north. George had a stroke, and at the time, his blood sugar was 750. That was 13 years ago. George is now 73 years old and has been coming to the center for nine years.

Patients Participating in Small Group Sessions

Sonya. Sonya is a social worker who was diagnosed with diabetes two years ago. She has had some other health issues, which she attributes to her stressful job and her family responsibilities. She works as a child welfare officer with a large case load, and she also takes care of her elderly mother. This has led her to decide she has to "let this job go." She is embarking on a huge life change, and part of that change is learning to manage her diabetes.

Linda. Linda was diagnosed with pre-diabetes in 2005 or 2006, noting that she was uncertain of the exact year. She became the caregiver for her dad as well as working full-time and was diagnosed with diabetes in 2009. She had been coming to the center for approximately six weeks and had just started attending group sessions.

Teresa. Teresa was diagnosed with diabetes approximately two years ago. She had recently retired after 24 years of work as a waitress. She is hoping the center participation will help her get back on track since she had been doing well until a family crisis created high levels of stress.

Martin. Martin is an English professor at an area college. He has had diabetes for about 18 years and shared that he hoped this group program could help him get his blood sugar under control.

Data Sources and Data Collection

Primary data sources were observations, field notes, interviews, audio recordings, and artifacts. In addition, I maintained a researcher log throughout the collection and analysis process that included ongoing memos to myself (e.g., thoughts I had while at the center, ideas to explore).

Analysis

My data analysis proceeded through a series of three phases. I provide a brief description of each phase here and a more detailed description of each phase with examples in the sections that follow. Phase I took place during data collection and organization. During this phase, I observed patient education sessions, interviewed staff and patients, and took field notes. After each observation, I wrote analytic memos, organized the data I collected, and transcribed the sessions and the interviews as soon as possible. Phase II involved coding data to make sense of key activities and focal areas. During Phase II of my analysis, I finished transcribing all sessions and interviews, combined my field notes and my session transcriptions into one document, reviewed my analytic memos, and wrote further notes on anything that seemed relevant to answering my research questions.

During Phase III of my analysis, I put the pieces back together in an attempt to see the bigger picture. Using the activity triangles I developed of each practice, I was able to develop a model of an intersecting activity triangle (see Figure 13.1) describing literacy practices at the center and the patients' homes. I was then able to look within and across the activity systems for evidence of tensions between activity, systems, and/or subjects.

In activity theory, tensions are essential elements of understanding an activity system and critical to change and learning. As Yamagata-Lynch (2010) states, "tensions arise when conditions of an activity put the subject in contradictory situations that can preclude achieving the object or the nature of the subject's participation in the activity while trying to achieve the object" (p. 23). To determine tensions, I reviewed transcripts of interviews, sessions, and my field notes for times when patients discussed things that got in the way of their diabetes management.

Patient Profiles

The patients and their experiences are an essential element of this study. During the process of coding, which essentially involves breaking down large amounts of data into small pieces, I realized I required one place in which I could provide a detailed portrait of the patients in this study. The patient profiles provided me that space and allowed me to offer a detailed description of the patients willing to participate in the study, sharing their time and experiences with me. I don't have the space here to share these profiles, but they helped me not to lose sight of the fact that these are real people with real struggles, not just a series of literacy events.

The Complexity of Health Literacy

In terms of literacy practices, data analyses suggest three findings. First, literacy events constitute the majority of events taking place during the sessions. Second, practices surrounding the events function through use of specific tools and rules, and the way tools were used within the practice were influenced by the rules of the practice. Third, practices engaged in by patients to manage

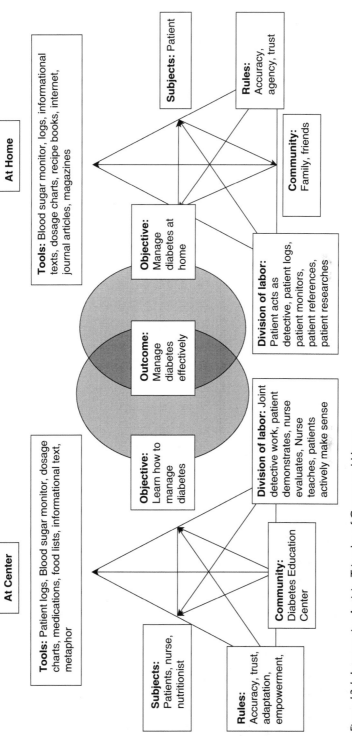

Figure 13.1 Intersecting Activity Triangles of Center and Home

their diabetes at home and at the center differ; only one practice – Detective Work – occurs in both settings.

Patients engage in different literacy practices at home and at the center. These practices follow rules and use specific tools. The ways in which the tools are used are influenced by how the rules are enacted. The literacy practices patients engage in at home are complex and varied. Patients must engage in these practices independent of the center. This places significant literacy demands on patients at home. Patients, however, do not mention these literacy demands when discussing tensions they experience when managing their diabetes. Instead, they struggle with tensions they experience within themselves and with societal factors.

Regarding the interconnectedness of the activity settings, analyses of the data suggest the two key activity systems (patients' homes, the center) are intersecting and interdependent. This connectedness is seen in both literacy practices and authorship and use of tools.

Finally, tensions existed between the activity systems and the larger society context in which they operated, specifically in the authorship of tools provided to patients by the center. Further, additional tensions experienced by patients get in the way of patients achieving their desired outcome of managing their diabetes.

Center Literacy Practices

I identified four literacy practices that patients engaged in at the center: Detective Work, Demonstration, Making Sense, and Just the Facts.

Detective Work

I defined Detective Work occurring during the session at the center as investigative work completed during the session with the assistance of the nurse practitioner or nutritionist and the patient. While engaging in the practice of Detective Work, patients and staff used patient created tools to determine how a particular food or medicine affected the patient's blood sugar. These investigative sessions were often the substantive part of each session with both nurse or nutritionist and patient poring over the patient's logs to examine them in detail.

Demonstration

The practice of Demonstration is the practice of patients showing competency in a newly learned skill or task. This practice is a complicated dance in which the patient, nurse, and nutritionist adapted both tools and behaviors.

Adaptations were made when patients were empowered to suggest adaptations and/or the nurse and nutritionist made adaptations based on the patient's needs. In this practice, patients needed to demonstrate their ability to use multiple tools including syringes, blood sugar monitors, and dosage charts.

Making Sense

Making Sense is the practice of trying to understand the physiology of diabetes. This practice involved the nurse using a text to explain to the patient the way diabetes works at a cellular level. This involved the tools of metaphor and informational text and the rule of adaptation.

Just the Facts

Just the Facts is the literacy practice during which the medical staff presented factual information, such as lists of foods with low carbohydrate counts, while the patient listened to the presentation. Tools included food lists and instruction sheets about dosages of medicines.

Home Literacy Practices

Patients engage in five literacy practices at home to manage their diabetes: Detective Work, Monitoring, Logging, Referencing, and Researching. The practices involve the use of specific tools and follow certain rules. These practices are complex and are engaged in by patients at home without the support of medical staff. The literacy practices of the center and home occurred in different activity settings, but they built on each other and supported each other.

For each literacy practice patients engaged in at the center, there were associated home practices. All the literacy practices of the center were dependent on literacy practices engaged in by patients at home. The reverse was also true. Literacy practices patients engaged in at home were based on literacy practices that took place at the center.

Detective Work

Detective Work as a home practice is investigative work completed at home by the patient. This investigative work involved the same tool as Detective Work at the center (patient logs). This home practice shared the rule of accuracy but, instead of trust, employed the rule of agency.

Monitoring

Monitoring is the practice of patients being aware of the ways in which new treatments affect them and responding as needed. This practice focused on patients being aware of their body's responses and either treating those responses using their own judgment (and based on what they had learned at the center) or informing the center when needed. Monitoring is a high-stakes literacy practice. When a patient receives a new treatment (e.g., medication, adjusted dosage) the medical staff cannot be sure how the patient's body will react. The patient, at home, must monitor his or her reaction and respond to it appropriately. The practice of Monitoring required patients to use a variety of tools, including blood sugar monitors, informational texts, and logs. It also required they follow the rules of accuracy and agency.

Logging

Logging is a practice at home in which patients keep a log, written or electronic, of their blood sugars and/or food intake. This logging involved specific tools: blood sugar monitors, logs, and rules for accuracy. This practice is heavily interconnected to the practice of Detective Work both at home and at the center, as well as Monitoring.

Referencing

Referencing is the literacy practice of patients referring to tools used during their patient education sessions at home. These tools included informational texts from pharmaceutical companies regarding their medication, information texts about how to administer medications, information texts about how to handle side effects of medications, or informational texts such as food lists with carbohydrate counts.

Researching

Researching is a home literacy practice in which patients actively and independently pursue new information about diabetes independent of the center and its staff. This differs from referencing, which emphasized patient's use of information distributed by the center.

Tensions Experienced by Patients

In this section, I share the findings on tensions patients had experienced. Determining the tensions within an activity system is an important part of understanding the system and how it functions (Yamagata-Lynch, 2010). By identifying the tensions patients experience within the activity system, we can understand what might get in the way of their diabetes management and effective tool use. As Yamagata-Lynch (2010) states "tensions arise when conditions of an activity put the subject in contradictory situations that can preclude achieving the object or the nature of the subject's participation in the activity while trying to achieve the object" (p. 23).

Patients experienced a variety of tensions as they were attempting to achieve their objective of managing their diabetes. These tensions got in the way of patients using tools effectively to manage their diabetes. Interestingly, no patients identified a lack of literacy skills as a tension they experienced that got in the way of their diabetes management. The tensions patients identified were all related to either tensions within themselves (Knowing vs. Doing) or tensions between themselves and the larger societal context in which the activity setting of Home existed (Stress vs. Doing, Time vs. Doing, Support vs. Doing).

Discussion

Health literacy is a concept in flux. The fields of clinical health, public health, and literacy have all added their perspectives to our understandings of health literacy and what it means to be health literate. Of these studies, little research has focused on the lived reality of patients as they navigate the multiple activity systems of the medical and home settings to manage their health. This study supports the perspective that health literacy is a complex, situated social practice that should be studied within the context in which it is used.

Health literacy as a construct cannot be divorced from disease management. In fact, in this study I found that all the events related to diabetes care that took place during patient education sessions were literacy events. That means literacy is absolutely central to patient education. As Papen (2009) found, health care environments are what she called "textually mediated worlds" (p. 23), but the tools patients use as they learn to manage their health go beyond text. Drawing on the work of Hodge and Kress (1988), this study broadened the definition of "tool" to include multiple semiotic modes of communication, including physical tools such as syringes and blood sugar monitors. Including these tools in our definition of health literacy is vital to understanding the literacy demands health education places on patients. Health literacy is not *an add-on* to disease management; it *is* disease management. Understanding how patients use and understand tools in health care settings and at home is essential to supporting patients as they learn to manage their health.

Health literacy is not a basic literacy. Currently, we often study health literacy as a separate construct from disease management, focusing often on those patients we've identified as "low-literacy," but we cannot assume someone who can decode basic health related words is health literate. Health literacy is complex and highly situated. The literacy practices patients engaged in at the center and at home were tied to the management of diabetes. The practices involved negotiating specific rules and using a variety of tools, even including tools patients were required to author themselves. Engaging in practices such as Detective Work involved using blood sugar monitors, creating and using blood sugar and food logs, using that information to investigate how different foods affect your blood sugar, and making adjustments as needed. This was a complex process that is specific to the management of diabetes.

Not only is the experience of managing diabetes high-stakes and complex for patients, the findings of this study show they also must navigate a variety of life tensions. These tensions included stress, lack of time, lack of support, and difficulty enacting the knowledge of how to manage their diabetes. Papen (2009) writes that issues other than literacy, such as emotions, can get in the way of patients managing their diabetes. She suggested that, if medical staff are not aware of the reason patients are not using the provided tools, they may believe it is related to a lack of literacy skills when the cause may actually be something quite different.

A second area where patients need support is when they engage in literacy practices at home. One of the findings of this study was that the home and center literacy practices of patients differed, with only Detective Work overlapping both settings. Further, these practices were interdependent. In other words, the literacy practices the patients used at home supported those used at the center and vice versa. This means the practices in both settings are critical to one another. It also means patients were engaging in complex and different literacy practices at home but potentially lacking the support they needed and experienced at the center. This places a considerable responsibility on the patient and requires patients to be able to manage significant literacy demands independently.

This study challenges the reductionist definitions and assessments of health literacy. Word list tests and cloze procedures cannot possibly capture what it means to be health literate. Health literacy is complex and socially situated and should be studied and assessed in a way that captures that complexity. If we choose to ignore this complexity, we are choosing to ignore the needs of the patients we hope to serve.

References

Barton, D., & Hamilton, M. (2012). *Local literacies: Reading and writing in one community*. Routledge.

Black, S. (2012). Diabetes literacy: Health and adult literacy practitioners in partnership. *Australian Journal of Adult Learning, 52*(1), 89.

Engeström, Y. (1987). *Learning by expanding: An activity-theoretical approach to developmental research.* Retrieved February 24, 2017, from http://lchc.ucsd.edu/mca/Paper/Engestrom/Learning-by-Expanding.pdf

Engeström, Y. (2001). Expansive learning at work: Toward an activity theoretical reconceptualization. *Journal of Education and Work, 14*(1), 133–156.

Hodge, R., & Kress, G. R. (1988). *Social semiotics*. Cornell University Press.

Knobel, M., & Lankshear, C. (Eds.). (2007). *A new literacies sampler* (Vol. 29). Peter Lang.

Papen, U. (2009). Literacy, learning and health: A social practices view of health literacy. *Literacy and Numeracy Studies, 16*(2 and v. 17 no. 1), 19.

Pleasant, A., & Kurkuvilla, S. (2008). A tale of two health literacies: Public health and clinical approaches to health literacy. *Health Promotion International, 23*(2), 152–159.

Rogers, R. (2003). *A critical discourse analysis of family literacy practices: Power in and out of print.* Routledge.

Rogoff, B. (1990). *Apprenticeship in thinking: Cognitive development in social context.* Oxford University Press.

Sørensen, K., Van den Broucke, S., Fullam, J., Doyle, G., Pelikan, J., Slonska, Z., & Brand, H. (2012). Health literacy and public health: A systematic review and integration of definitions and models. *BMC Public Health, 12*(1), 80.

Yamagata-Lynch, L. C. (2010). *Activity systems analysis methods: Understanding complex learning environments* (pp. 63–79). Springer.

Yin, R. K. (2014). *Case study research: Design and methods* (5th ed.). Sage.

Chapter 14

Little Free Libraries

Fostering Access to Reading Materials While Developing Community Ties

Peggy Semingson and Karabi Bezboruah

Author Note

Peggy Semingson: https://orcid.org/0000-0002-7446-4399

Karabi Bezboruah: https://orcid.org/0000-0001-6070-2010

This chapter is based on the interests of the authors in fostering access to books through community and civic engagement in Little Free Libraries (LFLs). We are especially interested in coming to know more about developing partnerships and LFLs that are designed to take place in visible and public environments. While we are interested in partnerships to foster literacy and education in public spaces (e.g., schools, non-profits, and even airports), there is also a lot of promise for LFLs situated in front of homes and households. The focus of this chapter will be on defining the Little Free Library (LFL) book exchange process, building on the non-profit "parent" organization Little Free Library (https://littlefreelibrary.org/), ways to get started, caveats and cautions in the process, and ways to use creative spaces and upcycling. Sarmiento et al. (2018) defined Little Free Library (LFL) as "semi-autonomous, spatially and relatively financially accessible, neighborhood book exchanges through units resembling birdhouses or oversized mailboxes," (p. 233) and considers it akin to a do-it-yourself (DIY) project.

DOI: 10.4324/9781003228042-18

Because we live in the large geographic region and mega-city of the Dallas-Fort Worth metroplex, we will draw on examples of both individual LFLs and partnership-based approaches to creation of libraries from our local geographic region. Examples can hopefully inspire others to recreate and/or envision partnerships and design of this type of micro-urban intervention in their own location (Sarmiento et al., 2018). LFLs rely heavily on financial sponsorship and oversight. Two questions that can guide thinking about LFLs are the following:

- Who are the types of sponsors of little free libraries at the community level (e.g., personal, non-profit, government, civic/city-based, etc.)?
- On what type of space (public or private) are little free libraries located (e.g., type of sector: public school, police station, firehouse, private property) – private versus community spaces?

Depending on whether you are an individual looking to champion and/or sponsor the broader LFL cause or looking to formally support and/or create partnerships, it helps to think of the LFL movement in terms of who is doing the basic sponsorship of the materials, design, and maintenance. We provide concrete examples of the various types of sponsorship and locations of LFLs in this chapter.

We draw on the research literature, hands-on experiences, and observations of LFLs in the local region and our respective fields. Peggy is in TESOL education while Karabi is engaged in teaching and research in the field of public policy and non-profit management. The first author has visited and documented dozens of official "Little Free Libraries" over the last several years in pictures and videos (mainly those formally registered with the official Little Free Library organization) in the Dallas-Fort Worth area as well as other major cities in Texas during road trips, primarily before the COVID-19 outbreak. Additionally, the first author is in the Facebook group for Little Free Library stewards. We recommend that others who are interested in both individual LFLs in their yard or in developing a partnership based LFL also do such participatory engagement in their communities before getting started. This might include:

- Using the LFL location map to scout out LFLs in your area to visit and get ideas. The map for the LFL organization can be found here: https://littlefreelibrary.org/ourmap/.

- Join the LFL steward group on Facebook and follow the LFL organization on social media such as Twitter, Facebook, and Instagram. This group is only for those who have LFLs registered with the official LFL organization.
- Look up examples of LFLs on Google Images, Twitter, and Instagram to compare different visual examples.
- Bookmark the official LFL website to learn more about the official branded program: https://littlefreelibrary.org/

Through such browsing online on the topic of LFLs, inspiration can be drawn on for the design and building of LFLs in one's own community.

Key Concepts Driving the Book Exchange Movement

In this section we describe some key fundamental concepts that underlie the LFL movement and why it matters. Although the concept of book exchanges has been around since the beginning of mass literacy and written texts, the specific LFL concept is much more recent. There are three concepts that relate to the LFL global movement. The first is the idea of local literacies and a do-it-yourself (DIY) approach to literacy supports outside of sanctioned and supported institutions such as public libraries (Sarmiento et al., 2018). Additionally, the notion of literacy sponsorship requires that a LFL sponsor or group of sponsors invest time, some money (materials), and intellectual and social capital to launch and maintain the project.

Second, the LFL movement is a global one, which spread around the globe to not only provide access to books but to foster the idea of reuse and celebration of books in community. Inherent in the LFL movement is the notion of sustainability in such reuse of books and reading materials.

Third, a critical underlying concept is community engagement. Library stewards, who actively maintain and curate the library, connect with others, while "patrons" of the LFLs also engage with other people's texts, goodwill and generosity, and the motto and ethos of "take a book, leave a book" rendering a type of mutual aid and reciprocity for material items related to literacy in a neighborhood. Finally, during the COVID-19 outbreak when this chapter was written, the idea of reading in outdoor spaces was literally a safe place to read (Semingson & Kerns, 2021).

A crucial aspect for implementing LFLs in communities is the need to increase access to texts that are considered leisure reading to foster education and reading experiences in out-of-school learning contexts. Due to various structural inequities, geographic locations, socio-economic disparities, and more, not all communities have access to public libraries or other book outreach such as a bookmobile. Consequently, for those living in a community deemed as a "book desert," LFLs provide greater access to books and materials. A "book desert" can be defined as a location where there is not a lot of access to books or other print reading materials.

The Role of the Steward: Civic Engagement, Curation, Maintenance

A key aspect of LFLs is the ongoing maintenance of the library, beyond the initial design, conceptualization, and "planting" of the LFL. Like an actual house or library, the LFL needs a caretaker who understands the role of the steward. In the first author's experiences as a steward to the four LFLs at The University of Texas at Arlington, observation of steward chat in public discussion forums on Facebook, as well as information gleaned from the LFL website page for stewards, the job description of a steward can be seen as follows:

1. Oversight. Check in on the library periodically. Note if the library needs to be restocked with books and the general maintenance of the library.
2. Keeping the books well stocked. In addition to people in the community donating books, replacing books borrowed, and returning books read, there are other ways that a steward can secure books for the library. Sometimes people will leave a box of books next to the library to donate. The steward can also request that people donate books and then store those books in their garage or some other area for later restocking. Outreach to local community groups can also help. For instance, the first author collaborated with the Junior League of Arlington to conduct a book drive where a wide variety of books were collected for the four LFLs at The University of Texas at Arlington.
3. Curating the books. Because donations can be random, it is important for the steward to actively curate the books. This may mean going through books and weeding out books that may be dirty, extremely outdated, in bad shape, or otherwise unreadable. This can be a contested and debatable area as some may suggest that overly curating books can border on censorship. An often-discussed area of curation is whether to remove religious materials in the LFLs or take them out. This area is not without debate as

to what should be curated and what constitutes quality books. Curation can be a highly subjective area and one that generates contention on discussion forums when stewards are talking about what should go in the library and what should be removed. Protecting against vandalism and theft can be done by installing a secure and visible camera on the site with a note that the library is monitored. Another tactic is stamping the inside of the books with a stamp with directions on how to return books to the LFL. This is a deterrent against those who swipe books for resale.

4. Promoting the library itself. There are two aspects to promoting the LFL. First, when the LFL is being created and opens, there should be a launch party. A small gathering celebrating the launch of the library can generate interest in awareness of the library. Other digital forms of marketing the library can take place on social media such as the creation of a Facebook page about the library.

5. Learn the steward role. Stewards maintain the LFL. We suggest that LFL stewards also visit the LFL steward page to learn more about the role of the steward. Joining discussion forums such as on Facebook that are specifically for LFL stewards can help. The steward groups can really help troubleshoot such as when a LFL is wiped out by people who are not generous and take all the contents. Another theme of concern for stewards is when the LFL is graffitied or vandalized, which can be very upsetting. Suggestions for what to do, such as installing a camera, are often discussed in discussion forums.

Process and "How To": Steps to Getting Started

In this section, we describe the concrete process of getting started with the LFL concept. At its most basic, creating one LFL in a household would be the simplest beginning, or a multisite and multi-partner collaboration would be the most complex. The LFL project (four LFLs) that took place in 2015 at The University of Texas at Arlington would be something in between. In all cases, the project starts with grassroots efforts when one or more people become interested in replicating the concept in their own neighborhood. Some people are simply enamored with the diminutive nature of the libraries and the aesthetic appeal while others want to provide access to books in a no-nonsense book exchange format. Nevertheless, the process basically stays the same whether it is an individual household or a partnership in terms of the sequence of events, which we will describe later. Often, the design and creation of a LFL can be a good scouting project for youth or a non-profit. The steps involve: (a) conceptualizing the project, (b) selecting a location and securing permissions (if needed), (c) designing and building the LFL, and (d) ongoing stewardship and care of the LFL. We recommend you visit the "how to" directions on the official Little Free Library website (https://littlefree library.org/).

The Importance of Sponsorship

Sponsorship of the libraries is a crucial consideration. At the beginning of the chapter, we posed the question, "Who would be sponsoring the project and where would the spaces be for the LFL?" The types of sponsors beyond the individual level are largely religious in nature, non-profit or charitable organizations, or those typically part of a civic agency (such as a school, library, police station, etc.). At the household level, individuals typically fund these. Scouting projects can also take on all aspects of the LFL. Later we will discuss the role of partnerships in creating the initiative and implementation of the LFL with multiple stakeholders. Locations are usually in the front yard of a household or in a visible space of the non-profit, charitable group, religious organization, etc.

The first author has been a library steward of four official LFLs that were developed in 2015 at The University of Texas at Arlington, the university affiliation of both authors. As a bit of context, these official LFLs were developed in collaboration with a librarian, Evelyn Barker, then at UT Arlington, and sponsored by a known local philanthropist and political science faculty member, Dr. Allan Saxe (see: www.facebook.com/UTAFreeLittleLibraries/) for a compilation of photos promoting the project).

Dr. Saxe was an enthusiastic and generous community supporter already, and after funding the four LFLs at The University of Texas at Arlington, he was inspired on his own to start several more LFLs at nearby community colleges in his name, as well as sponsor LFLs in noted areas of the city of Arlington in conjunction with a non-profit called Arlington, Proud to Call it Home (led by Mark Joeckel). The name of the project that ensued in the broader community was called the Allan Saxe Caravan of Books. In a follow-up informal video with Dr. Saxe, documented by the first author on YouTube ("Dr. Allan Saxe on Little Free Libraries, Literacy, and Reading!" located at www.youtube. com/watch?v=98-CoTR9czg), Saxe states that he is inspired by his own life as a reader to want to help others. In this excerpt from the video transcript, Dr.

Saxe discusses the "why" of what motivated him to support little free libraries on campus at UT Arlington:

PEGGY SEMINGSON: Tell us the "why" behind your interests.

DR. ALLAN SAXE: I watched a program on television one time on a Sunday morning, and I had never heard of a Little Free Library. And they were talking mostly about free libraries in other parts of the country, and I said, "That's neat." You know, they build a little box and people put a book in, and then if you want to get that book, you can take it home and read it or learn, or whatever they want to do, and put another book of yours in and to return it or whatever. . . . But Little Free Libraries are very interesting things. First of all, it's free and people can go there. You can put any book you want in there and take it out, put another one in if you like or not. And it's just a wonderful way to get people to read in a very informal nice way . . . it's just a wonderful novel idea.

If possible, we recommend such documentation of the oral narratives and contributions of your sponsors (such as Dr. Saxe) in multimedia format (e.g., news, press releases, video, podcasts, etc.) for posterity and to help others understand the concept and potential impact. Thus, the initial project and sponsor sparked growth in the movement in the local immediate community with the proliferation of further libraries. We hope that, similarly, planting and establishing LFLs in your own community will inspire others locally and beyond.

Conceptualizing the Project and Securing Sponsors and Partners

The first step is envisioning the project, sketching out ideas, and looking at examples of current projects that you want to emulate. The project should be discussed with all stakeholders in the project. If it is a household project, involving everyone in the household can be an engaging activity. Partnership-based LFLs (not an individual household) are typically at K–12 schools, civic locations (e.g., parks, police stations), universities, or in a non-profit (as a donation or charity contribution). Deciding on the budget, timeline, and decor/aesthetic ideas for the LFL is crucial as points of discussion. A key decision is deciding whether to build the library from scratch, upcycle something else (e.g., an old newspaper stand or a phone booth), or order one already built and ready to be painted from the LFL organization.

   Working solo versus working with partners will require a different set of discussions and timeline. In fact, partnership-based projects (discussed later) will be more complex as multiple stakeholders are involved. On the other hand, participants can involve highly skilled people such as architects, who can be an asset for the design. If the library is built to honor someone or commemorate people, it may invite the participation of many. For instance, in our region of the Dallas-Fort Worth Metroplex, five LFLs were planted in 2017 in Dallas in honor of the five fallen officers ambushed in 2016. The project was done in collaboration with many diverse stakeholders across the community. (See: www.bcworkshop.org/posts/tag/Little+Free+Library).

Locations and Learning the Municipal Constraints to Start the Project

One of the main constraints of selecting the location of a LFL would be municipal codes that may constrict whether little free libraries can be placed at all in public areas. If the LFL is placed in a public area, permissions must be secured. The common locations of LFLs and book exchanges are the following:

- Front yard of a house or apartment, near the street,
- Central location in a university in a high-foot trafficked and visible area (e.g., next to the student dorms, centrally located common areas where students gather),
- Central location near the street or drop-off area of a K–12 school,
- Central location at a religious place of worship such as the front lobby or near the front door,
- In a public park adhering to city permissions, or
- Civic location such as a city hall, community center, police station, fire station, community garden, or other municipal location.

Key considerations in selecting a location are high foot traffic, a place that is secure from the elements, visibility, and zoning rules. Meaningfulness to the community is also crucial such as when the LFL is created to honor a person or group of people.

Design: Creation from Scratch versus Upcycling and Aesthetic Considerations

Purposes (not mutually exclusive) of providing the LFL can also determine the design. Some typical purposes include providing access to books, in tribute to someone or a group of people, something of aesthetic or architectural interest, replica of a nearby area, and/or genre-specific (e.g., mainly children's books). A few types of design are included in the following list.

- Basic: The most basic library is simply a wooden or other sturdy container on a post that is planted in the ground to provide access to books. It should have a sign on it indicating what it is and how it works. The basic libraries can be obtained from the LFL organization or built from scratch.
- Upcycled: Some people have converted an old newspaper container or even an old tree into a book exchange spot.
- Aesthetically interesting: Some LFLs are visually colorful or take on a theme such as a Book Bot (robot in appearance) or even a nod to popular culture such as a converted phone booth that resembles something from Dr. Who. In the Dallas Fort Worth area, there is a mid-century modern LFL that is almost identical to the homeowner's mid-century modern house.
- Re-creation of a local building that is a nod to the region "hyper-local." In Bedford, Texas, a citizen created a replica LFL of the Bedford Boys Ranch as her book exchange.
- LFL "plus": Some book exchange areas include an adjacent small bench and small garden area to read.

Partnerships

There are over 15,000 registered LFLs in communities around the world. This originated in New York as a design competition for architects and soon easy-to-assemble LFLs popped up around the city. Traditional public libraries are also beginning to see the benefits of having LFLs or pop-up ones to cater to the needs of the underserved population in urban and rural areas. A case in point is a community by the name of Vinton in El Paso County, Texas as cited in Schmidt and Hale (2017). In 2014, due to budget cuts, the public library decided to charge a $50 fee for nonresidents to access the El Paso Public Library. In order to address this fee and to provide library services to the village of Vinton, the state representative and the Mayor of Vinton installed five LFLs. These were done in collaboration with several community organizations, the El Paso public library, and support from the government. However, the community was charged with the maintenance and stocking of books. Schmidt and Hale (2017) argue that this could be a move "to privatize a public service and an absolution of government responsibility to provide the service as a societal need" (p. 21). Some important outcomes of the LFLs are collaboration within neighborhoods, partnerships with airports and train stations to provide some reading materials to travelers and encouraging literacy, and building communities (Kozak, 2017). With the heightened interest in digital books and literary resources, some pop-up libraries are also increasingly offering electronic books and magazines. Such partnerships with other entities are making books and reading materials easily accessible either in underserved communities or at transit stops.

LFLs at Transit Stops

These are LFLs at airports to provide travelers with no-cost entertainment. Travelers can take a book or share a book from the *flybraries* and encourage others to read and pass their time while waiting for their flights. These are usually placed in high visibility and high traffic areas without being obtrusive. For instance, Philadelphia airport and Seattle Tacoma airport in the United States, Thunderbay Airport in Canada, Cape Town airport in South Africa, and Vantaa airport in Finland have flybraries that are very popular. These flybraries are designed in a way that provides a comfortable place for travelers to relax and enjoy their books. These are established in partnerships with the airports and encourage literacy among adults and children and promote sustainable use of books. Similar libraries have become popular in train, tram, and bus stations.

Community Groups

LFLs are generally established in underserved areas also known as *book deserts* and are operated on a volunteer basis. Individuals and community groups then become critical in ensuring that the LFLs are operating well and have a constant supply of books and other reading materials, the upkeep of the bookstore and aesthetics, and following local zoning codes and ordinances regarding location of the LFL.

Technology Companies

The interest of technology companies in LFLs is also evident in the move to digital books and resources through kiosks at transit stations. Pop-up or LFLs combine e-readers, e-books, and smart devices to provide a host of services such as books, reading materials, or games. Seattle Tacoma airport in the U.S.

has e-books for free download. In a Bucharest subway station, the telecom company Vodaphone collaborated with a publishing house to provide commuters with freely downloadable e-books by scanning a QR code (Davis et al., 2015).

Thus, partnerships can be with public, private, and non-profit organizations, and each plays a vital role in the development and operations of the LFLs. It is important to understand that LFLs work when there are partners invested in its success, as someone must maintain these. Unlike public libraries that have professional librarians to organize and catalog and maintain their repository, LFLs are primarily community driven, low-scale operations that can add value when established in rural or underserved urban neighborhoods or in transit stations and have the potential to be offered in shopping malls and convenience stores. It can also be a way to address social justice issues (Davis et al., 2015; Findlay-King et al., 2018) by taking literacy beyond the physical space of a library to the communities that might otherwise not have access to these resources.

Criticisms and Caveats

LFLs often encounter zoning ordinance issues when created in high traffic areas that prevent people from using the sidewalks or bus stops (Kozak, 2017). The argument for establishing LFLs also run counter to the arguments for more support for traditional public libraries. Research suggests that, due to the popularity of LFLs, public libraries may receive less funding and support more local control of libraries through freely available ones and may even be privatized as evident in the 2012 Localism Act in the UK, which devolved responsibility of library operations to local community groups primarily comprised of volunteers (Findlay-King et al., 2018; Kozak, 2017). Similarly, the village of Vinton in Texas, as noted previously, established Little Free Libraries after a budget cut to the city library, and the free libraries had to be maintained by community volunteers.

Conclusion

In this brief chapter, we discussed a broad overview of the purpose and mission of the LFL global movement. We drew upon resources across recent research literature, our own experiences with LFLs in the local Dallas-Fort Worth metroplex, social media forums, our own backgrounds as education and public affairs focused experts, as well as gathered insights from a local philanthropist who has funded a few free libraries. We conclude that LFLs can have several designs and ways of operations as seen in this discussion. Some are established in small birdhouses, whereas there are others located in fancy nooks within airports or offered as an e-book that is downloadable on personal mobile devices. This provides more flexibility and takes books to consumers or readers and encourages literacy. Another conclusion is that partnerships with other public, for-profit, and non-profit organizations are important for the maintenance and operations of the LFLs. As evident, these LFLs are volunteer-based, and therefore, continuity and sustainability are based on the commitments of the volunteers. The complexity of starting the process comes when multiple stakeholders are involved. However, it is a very rewarding experience to work with motivated partners to establish a LFL as a hyperlocal project. The process involves having a vision, designing the library, selecting a strategic location, stocking and maintaining the library, and promoting its use in the community. Library stewards have a unique role and oversight for the library. Municipal constraints, if any, should be vetted ahead of time to make sure there are no glitches in the setup process. We hope that people can establish these little book exchanges in their own community and inspire others to do the same.

References

Davis, A., Rice, C., Spagnolo, D., Struck, J., & Bull, S. (2015) Exploring pop-up libraries in practice, *The Australian Library Journal, 64*(2), 94–104. https://doi.org/10.1080/00049670.2015.1011383

Findlay-King, L., Nichols, G., Forbes, D., & Macfadyen, G. (2018). Localism and the Big Society: The asset transfer of leisure centres and libraries – fighting closures or empowering communities? *Leisure Studies, 37*(2), 158–170.

Kozak, N. I. (2017). Building community, breaking barriers: Little Free Libraries and local action in the United States. *M/C Journal, 20*(2). https://doi.org/10.5204/mcj.1220

Sarmiento, C. S., Sims, J. R., & Morales, A. (2018). Little Free Libraries: An examination of micro-urbanist interventions. *Journal of Urbanism: International Research on Placemaking and Urban Sustainability, 11*(2), 233–253.

Schmidt, J., & Hale, J. (2017). Little Free Libraries®: Interrogating the impact of the branded book exchange. *Journal of Radical Librarianship, 3*, 14–41.

Semingson, P., & Kerns, W. (2021, May/June). Leveraging nature: Creating reading and writing opportunities outdoors during COVID-19. *Literacy Today, 38*(6), pp. 22–23. http://viewer.zmags.com/publication/8854c52f?fbclid=I-wAR24d2ncqh_4f-2QmIcCP4UnMBDFwiYLe7X4qVmYE-vF5ol_TaxbMVKDKlU#/8854c52f/24

Chapter 15

Indigenous-Led, Community-Based Language Reclamation and Regeneration Initiatives

M. Kristiina Montero, Spy Dénommé-Welch, and Stanley R. Henry

Author Note

M. Kristiina Montero: https://orcid.org/0000-0002-1692-6110
Spy Dénommé-Welch: https://orcid.org/0000-0002-8860-4647
Stanley R. Henry: https://orcid.org/0000-0003-4906-5561

We begin this chapter that explores Indigenous-led, community-based language reclamation and regeneration[1] efforts by first acknowledging the traditional lands of the Anishinaabeg, Hodinohsyó:ni, and the Neutral Peoples on which we are writing and collaborating. Indigenous and non-Indigenous peoples of these lands are joined by the Gä:sweñta' Covenant or the Two Row Wampum-Covenant Chain Treaty of 1613, the oldest known treaty between

DOI: 10.4324/9781003228042-19

incoming Europeans and Indigenous North Americans (Hill & Coleman, 2019). Symbolized on the Wampum Belt are two vessels traveling down the same river, side by side, in parallel. The agreement outlines that each party is equal and, collectively, is to keep their beliefs and laws in their separate vessels; neither party shall attempt to interfere in the other's ways so that all can live in interdependent autonomy in friendship and peace (Hill & Coleman, 2019).

Additionally, we acknowledge that as Indigenous (Dénommé-Welch and Henry) and non-Indigenous (Montero) authors of this chapter, we embody the Gä:sweñta' Covenant. We come together as life-long language learners: Henry is a Gayogoho:nǫ'néha (Cayuga language) learner, speaker, and teacher; Dénommé-Welch is an ongoing learner of Anishinaabemowin working to bridge language, expression, and the arts, and an English-French bilingual; and Montero learned and maintained her heritage languages – Finnish and Spanish – in addition to English and French. Together, we raise awareness that the long-standing Gä:sweñta' Covenant has not been honored, as evidenced by the massive language shift and loss of many Indigenous languages. As Indigenous communities mobilize to reclaim and regenerate their living languages, we remind readers to allow and enable the canoe to travel along its part of the river without interference.

Language shift, leading to language loss, (Fishman, 1991) describes a social phenomenon of one people's language being replaced with that of another, when the majority language overtakes the original language at all levels of public and private life. Indigenous language shift and loss have occurred across the globe and continue to occur at alarming rates due to the consequences of colonization and neocolonization. Of the 7,139 languages currently used worldwide (Ethnologue, 2021b), over 40% are considered endangered, meaning that the language users have begun to teach and speak the more dominant language(s) to their children (Ethnologue, 2021a). Linguists estimate that a language goes dormant (or extinct) every two weeks; the majority are Indigenous languages (Office of the High Commissioner of Human Rights (OHCHR), 2019). UNESCO predicts that approximately 90% of the world's languages may be replaced by globally dominant languages such as English, Mandarin, or Spanish by the end of the 21st century, in less than 80 years (Brenzinger et al., 2003).

The Hän language, for example, is endangered, meaning that the speaker population is small, and children no longer learn and use the language. Hän was traditionally used by the Tr'onkëk Hwëch'in Peoples (Trans: People of the Klondike River) located on the lands of what is now known as Eagle, Alaska (USA) and Dawson City, Yukon (Canada). A relatively short jaunt down the Yukon River once connected the Tr'onkëk Hwëch'in; however, they are now separated by over 1,700 kilometers (1,050 miles) and a border crossing requiring nation-state passports for passage. Before and during the height of the Gold Rush of 1898, Hän was the lingua franca used by several Indigenous communities (Creed et al., 2020) but experienced a rapid shift toward English mainly due to the influx of non-Indigenous people (Yukon Native Language Centre, 2020).

As of 2010, it was estimated that there are fewer than 50 fluent Hän speakers (UNESCO, 2010). Percy Henry is one of the last known fluent Hän speakers (White, 2021). Henry continues to collaborate with The Council of Yukon First Nations to keep the Tr'onkëk Hwëch'in Peoples connected to their rich heritage through language learning communities and the preservation and dissemination of Hän words, phrases, songs, dances, and stories documented in audio lessons, storybooks, and other supporting pedagogical materials. While intergenerational language transmission of Hän may be multiple generations away, these community-led efforts lay the groundwork for total language regeneration.

Language loss is detrimental to Indigenous peoples: Indigenous languages are critical to preserving and carrying forward Indigenous Knowledges, worldviews, identities, ceremonies, linguistic and cultural self-determination and autonomy, access to spiritual and cultural practices (Romero-Little & Blum-Martinez, 2012), and advancing Indigenous creative expression and traditional and contemporary arts practice (Alie, 2016). Indigenous languages and knowledges are also important to global knowledge systems: Linguistic diversity is linked to biological diversity (see for example Upadhyay & Hasnain, 2017). When an Indigenous language goes dormant, so does an elaborate classification system of the natural world (UNESCO, 2017). Indigenous language reclamation and regeneration, a human right (United Nations, 2008), is also an act of resistance to intentional attempts of erasure.

Intentional Erasure of Indigenous Languages and Worldviews

Turtle Island (North America), Aotearoa (New Zealand), and Australia, lands with European (British, French, and Spanish) colonial histories, have directly contributed to the demise of Indigenous languages, identities, family structures, artistic expression (dance, song, arts), cultures, and economies because of their intentional and violent assimilationist policies and related practices designed to "get rid of the Indian problem" (Titley, 1986, p. 50). These policies of Indigenous erasure were enacted through aggressive and state-orchestrated education systems as witnessed in Residential and Indian Boarding Schools across Turtle Island and child welfare policies that saw the forced removal of Indigenous children from their families and communities.

Furthermore, when nation-states enforce language policies that discourage or prohibit the teaching and use of Indigenous languages in public spaces, Indigenous peoples are led to feel shame for their languages, cultures, and identities. Across Turtle Island, numerous testimonials account for the acts of physical and psychological violence inflicted on children who used their Indigenous language. For protective reasons, many fluent speakers of Indigenous languages restricted or altogether ceased intergenerational language transmission, further reducing the number of fluent language speakers. In Canada, for example, only 3 of the over 60 Indigenous languages – Cree, Inuktitut, and Anishinaabemowin – have enough fluent language speakers to be sustained indefinitely through uninterrupted intergenerational transmission (Walker, 2017).

Influential Indigenous-Led Language Reclamation and Regeneration Initiatives

The protective factor against language shift and loss is intergenerational language transmission. It is much easier to see a language through dormancy than witness its complete regeneration. Hebrew and Hawaiian are well known for having regenerated their languages from a dormant state. In both cases, a turning point was when the language was taught and used in public education (Shah & Brenzinger, 2018). To sustain intergenerational language transmission there must be an intentional focus on the life of the language and its relationship to the culture (Fishman, 2007). Furthermore, the language requires a critical mass of language speakers, community interest and support, individual and collective identification with the language, and a sustainable language transmission infrastructure, including significant investment by the nation-state (Hinton, 2011a).

Understanding Indigenous language reclamation and regeneration efforts must occur at the community level because Indigenous languages are invariably rooted to the Land (Galla, 2016). Indigenous language reclamation and regeneration efforts may include learning keywords and phrases for ceremonial purposes, maintaining language archives to preserve linguistic records (e.g., sound recordings, oral histories, stories, songs, dances), or teaching the language to children and adults (Hinton, 2011b). The kind of language reclamation and regeneration efforts and their success depends on available resources (financial, human, and linguistic capacity), community interest, and motivation. However, grassroots movements in and of themselves are not sustainable long term because the resource burden lives within the communities and on the backs of goodwill. Next, we briefly describe three community-led language reclamation and regeneration initiatives that experience various degrees of intergenerational language transmission: Indigenous language nests, master-apprentice language learning programs, and digital technologies that support language reclamation and regeneration efforts.

Language Nests

In the 1980s, the Te Kōhanga Reo or "language nests" began in Aotearoa (New Zealand) and have become the model for many language nests across the globe (McIvor & Parker, 2016). The goal of language nests is to establish Indigenous language futurity by building capacity for sustainable intergenerational language transmission beginning in early childhood. Language nests are founded on the principles of full language and cultural immersion led by fluent language speakers. They depend on an extensive network of fluent language speakers and a commitment from the parent generation to promote and use the nest language with their children. Language nest teachers provide highly interactive language learning opportunities so that children experience the relevance in the nest language (McIvor & Parker, 2016). For language nests to be successful the teaching staff must only use the nest language in the teaching context and direct and redirect children to use the nest language. Language nests can take place in homes and home-like settings or in settings that might resemble a mainstream preschool structure.

Master-Apprentice Language Learning Programs

Master-apprentice language learning programs were developed in the early 1990s to build fluent language speakers in Indigenous language communities in California with few living fluent speakers. These programs taught Indigenous languages to the "missing generations" who could potentially go on to teach children in contexts where school-based immersion programs were not possible due to the low number of fluent language speakers (Hinton, 2011a). The model, while conceptually simple, was proven difficult to implement because of its reliance on volunteer (or poorly compensated) teachers and learners. The idea behind master-apprentice language learning programs was to create partnerships between a fluent (master) and nonfluent language speaker (apprentice) and immerse them in everyday activities (e.g., cooking, washing clothes, gardening, traditional ceremonies) sustained over time (10–20 hours per week over several months) where only the target language was used. The focus of the program was on oral language transmission; in fact, print literacy was not encouraged because "writing words down diminishes the language being uttered in any given unit of time and also diminishes interaction and real communication" (Hinton, 2001a, p. 221). The goal was to develop conversational fluency in the apprentice. (For a fulsome description of the principles of the master-apprentice program see, Hinton, 1997).

Digital Technologies Supporting Indigenous Language Reclamation and Regeneration

Indigenous peoples are becoming more accepting of digital technologies to support language reclamation and regeneration efforts (Galla, 2018). The digital environment creates spaces where Indigenous peoples can have autonomy over the resource creation and dissemination and allow learners to engage with the language according to individual schedules and without feeling embarrassment or shame (Smith et al., 2018). Additionally, digital technologies facilitate the preservation of linguistic artifacts (e.g., audio recordings of Elders speaking, transcripts of oral language, language documents such as dictionaries). When a language community is motivated to reclaim and regenerate the language but is without living fluent language speakers, digitally assisted tools can effectively support regeneration efforts. An example can be seen among people of the Gamilaraay language community in Australia that, since the mid-1990s, has experienced a significant regeneration movement where community members use digital technologies to develop and disseminate word lists, dictionaries, and teaching materials.

Digital technologies such as social media, online video streaming, texts, and chat forums create new domains in which languages can exist, enable people to engage with languages via new modalities, and extend the reach of local languages once limited to geographic regions (Galla, 2016). Furthermore, digital technologies may elevate the status of the language among younger language learners whose daily lives are heavily influenced by digital technologies (Wagner, 2017). While digital technologies should be integral to language reclamation and regeneration movements because of their potential to create new social ecologies in which languages can be actively used (Wagner, 2017), they should not be considered a panacea to reversing language shift and loss. Missing from many digital language learning tools is the lived experience of the language, which is a critical component for sustained language regeneration.

Lessons from the Koru: Pushing Language Learning and Expression in New Directions

Speaking to the evolutionary nature of language regeneration, Hohepa (2006) underscored that "nothing regrows in exactly the same shape that it had previously, or in exactly the same direction" (p. 294). For example, when describing master-apprentice programs, Hinton (2011a) explained that language-learning teams would sometimes need to coin new language to speak about the contemporary world. In this way, language regeneration is like a *koru*, a new shoot of a fern, that Hohepa used to symbolize the growth and regrowth, development and redevelopment of language: "The *koru* first circles back towards itself, then, unfurling from itself, spreads out in different directions, the frond connected back through the strength and stability of its trunk into the nurture of *Paptuanuku*, our Earth Mother" (Hohepa, 2006, p. 295). To this end, we next present two examples of how language regeneration emulates the *koru* by coining innovations that push language learning and language expression in new directions.

Indigenous Language Teaching and Learning Innovations

Gayogǫho:nǫ'néha (Cayuga language), from the Iroquoian Language Family that includes languages of the Mohawk, Seneca, Oneida, and Onondaga Nations, is used by members of the Hodinohsyó:ni Confederacy located across Turtle Island. Originating from Upstate New York, Gayogǫho:nǫ'néha is now widely spoken by members of the Six Nations of the Grand River Territory and is taught in K–12 immersion and post-secondary programs. Similar to many Indigenous languages across the globe, Gayogǫho:nǫ'néha is critically endangered with only about 50 people who speak Gayogǫho:nǫ'néha as their mother tongue (Green, 2017). Gayogǫho:nǫ'néha reclamation movements are gaining momentum; there are more speakers and learners of Gayogǫho:nǫ'néha as a second language than mother tongue speakers (Green, 2017).

Henry, one of the coauthors of this chapter, teaches an introductory course on Gayogǫho:nǫ'néha language in a university setting. The course offers over 72 instructional hours, currently offered remotely. Henry's pedagogy is informed by his personal experiences with the Gayogǫho:nǫ'néha language and lessons learned over 20 years. Acknowledging the life of the language, Henry teaches Gayogǫho:nǫ'néha based on principles of holism that view the language as a vehicle for communicating and transmitting Indigenous Knowledges intergenerationally, pushing language pedagogy beyond vocabulary and grammar.

However, teaching Gayogo̱ho:nǫ'néha in the higher education classroom, whether online or face-to-face, will likely not create fluent speakers. In fact, in a study of language regeneration efforts on Six Nations of the Grand River Territory, Green (2017) noted that online learning and Native as Second Language learning are the least effective ways to support the regeneration of Hodinohsyó:ni languages.

Henry developed a holistic, circular pedagogical framework titled *Teaching from the Threshold*. The framework underscores how the Gayogo̱ho:nǫ'néha language is entrenched in Hodinohsyó:ni land relationality, individual and collective identity, futurity and worldview, plus the underpinnings of Hodinohsyó:ni philosophy and ways of being. Gayogo̱ho:nǫ'néha (or any Indigenous language) can only be taught by integrating these elements into language pedagogy; Indigenous languages must be taught holistically so that learners can experience the living knowledge of Indigenous cultures through language.

Henry begins each class with the ohę:dǫ' gaihwadegǫ' ganǫhǫnyǫhk (thanksgiving address), spoken words that offer thanks to all Creation. In isolation and without cultural context, the meaning of the words would remain superficial. However, by integrating storytelling and holism – underpinnings of the theoretical framework described earlier – the speaker infuses the oral language with cultural context. For example, to acknowledge relationality with the sun, the Hodinohsyó:ni say *shedwaj'ia'*, which roughly translates to "our elder brother" in English. Absent from Hodinohsyó:ni cultural context, *shedwaj'ia'* could be reduced to describe kinship between siblings. Although true, this generalization does not embrace the relational significance in Hodinohsyó:ni worldview, thus, the *Teaching from the Threshold* pedagogical framework prevents erasure of cultural knowledge. When studying the word *shedwaj'ia'*, Indigenous Knowledge emanates and extends meaning beyond sibling kinship to kinship. When teaching language through Indigenous worldviews, philosophies, and relationship, learners are given access to the *skeleton key* (Porter, 2008) that unlocks doorways to remedy the long-term impact of colonization that sought to extinguish Indigenous people's kinship with Land and Creation.

Indigenous Arts-Based Language Reclamation and Regeneration Innovations

In a 2012 report titled *We Have To Hear Their Voices* commissioned by the Canada Council for the Arts on Indigenous language and the arts, Sinclair and Pelletier (2012) wrote:

In our Aboriginal languages, many of the fluent speakers have pointed out the fact that there is no specific word for art, but there are literally hundreds of 'verbs' that describe an artistic activity. These descriptive verbs in Cree or Mohawk or Haida have incredible ranges and are all related to different aspects of traditional life and culture: from singing to the child in the mother's womb, to dancing, to welcoming the sun or the rain or the thunder beings.

(p. 1)

The idea of integrating and combining Indigenous languages and art serves as a central motif in the work of various Indigenous artists across Turtle Island. Notable examples include the music of Innu band Kashtin, a duo that emerged in the 1980s and 1990s and released numerous albums written and sung in the Innu-aimun language. Also, the group, The Jerry Cans, from Iqaluit, Nunavut, Canada, produces and performs music in Inuktitut, combining folk, rock, and throat singing. Meanwhile, electropop artist Riit blends Inuktitut lyrics, throat singing, and electronics to produce atmospheric songs that articulate contemporary forms of cultural expression and language through music. Riit explained that Inuktitut is a strong component of her life and work. She noted that "Inuktitut in Pang [her hometown] is very strong" and that she "barely spoke in English except in school" (Williams, 2019, n.p.).

The resurgence of language is influential on the work of Indigenous artists from across the field. Indigenous artists are developing innovative ways to incorporate their language(s) in their works, which in turn disrupts linguistic hegemony and decenters imposing colonial languages while moving toward reclaiming, recuperating, or recentering Indigenous languages. For instance, in a 2017 exhibition at Gallery 101 in Ottawa, Ontario, Canada titled *Language of Puncture*, curator Joi T. Arcand (néhiyaw/Muskeg Lake Cree Nation) worked with Indigenous artists to investigate the implications of language sovereignty and representation in art. The exhibit critiqued the colonial barriers used to methodically interrupt Indigenous languages while looking at new ways to rebuild and restore them. As explained on Gallery 101's website (2017):

The artists in Language of Puncture are writing language anew – often employing humour, slang, and vernacular drawn from shared, everyday experiences. They are creating new typographies and Indigenizing fonts, whispering Anishinaabemowin through spray painted letters, beading secrets out of slang, and letting letters carry the weight of not knowing one's language.

(n.p.)

Increasingly, efforts to regenerate Indigenous languages through art and performance are becoming a critical form of art intervention that offers a space to reclaim and reassert Indigenous aesthetic and expression. Arcand, for example, creates a form of wearable art and a way of reimagining new forms of literacy and Indigenous art aesthetics through laser cut jewelry using Cree words and syllabics. Arcand also recenters the Cree language and forms of visual culture to explore Indigenous expression and articulations in public space.

Arcand's work ▽ᑲᐃᐧᐊᑲᐧᕠᒧ (Trans: Don't Speak English, 2017) visually signifies Indigenous language expression as a form of resistance to imposed colonial settler structures. By strategically placing vinyl-cut words written in Cree syllabics on a staircase in the gallery, Arcand critiqued the impacts that colonial languages have had on Indigenous Knowledge systems. Writing about Arcand's work, Hampton (2018) noted that her "media makes hyper-visible that which has historically had low visibility in dominant culture" (n.p.). Indeed, Arcand's work guides the public to rethink and reconsider the effects of linguistic colonialism and how this space can be disrupted and challenged. Hampton (2018) explained:

> Arcand doesn't always make English translations of her work readily available. 'Why should I make it easy for anybody?' she asks. In a predominantly Anglophone country like Canada, English speakers often express an entitlement over communications and their access to it. Arcand's work challenges these presumptions: If you want the answers, you have to look, you have to do the work. At WAG, she placed translations strategically in the elevator: 'I always say, if you want the easy way, you take the elevator.'
>
> (n.p.)

The visual significance of this work further drives home the implications of accessibility and how Indigenous people have been limited by the colonial forces and dominant mindsets, which have been gravely undervalued and underprivileged. Furthermore, the Cree words become a conscious and deliberate signifier of the barriers faced by Indigenous people and (in)access to their languages. Making the Cree language visible and present is also a form of resistance against expectations that Indigenous languages be translated for dominant society. The notion of reclaiming, preserving, and maintaining Indigenous languages such as Cree or Anishinaabemowin, among many other threatened languages, is a sharp reminder of the deliberate need to take action in how we interact and respond to this urgent call toward language reclamation and regeneration.

Concluding Thoughts

The journey toward Indigenous people's reclamation and regeneration of Indigenous languages is a resiliency narrative. Resilient because, despite the best efforts from nation state's assimilationist policies that sought to extinguish Indigenous languages and cultures, Indigenous peoples persist. Resilience is witnessed by the way Indigenous people are reclaiming their languages in ways that counteract language shift and loss by connecting and reconnecting themselves and the world to a polyphony of languages, sounds, songs, stories, and dances. There is an urgency to reclaim and regenerate the languages as more and more fluent language speakers are passing on to the Spirit World. Colonialism, or "the process by which Indigenous cultures are subverted and ultimately destroyed" (Mohawk, 2010, p. 55) have strained Indigenous people's relationship with the spirit of their languages, but Indigenous peoples worldwide are actively reclaiming and regenerating their languages. Like the *koru* that circles back toward itself, we return to the beginning of our chapter where we reminded readers to allow and enable the canoe to travel along its part of the river without interference. For Indigenous readers, we support your efforts. For non-Indigenous readers, we call on you to continue to learn about the Indigenous languages in your local area, and the next time you see an Indigenous word in a public space or hear the melody of Indigenous words, reflect on their significance, and join in solidarity with the Indigenous language reclamation and regeneration movements underway.

Note

1. Instead of using mainstream terms such as language revitalization, revival, and language extinction, we deliberately use the terms language reclamation to recognize the necessary efforts to reclaim Indigenous languages after attempted linguistic and cultural erasure through colonization (Hinton, 2011b; McCarty & Nicholas, 2014); language regeneration to reflect the life inherent in language and the idea that living languages are constantly being grown, regrown, developed, and redeveloped (Hohepa, 2006); and sleeping or dormant languages (as opposed to extinct) to refer to languages with no living speakers (Hinton, 2001b).

References

Alie, R. (2016). Aboriginal performance cultures and language revitalization: Foundations, discontinuities, and possibilities. *The University of Western Ontario Journal of Anthropology*, 24(1), 30–43. https://ojs.lib.uwo.ca/index.php/uwoja/article/view/8965/7159

Brenzinger, M., Dwyer, A. M., de Graaf, T., Grinevald, C., Krauss, M., Miyaoka, O., Osteler, N., Sakiyama, O., Villalón, M. E., Yamamoto, A. Y., & Zepeda, O. (2003). *Language vitality and endangerment.* International Expert Meeting on UNESCO Programme Safeguarding of Endangered Languages, Paris, France. https://unesdoc.unesco.org/ark:/48223/pf0000183699

Creed, M., diSuvero, V., & Kellie, C. Q. (2020). *Alaska native languages: Hät gotan.* Alaska Native Language Center. https:www.alaskanativelanguages. org/about

Ethnologue. (2021a). *How many languages are endangered?* SIL International. Retrieved March 1, 2021, from www.ethnologue.com/guides/how-many-languages-endangered

Ethnologue. (2021b). *How many languages are there in the world?* SIL International. Retrieved March 1, 2021, from www.ethnologue.com/guides/how-many-languages

Fishman, J. (1991). *Reversing language shift: Theoretical and empirical foundations of assistance to threatened languages.* Multilingual Matters.

Fishman, J. (2007). What do you lose when you lose your language? In G. Cantoni (Ed.), *Stabilizing Indigenous languages.* Northern Arizona University.

Galla, C. K. (2016). Indigenous language revitalization, promotion, and education: Function of digital technology. *Computer Assisted Language Learning, 29*(7), 1137–1151. https://doi.org/10.1080/09588221.2016.1166137

Galla, C. K. (2018). Digital realities of Indigenous language revitalization: A look at Hawaiian language technology in the modern world. *Language and Literacy, 20*(3), 100–120.

Gallery 101. (2017). *Language of puncture.* Gallery 101. Retrieved March 1, 2021, from https://g101.ca/exhibits/language-puncture

Green, J. (2017). *Pathways to creating Onkwehonwehnéha speakers at Six Nations of the Grand River Territory.* Six Nations Polytechnic. www.snpolytechnic.com/sites/default/files/docs/research/pathways_to_creating_speakers_of_onk wehonwehneha_at_six_nations.pdf

Hampton, C. (2018). *Reflections on language: Joi T. Arcand in Sobey art award 2018.* National Gallery of Canada. Retrieved March 1, 2021, from www. gallery.ca/magazine/artists/sobey-art-award/reflections-on-language-joi-t-arcand-in-sobey-art-award-2018

Hill, R. W., & Coleman, D. (2019). The two row Wampum-Covenant chain tradition as a guide for Indigenous-University research partnerships. *Cultural Studies Critical Methodologies, 19*(5), 339–359. https://doi.org/10.1177/1532708618809138

Hinton, L. (1997). Survival of endangered languages: The California master-apprentice program. *International Journal of the Sociology of Language, 1997*(123), 177–191. https://doi.org/10.1515/ijsl.1997.123.177

Hinton, L. (2001a). The master-apprentice language learning program. In K. L. Hale & L. Hinton (Eds.), *The green book of language revitalization in practice* (pp. 217–226). Brill.

Hinton, L. (2001b). Sleeping languages: Can they be awakened? In L. Hinton & K. L. Hale (Eds.), *The green book of language revitalization in practice* (pp. 413–417). Brill.

Hinton, L. (2011a). Language revitalization and language pedagogy: new teaching and learning strategies. *Language and Education, 25*(4), 307–318.

Hinton, L. (2011b). Revitalization of endangered languages. In P. Austen & J. Sallabank (Eds.), *The Cambridge handbook of endangered languages* (pp. 291–311). Cambridge University Press.

Hohepa, M. K. (2006). Biliterate practices in the home: Supporting Indigenous language regeneration. *Journal of Language, Identity, and Education, 5*(4), 293–315.

McCarty, T. L., & Nicholas, S. E. (2014). Reclaiming Indigenous languages: A reconsideration of the roles and responsibilities of schools. *Review of Research in Education, 38*(1), 106–136.

McIvor, O., & Parker, A. (2016). Back to the future: Recreating natural Indigenous language learning environments through language nest early childhood immersion programs. *The International Journal of Holistic Early Learning and Development, 3,* 21–35. https://ijheld.lakeheadu.ca/article/view/1444

Mohawk, J. (2010). Indigenous economics: Our strategy for survival. In J. Barreiro (Ed.), *Thinking in Indian: A John Mohawk reader* (pp. 53–58). Fulcrum.

Office of the High Commissioner of Human Rights (OHCHR). (2019). *Many Indigenous languages are in danger of extinction.* Retrieved March 1, 2021, from www.ohchr.org/EN/NewsEvents/Pages/Indigenouslanguages.aspx

Porter, T. (2008). And grandma said . . . *Iroquois teachings as passed down through the oral tradition.* Xlibris Corporation.

Romero-Little, E., & Blum-Martinez, R. (2012). In retrospect, revitalizing the Cochiti language – A proposal for community re-engagement in collective spirit and mutual respect. *Journal of American Indian Education, 51*(3), 95–103. www.jstor.org/stable/43608640

Shah, S., & Brenzinger, M. (2018). The role of teaching in language revival and revitalization movements. *Annual Review of Applied Linguistics, 38,* 201–208. https://doi.org/10.1017/S0267190518000089

Sinclair, B. E., & Pelletier, D. (2012). *We have to hear their voices: A research project on Aboriginal languages and art practices.* https://canadacouncil.ca/research/research-library/2012/05/we-have-to-hear-their-voices

Smith, H. A., Giacon, J., & McLean, B. (2018). A community development approach using free online tools for language revival in Australia. *Journal of Multilingual and Multicultural Development, 39*(6), 491–510. https://doi.org/10.1080/01434632.2017.1393429

Titley, E. B. (1986). *A narrow vision: Duncan Campbell Scott and the administration of Indian Affairs in Canada.* UBC Press.

UNESCO. (2010, March). *UNESCO atlas of the world's languages in danger.* United Nations Educational, Scientific, and Cultural Organization (UNESCO). http://www.unesco.org/languages-atlas/index.php

UNESCO. (2017). *Biodiversity and linguistic diversity.* UNESCO. Retrieved March 1, 2021, from www.unesco.org/new/en/culture/themes/endangered-languages/biodiversity-and-linguistic-diversity/

United Nations. (2008). *United Nations declaration on the rights of Indigenous peoples.* United Nations. www.un.org/esa/socdev/unpfii/documents/DRIPS_en.pdf

Upadhyay, R. K., & Hasnain, S. I. (2017). Linguistic diversity and biodiversity. *Lingua, 195,* 110–123. https://doi.org/https://doi.org/10.1016/j.lingua.2017.06.002

Wagner, I. (2017). New technologies, same ideologies: Learning from language revitalization online. *Language Documentation & Conservation, 11,* 133–156. https://scholarspace.manoa.hawaii.edu/bitstream/handle/10125/24730/wagner.pdf

Walker, N. (2017). Mapping Indigenous languages in Canada. *Canadian Geographic.* A magazine of the Royal Canadian Geographic Society. www.canadiangeographic.ca/article/mapping-indigenous-languages-canada

White, D. (2021, February 28). *Hän-language childrens' book pays tribute to beloved Yukon elder.* Canadian Broadcasting Corporation. https://www.cbc.ca/news/canada/north/han-language-book-sh%C3%ABtsey-grandpa-1.5930317

Williams, M. (2019). Inuk throat-singing electro-pop artist Riit is ready to shine. *The Fader, Spring, 2019*(116). www.thefader.com/2019/04/02/inuk-throat-singing-electro-pop-artist-riit-is-ready-to-shine

Yukon Native Language Centre. (2020). *Hän language lesson and learning resources.* Council of Yukon First Nations. http://ynlc.ca/languages/han.htnl#dlr

Chapter 16

Of Pirates and Superheroes

826 National and Hybrid School-Community Writing Spaces

Susan Cridland-Hughes and Mary-Celeste Schreuder

Author Note

Susan Cridland-Hughes: https://orcid.org/0000-0002-4209-5197

Mary-Celeste Schreuder: https://orcid.org/0000-0002-5893-1292

Writing never occurs in a vacuum – it is always a complex dance among individual goals, skills, and spaces where writing is welcomed and valued. When conceptualizing how youth develop habits and skills of writing, we often focus on the work of schooled writing (Applebee & Langer, 2011). However, much work has been done to explore how out-of-school writing spaces and hybrid writing spaces intersect to support chosen spaces of writing (Dyson, 2003; Fisher, 2007; Hess et al., 2019). These chosen spaces allow youth to imagine themselves in a range of writing experiences, nurturing a desire to write that extends beyond assessment and evaluation and into true communication.

826 National is a collection of chapters and affiliated writing centers that work to support students in the doing of extraordinary things in writing. In

DOI: 10.4324/9781003228042-20

this chapter, we explore the 826 National network as both a space welcoming collective writing and as a space focused on individual goals for writing.

Supplying Pirates, Supporting Students

In 2002, author David Eggers (2000) and educator Nínive Calegari conceived of opening an unconventional writing and tutoring center for students in an under-resourced area of San Francisco. Eggers and Calegari's experienced city schools as under-staffed, under-resourced, and under-funded and desired to improve their community by connecting students to professionals through one-on-one writing and reading instruction. Knowing individualized support is not often possible in school, Eggers enlisted his community of writing friends, with flexible work hours, to support student literacy learning during out-of-school hours. Eggers and Calegari chose 826 Valencia Street – a commercial location zoned for retail. In order to adhere to regulations, they transformed their chosen space, 826 Valencia, into a whimsical Pirate Supply Store with a tutoring and publishing center in the rear (826 National, n.d.).

Due to the success of the original store, the 826 National network was founded in 2008 and has grown to encompass 9 chapters, over 50 affiliated organizations, and is now the "largest youth writing network in the country" (826 National, n.d.). Chapters continue to value urban spaces, choosing under-resourced locations with strong neighborhood ties in order to reach students within their own communities. With storefronts transformed into superhero, robot, or magic supply companies, 826's purpose is "the exploration of endless possibility" to encourage student imagination "through the power of writing" (826 National, n.d.).

Writing as "Boundless Optimism" and "Possibility of Creativity"

The 826 National network has specific markers for the mission, purpose, and scope of the program. Eggers said in his 2008 TED talk that the principles of these affiliates are "one-on-one attention, complete devotion to the students' work and a boundless optimism and sort of a possibility of creativity and ideas" (Eggers, 2008, 01:22). First, the goal of the 826 National network affiliates is to establish the programs in areas where they can be of most good to the neighborhoods and youth they serve. This focus makes each of the affiliates responsive to the placemaking of the individual community (Kinloch, 2009).

The embedded nature of the writing and tutoring center places these areas of creativity and joy at the heart of the community.

At the end of Eggers' TED talk (2008), he gives a call of action to the audience:

> The schools need you. The teachers need you. Students and parents need you. They need your actual person: your physical personhood and your open minds and open ears and boundless compassion, sitting next to them, listening and nodding and asking questions for hours at a time.
>
> (23:22)

The heart of the 826 National network is the development of relationships and connections between youth and adults, across the clear lines between community and school. These connections see the identities of teacher and student as the central roles around which all other relationships revolve.

Paying Back Part of the "Education Debt"

Kinloch et al. (2017) make the argument that public schools do not offer equal education opportunities to students from historically marginalized groups. Although the vision of public school is egalitarian and equalizing, vast amounts of research demonstrate the resourcing gap between monolingual, predominantly middle-class schools and schools with large numbers of diverse students, including linguistically, racially, and economically. This gap has manifested in what Ladson-Billings terms the "education debt" (2006).

This lens is key for understanding the role the 826 National network plays in addressing that debt. Philosophically, the organization positions itself as a hybrid school-community space where resources, specifically volunteers, one-on-one attention, and language practice, can be provided to all youth, particularly those who learn and live in under-resourced communities. The idea of bridging, of offering a space and program that is simultaneously in and out of schools that works both independently and in conversation with teachers, is grounded in a theory of change that involves key components of "Third Space" and a "culture of creativity" (826 National, n.d.).

How Do Third Space and a Culture of Creativity Intersect in 826 National?

Gutiérrez (2008) describes the evolution of Third Space as beginning in the notion of shared meaning making and, more recently, moving into the idea of a "collective Third Space as interactionally constituted, in which traditional conceptions of academic literacy and instruction for students from nondominant communities are contested and replaced with forms of literacy that privilege and are contingent upon students' sociohistorical lives" (Gutiérrez, 2008, p. 148). This shift moves the location of shared interactions away from the engagement of two individuals and into the systems that govern education and the places where education is formalized. For this Third Space to emerge, there must be a flattening of power relations and a commitment to literacy in context.

While Third Space is well known in literacy circles, 826 National simultaneously embeds a commitment to creativity within the shared interactions and exploration of writing as a creative process. The community, whether based at a center or through an affiliate, prioritizes specific norms for both youth and volunteers: "experimentation and risk taking for student writing; respect for diversity of learning styles, honoring diversity of opinion, race, ethnicity, and culture; and experimentation for tutors in working with students on homework and writing" (Fried & Taylor, 2014, p. 1). Broadly speaking, a space framed around shared creative risk-taking for both students and adults requires the redefinition of what multigenerational spaces can and should look like. Although there is support and guidance, students and volunteers negotiate what this collaborative endeavor includes and how best to support the young people participating. Students and tutors are reminded that discipline is not the goal, but rather invention.

A Tale of Two Contexts: How 826-Inspired Writing Centers Adapt to the Local Environment

The 826 National network mostly serves students aged 6–18 through numerous free-of-charge programs, including after-school tutoring, field trips, in-school assistance, writing workshops, and the Young Author's Book Project (YABP). Beyond the original San Francisco location, chapters have been established in nine major cities, reaching over 80,000 low-income youth living in these urban centers (826 National, n.d.). Before a chapter is established, the needs of the target community are rigorously researched, and in-depth information about neighborhood demographics, local schools, and possible community partnerships are identified. For this reason, each chapter differs in their target audience; for instance, the 826 chapter in San Francisco mostly serves a Latinx population, while the Minneapolis chapter serves a large refugee population. With free and purposefully adaptable curriculum, 826 encourages each chapter to focus on the needs of their unique setting (826 National, n.d.).

To this point, this chapter has focused on urban scaling up of the 826 National network model. However, more than a quarter of public-school students attend rural schools, and of those students almost one half are identified as from low-income families (Showalter et al., 2017). These statistics highlight the need for resources such as the 826 National network in areas that do not benefit from a concentrated population of city-dwellers with access to public transportation and a deeply held sense of individual community. In this section, we contrast the story of 826 Valencia with the story of one network affiliate working in a more rural context.

The Wordmobile

In a rural area of the Southeastern United States, writer and educator Adrienne Burris reconceptualized the 826 model and curriculum to reach students in an expansive county of over 795 square miles (U.S. Census Bureau, 2018). During her process of adapting the urban design of 826 for a rural area, Burris determined one central location would not be sustainable for such a dispersed community. Consequently, in 2012, Burris raised over $18,000 to purchase and renovate an old school bus, transforming it into The Wordmobile – a whimsical writing space with hanging plants, fairy lights, and a reader's stage (See Figures 16.1 and 16.2).

Figure 16.1 Image of Entrance to the Wordmobile

Figure 16.2 Image of Interior of the Wordmobile

As a tutoring center on wheels, Burris drove to rural areas most in need of academic support, tailoring workshops and activities to the diverse demographics of each neighborhood. In the 2019 Annual Report, Burris talked about her 826 National affiliate spaces as a shared endeavor, describing plans to "[expand] our Open Bus program to guest writers/teachers, making our Wordmobile more accessible to the community than ever before" (*Greenville Wordsmiths*, p. 7). As the Wordmobile continued to grow, however, Burris' model required regular modification and innovation to maintain the integrity of a community-based organization. In Burris' words, "Greenville is a quickly gentrifying town, with communities in a state of constant flux. When I had the idea for creating The Wordmobile, it was with that in mind: something could move where the people move." The Wordmobile became a staple of the community, where "the wonder of having a creative, designated space for writing [kept] people coming back again and again" – showing the power of evolving, innovative spaces to meet the specific needs of communities (A. Burris, personal communication, August 28, 2019).

We share the experiences of Burris in this section to describe the range of ways people have connected with the ideals and goals of the 826 National model. Although there is magic in the original conception of a dedicated community storefront with a publishing house in back and constant contact with practicing authors, the challenges of maintaining a space and the costs associated with those spaces have reshaped the continuum of program provision. New affiliates with smaller footprints and less access to funding have infused the creativity, whimsy, and sense of chosen space of the original 826 Valencia within mobile writing labs and push-in workshops at schools. Although these lack the sense of community that a standalone building provides, they do offer the opportunity for school spaces to be reimagined as areas that privilege imaginative writing.

How Does 826 National Facilitate Writing, Really?

There are specific models of instruction built into the 826 National network curriculum, and each of these models offers particular strengths for developing students as writers. In this section, we detail these models and provide examples of how each model functions within one of the affiliates.

Collaborative Writing

One of the models used by the 826 National network is that of collaborative writing. Collaborative writing as a structure has been found to "[improve] the metalinguistic activity of learning to write" (Corcelles Seuba & Castelló, 2015, p. 159) In Adrienne Burris' Wordmobile, this consisted of students designing a shared story. While students had individual responsibility for aspects of the story, elementary and middle school youth worked together to shape the final product.

Adult-Modeled Creative Writing

826 Valencia is one of the spaces where the adult modeling of creative writing occurs most frequently. While modeling of writing is commonly emphasized for argumentative writing, there is less research on how modeling operates in the structure of creative writing. Still, as is the case at 826 Valencia, students see adults engaging in creative writing in a professional setting, and they observe the products that emerge from the shared space. In this way, the modeling of writing as integral to life helps students imagine what is possible (826 Valencia, n.d.).

Publication (Both Digital and Physical)

This model of writing, referred to as a "project-based model" of writing, is consistent across the 826 National affiliates (826 Valencia, n.d.). Youth produce something that can be read and viewed by others. For 826 Valencia, this has included partnerships with author Khaled Hosseini, Amy Tan, Isabel Allende, and performer Robin Williams, all of whom wrote forewords to books written and published by students. For Adrienne Burris, the publication process includes both publication of class books from in-person workshops and the offer to publish for teachers as their classrooms work together on a shared project (*Greenville Wordsmiths*, 2019).

While these three models do not seem that different from how writing is traditionally taught in classrooms, the writing the 826 National network prioritizes is creative writing – a skill that is still largely reserved as an out-of-school intervention, even though research shows creative writing develops student engagement and critical thinking skills (Howe, 2016; Hunt, 2009). Creative writing is often pushed out of schools as the model becomes standardization and assessment; as such, students are often hesitant to embark on writing that they are not confident will be "right" (Magrath et al., 2003). Therefore, the 826 National curriculum works to develop students' writing confidence by exposing the fallacy that there is only one "right" way to write.

"Writing is Fun": Evaluating 826 National

External research on the 826 National network is close to nonexistent, with one study conducted by the Wallace Foundation in 2013. The study focused on eight community-based out-of-school time (OST) arts programs geared toward tweens and teens in low-income, urban areas. Relying on a qualitative study design, ten principles of success were identified and utilized for analysis of the eight OST programs, and 826 Valencia achieved all ten principles of success (Montgomery et al., 2013). The report specifically mentioned 826 Valencia's dedication to helping students see themselves as writers "by having them create author biographies and giving the now-published young scribes a table full of their books to sign for their fans" (p. 88).

Beyond outside evaluations, the 826 National network also conducts their own internal evaluations on their chapters using chapter reports, assessment outcomes, and survey data conducted by a hired research firm, Arbor Consulting Partners. In 2012, Arbor Consulting evaluated the impact of 826 Boston's Young Author's Book Project (YABP) – a program centered on teaching memoir writing to eleventh-grade ELL students. Through quantitative surveys and pre-and post-focus groups, results showed 96% of YABP participants felt they had developed into a "good writer," with a statistically significant increase in participants' belief that "writing is fun" (Fried & Taylor, 2013, p. 3). In 2013, Arbor Consulting evaluated the impact of the, at the time, seven 826 chapters' after-school tutoring programs (Fried & Taylor, 2014). Utilizing a mixed-methods design and triangulating over 1,700 student, parent, and volunteer surveys, findings showed an overwhelmingly positive academic impact on students when participating in the 826 tutor programs, including an increase in student homework persistence and writing self-confidence (Fried & Taylor, 2014).

While the results of the 826 National network evaluations are predominantly positive, 826 programs are not without challenges. As an example, Arbor Consulting found that 826 projects (such as YABP) are incredibly time consuming and only accessible to "teacher[s] who [are] willing to put in additional time for planning and follow-through during the project" (Fried & Taylor, 2013). Time continues to be a dwindling commodity in public schools, making the time necessary for 826 projects a luxury teachers may not be able to afford. In regard to volunteers, 826 Boston commented on the need for more training to improve volunteer communication with students and to combat high volunteer turnover rates and difficulties with retention (Fried & Taylor, 2013).

More research needs to be conducted on the 826 National network, especially as it continues to grow and develop. According to Howe (2016), the 826 program developed first "without any apparent intention of publishing results via formal educational studies" (p. 200), which reveals that conducting and reporting research on the 826 National network was of secondary importance to its curriculum and pedagogy. During its inception, focusing on the design of the program was vital; however, a lack of formal research limits "the program's ability to garner educational support and funding on a national level" (p. 200). To progress as a non-profit organization that relies on grants and donations, viable research must be disseminated on the 826 National network at the national and international levels.

Resourcing Without and Within Schools: Contextual Factors for Sustainability

The 826 National network also shows promising possibilities for stronger partnerships between schools and local communities through classroom placement of volunteers who support teachers and students on writing projects.

Relationships

In 2017–2018, almost 2,000 teachers were served and 434 in-school writing projects were conducted, showing the potential for community-based organizations to bridge the gap between in- and out-of-school literacies (826 National, n.d.). Resourcing is key to facilitating these partnerships. Prescheduled workshops can be planned and executed effectively with a small number of staff. However, with regard to volunteering in schools, as requests come in from teachers, someone needs to be available to immediately reach out to volunteers who are committed to sharing their time. For a small program such as Burris's Wordmobile, those requests may very well come in during a time that she is already facilitating workshops. Additionally, large cities have access to more volunteers than small cities and rural areas, and that can limit the outreach potential of an 826 affiliate.

Funding

Being a non-profit organization, 826 relies on fundraising and donations from individuals, partnerships, and national organizations. They also garner revenue from retail sales at their storefronts and writing events. With an expenditure of over 1.7 million, 826 receives most of their funding (70%) from foundations and corporations (826 National, 2019a), and since the inception of the network, their overall revenue has increased by 58% while their operating budget has grown by 43% (826 National, 2019b). Being a community-based organization, 826 relies on word-of-mouth advertising for donations and still remains relatively unknown to a large portion of the country. 826 has placed a limited focus on marketing, with the network relying on outside media, such as the *CBS This Morning* profile, to disseminate information about 826 and its programs (826 National, 2019b). While any exposure is beneficial, the issue remains that 826 is not nationally visible and, in the past, has not maintained a strategic vision for future marketing strategies and long-range plans. 826 is working to increase their marketing by hiring "a full-time marketing and communications role at the National office," with the hopes of becoming a visible member of the national education community (826 National, 2019b).

Sustainability

A sustainability issue for 826 is demand for the network's services. 826 reports that all of their chapters are outgrowing their locations with long waitlists for programming (826 National, 2019b). To address this issue, 826 is looking to expand their reach by increasing their online program – 826 Digital – and opening their latest chapter in Dallas, Texas. With ever-increasing demand outweighing supply, the 826 volunteer model also needs to consider new strategies to retain current volunteers and recruit new professionals. 826 is committed to maintaining individualized student support regardless of high demand; therefore, their future is dedicated to sustainability efforts that increase professional development for staff and volunteers, with greater focus on a "more proactive model of expansion" (826 National, n.d.). However, issues unique to the 826 space, such as increased gentrification in urban communities and the difficulty in replicating the rich community of writers and publishers in less urbanized areas, reveals potential challenges to the future sustainability of the 826 National network and its impact on community-based literacy.

Creating a Future for Creative Writing

In its 13 years of existence, 826 Valencia and the subsequent 826 National expansion have demonstrated that the particular emphasis on creative writing, whimsy, and project-centered writing are meaningful to teachers, students, and communities. The 826 affiliates have published hundreds of student-written books as well as countless other texts, but the constantly shifting nature of communities means that these models of community-based outreach will constantly shift as well.

While the 826 National network has moved toward providing its curriculum for free to teachers, the question remains whether teachers will access something if that requires additional time and a learning curve on their part. A model that does not allow teachers to cede that time in the classroom to facilitators relies heavily on classroom teachers to develop their own expertise. For some, this will be welcome, but there may be others who are stopped before they even start.

On the other hand, one of the challenges that all out-of-school literacy communities face when working within schools is the question of how to maintain the sense of independence in writing when youth see it as part of the classroom. This is not unique to 826 National; how community organizations operate betwixt and between schools is a part of the relationship to schools that will always need to be negotiated (Fisher, 2007). Connecting with schools offers the ability to directly support teachers, but some students thrive in spaces away from what they perceive to be a schooled environment.

Additionally, public schools continue to move inexorably toward more and more nonfiction writing. While this is in part traceable to Common Core, the reality is less time is allotted to things that are seen as peripheral to the curriculum, either because they are not assessed or because they are not valued. The 826 model of teaching writing is primarily a model that focuses on the joy and love of writing, and there is no standard for that.

In 2020, Burris transitioned to supporting writing as an employee of the school system. She still uses the same curriculum to provide workshops in teachers' classrooms and run after-school creative writing workshops, but the Wordmobile is parked. Ultimately, challenges of community engagement and non-profit funding compromised the ability to provide services in the mobile writing lab. The pandemic also limited the ability of community-based organizations to provide outreach, both in schools and in communities. Schreuder (2021) emphasized the difficulties of transitioning an in-person, out-of-school writing workshop for adolescent girls to a virtual meeting mediated through technology. Both the need for individual stability and the radical upheaval of the pandemic offers us very real challenges for the scaling up of the 826 model. What the 826 model reminds us, however, is that often our students are lacking joy in their education. The question we should be taking with us into the future is how to make school more magical. How do we create, within the walls of a classroom, a place where students are free to explore, fail, try again, and build beyond what they know to be possible?

References

826 National. (n.d.). *826 National.* https://826national.org/

826 National. (2019a). *826 National 2017–2018 annual report* [PDF file]. https://826national.org/wp-content/uploads/2019/05/826National_AR2018.pdf

826 National. (2019b) *Welcome to the future: Strategic plan 2018–20* [PDF file]. https://826national.org/wp-content/uploads/2018/09/826NatStratPlan2017.pdf

826 Valencia. (n.d.). *826 Valencia.* https://826valencia.org/

Applebee, A., & Langer, J. (2011). A snapshot of writing instruction in middle and high schools. *English Journal, 100*(6), 14–27.

Burris, A. (2019, August 28). Personal communication.

Corcelles Seuba, M., & Castelló, M. (2015). Learning philosophical thinking through collaborative writing in secondary education. *Journal of Writing Research, 7*(1), 157–200. http://dx.doi.org/10.17239/jowr-2015.07.01.07

Dyson, A. H. (2003). *The Brothers and sisters learn to write.* Teachers College Press.

Eggers, D. (2000). *A heartbreaking work of staggering genius.* Simon and Schuster.

Eggers, D. (2008, February). *My wish: Once upon a school* [Video]. TED. www. ted.com/talks/dave_eggers_makes_his_ted_prize_wish_once_upon_a_ school?language=en

Fisher, M. T. (2007). *Writing in rhythm: Spoken word poetry in urban classrooms.* Teachers College Press.

Fried, M., & Taylor, M. (2013). *I want you to have this: A collection of objects and their stories from around the world. An evaluation of 826 Boston's Young Authors' Book Project in partnership with Boston International High School 2012–2013* [PDF file]. 826 National. https://826national.org/wp-content/ uploads/2017/02/826-YABPEvaluation2013.pdf

Fried, M., & Taylor, M. (2014). *Ann Arbor Consulting Partners report on 826 National after-school tutoring programs* [PDF file]. 826 National. https://826national.org/ wp-content/uploads/2017/02/826-ASTEvaluationExecSummary2014-Web-Version.pdf

Greenville Wordsmiths (2019). *Greenville Wordsmiths 18–19 annual report* [PDF File]. www.greenvillewordsmiths.com/annual-report

Gutiérrez, K. (2008). Developing a sociocritical literacy in the Third Space. *Reading Research Quarterly, 43*(2), 148–164. https://doi-org/10.1598/RRQ. 43.2.3

Hess, J., Watson, V., & Deroo, M. (2019). "Show some love": Youth and teaching artists enacting literary presence and musical presence in an after-school literacy-and-songwriting class. *Teachers College Record, 121*(6), 1–44.

Howe, L. (2016). A review of creative writing workshop pedagogy in educational research: Methodological challenges and affordances. *Journal of Poetry Therapy, 29*(4), 195–206. https://doi-org/10.1080/08893675. 2016.1215379

Hunt, C. (2009). Creative writing as a tool for transformative learning. In *Proceedings of the eighth international transformative learning conference: Reframing social sustainability in a multicultural world* (pp. 172–177). Pennsylvania State University.

Kinloch, V. (2009). Literacy, community, and youth acts of place-making. *English Education, 41*(4), 316–336.

Kinloch, V., Burkhard, T., & Penn, C. (2017). When school is not enough: Understanding the lives and literacies of Black youth. *Research in the Teaching of English, 52*(1), 34–54.

Ladson-Billings, G. (2006). From the achievement gap to the education debt: Understanding achievement in U.S. schools. *Educational Researcher*, 35(7), 3–12. https://doi-org/10.3102/0013189X035007003

Magrath, C. P., Ackerman, A., Branch, T., Clinton Bristow, J., Shade, L. B., Elliott, J., & Williams, R. (2003). The neglected "R": The need for a writing revolution. *The National Commission on Writing*. College Entrance Examination Board.

Montgomery, D., Rogovin, P., & Persaud, N. (2013). *Something to say: Success principles for afterschool arts programs from urban youth and other experts*. Wallace Foundation.

Schreuder, M. (2021). *"We are girls. We are warriors. We are writers": Middle school girls and gender identity construction in an after-school writing workshop* [Unpublished doctoral dissertation, Clemson University].

Showalter, D., Klein, R., Johnson, J., & Hartman, S. (2017). *Why rural matters 2015–2016: Understanding the changing landscape*. Report of the Rural Schools and Community Trust.

U.S. Census Bureau. (2018). *Quick facts: Greenville County, South Carolina*. www.census.gov/quickfacts/greenvillecountysouthcarolina

Chapter 17

The May Literacy Center

A Child- and Community-Centered Approach to Teacher Education

Brian M. Flores, Amber Meyer, William Tignor, and Dixie Massey

Author Note

Brian M. Flores: https://orcid.org/0000-0002-8117-8024

Amber Meyer: https://orcid.org/0000-0003-2480-425X

William Tignor: https://orcid.org/0000-0002-9553-3007

Dixie Massey: https://orcid.org/0000-0003-0071-4559

Brief Historical Background of Literacy Centers

Multiple influences converged to support the creation of literacy centers within universities. In 1921, Grace Fernald established a clinic at UCLA for young readers who struggled in educational settings. Her method became known as the Fernald Method and utilized visual, auditory, and kinesthetic prompts to assist students. In the early 1920s, The Rockefeller Foundation financed a study by Dr. Samuel Orton, who shifted his attention from adults with brain damage to children. He wondered why students with normal

DOI: 10.4324/9781003228042-21

neurological function struggled to read, and he established a clinic to study this phenomenon. Donald Durrell was a student at the University of Iowa and worked with Dr. Orton on his studies of young children. Durrell then attended the Harvard Graduate School of Education and worked with Walter Dearborn in the Dearborn Psycho-Educational Clinic. The Dearborn clinic opened in 1917 and focused on the mental and psychological abilities of children. Strongly influenced by Dearborn and Orton, Durrell began working at Boston University in 1930, and in 1932 he established both an Educational Clinic and a graduate program in reading education. Local schools referred children with *learning problems* to the clinic where graduate students tested and tutored the children. These same graduate students often collected data in the local schools as part of their master's theses, which greatly influenced the design and norming of the Durrell Analysis of Reading Difficulty.

By the 1950s, many universities had reading clinics dedicated to helping teachers diagnose reading difficulties while assisting children to become better readers. Bond and Fay (1950) at the University of Minnesota reported that students in their clinic gained four times as much as was expected in reading growth, equating to several years of reading achievement. In this same timeframe, Ira Aaron created The University of Georgia Reading Clinic at the University of Georgia (UGA), one of the oldest continuously running reading clinics in the United States. Reflecting the 1950's era shift to focusing on children and teachers, the UGA Reading Clinic still offers university-based, one-on-one graduate-level tutoring to K–12th grade students every spring semester. With the 1950s and 1960s, the focus on children, practicing teachers, and/or teacher candidates was now the prevalent model for university-based reading clinics.

In 2019, Pletcher et al. (2019) provided a glimpse into ten university-based literacy centers in the U.S. and found most centers maintained similar programs to the University of Minnesota and UGA. Yet, there are nuanced differences for each center's funding, populations served, and tutors, information that is often difficult to come by on center websites and brochures. Since literacy center structures and programs are tricky to uncover, we felt it would be productive to provide a case-like description of the May Literacy Center (MLC), a university-based literacy clinic. In the remainder of this chapter, we discuss the MLC's populations served, programming, visions for the future, and growing partnerships.

The May Literacy Center: A Case Study

In 1990, Florence and John May established the Florence Simonds and John B. May Endowment at Salisbury State University (now Salisbury University).

This endowment endorsed community-based educational programs and research projects focused on children with learning exceptionalities and stemmed from Dr. John May's own struggles with dyslexia. Unfortunately, over the next nine years, no funds were allocated for such projects. Then in 1999, the May Literacy Center (MLC) was established.

The MLC is a university-based literacy center that provides year-round literacy instruction for local school children from grades K–8 in a student-centered learning environment. The current MLC mission states that we strive to:

> Support children's reading and literacy development from kindergarten through 8th grade. Support graduate and undergraduate students' knowledge of reading and literacy development and instruction through interactive learning experiences under the guidance of Salisbury University faculty.
>
> (Seidel School of Education, 2019)

The MLC boasts a children's library, two teacher resource rooms, set of iPads, a selection of leveled reading materials, three small one-on-one tutoring rooms, and three high-capacity classrooms. At the center, undergraduate teacher candidates develop customized instructional programs to help meet children's specific and individualized learning goals while building family and community relationships.

Target Populations Served

Teacher Candidates

Tutoring programs are part of the Department of Early and Elementary Education required literacy methods course sequence for initial educator certification through a Maryland Approved Educator Preparation Program. The Literacy Assessment and Intervention course provides teacher candidates with the introduction and application of formal and informal literacy assessment tools integrated with knowledge about a child obtained through conferences with families and caregivers to make appropriate culturally responsive, student-centered instructional decisions. The course content includes information and practices in administering research-based literacy teaching strategies to support instructional decisions for early literacy, phonemic awareness, phonics, vocabulary, fluency, comprehension, and writing.

During instruction, the teacher candidates engage in formal and informal conversations with the child and family/caregivers, administer assessments, plan individualized lessons, provide one-on-one literacy instruction over eight weeks, generate detailed reflections after each tutoring session, and provide a summative report to the family/caregivers after tutoring sessions.

Children and Families

Although the current political climate surrounding immigration in the United States is tumultuous, the number of languages spoken in U.S. schools is ever-growing (National Clearinghouse for English Language Acquisition, 2010; Pacheco & Miller, 2016). This trend is manifested in the local schools we serve, with a 230% increase over the last ten years in children whose primary language is something other than English, and there are now more than 33 languages spoken in our local schools (Wicomico County Public Schools, WCPS, 2019).

In a recent conversation with the Assistant Superintendent for Instruction-Chief Academic Officer from the local school district, he expressed concerns about schools meeting the educational needs of that rapidly growing English Language Learner (ELL) population. This prompted a partnership between the MLC and the school district's English for Speakers of Other Languages (ESOL) department, which resulted in the MLC's outreach materials being translated into Spanish and Haitian Creole (the two largest ELL populations in the district) and distributed to families through all the district's elementary and middle schools.

At first, this effort did not garnish the anticipated results; families/caregivers seemed hesitant to sign their children up for literacy tutoring services. Through ongoing conversations between the ESOL Department and the MLC Director, it was deduced that the hesitation was not due to a lack of interest in the programs. Families did inquire about the program, but they expressed concern over cost. There was a weekly fee for tutoring services, and parents could not incur the extra expense. A close look at the school district's demographic data showed that the number of children and families constituting at-risk populations, ELLs, special education, and students eligible for Free and Reduced Meals (FARM), was on the rise (WCPS, 2019). Therefore, we terminated the tutoring fees. The result of discontinuing fees was immediate, with more than 50% of the children admitted into the MLCs programs qualifying for ELL services. Therefore, demographic data shows that MLC enrollment on average consists of 50% Hispanic; 30% white; 10% People of

Color; and 10% Asian, Haitian-Creole, or undeclared. Additionally, 95% of enrolled children qualify for FARM.

This population shift caused instructors and tutors to deploy different teaching strategies to meet ELL children's needs along with revised approaches used during parent/caregiver conferences. Martínez (2018) states that,

> Bi/multilingualism is the norm worldwide. Somewhere between 60% and 70% of the world's population is at least bilingual. In other words, speaking two or more languages is the typical human condition. Yet, in the United States, we tend to treat bi/multilingualism as if it were a deviation from normal linguistic development.
>
> (p. 515)

The MLC seeks to meet the needs of the changing educational climate through translanguaging (García & Wei, 2012) and culturally sustaining instructional practices (Paris, 2012), with an understanding that a strong home language provides children a more significant advantage to learning a second language (Pacheco & Miller, 2016). Now that we have described the individuals we serve at the MLC, we can discuss our program's structure in the next section.

Instructional Programming

Tutoring at the MLC is the first high contact opportunity for teacher candidates to work with children. Tutoring is 1 hour and 15 minutes per week for 8 weeks, and, during this time, teacher candidates follow a rigorous, highly structured program that includes these components: administering assessments, planning lessons, reflecting on instruction, conducting parent conferences, and writing and sharing summative reports for parents/caregivers pertaining to the student learner. We feel it is essential to show the complex structure of our programs, because this information is not readily available when researching most reading/literacy clinics.

Throughout the eight-week tutoring sessions, course instructors coach tutors to use a balanced literacy approach by engaging students in their zone of proximal development (Vygotsky, 1978) within and across the areas of reading, writing, listening, speaking, and word study to meet their identified learning goals (Tompkins, 2015). Course instructors coach tutors on negotiating and evaluating how best to leverage MLC resources to encourage literacy development through strategic student learning goals without the requirement of a generalized scripted curriculum commonly mandated in a traditional classroom context.

New Visions Take Time, Effort, and Funding: Increasing the MLC's Impact

Once the May endowment was reallocated to create the university-based literacy tutoring program for local school children, the program became dependent solely on course enrollments. Thus, the number of children and families we impact is predicated on the ebb and flow of that enrollment. For instance, we average service to about 75 children in the fall, usually half that in the spring, and the number dips to single digits over the summer. So, how do we ‚enhance our programs and increase the number of children and families we serve at the center? We created three veins of program expansion initiatives, first, an advisory council; next, intra-university partnerships with the Department of Social Work and the English Language Institute; and finally, an alternative tutoring program.

Advisory Council

The creation of the Advisory Council was to increase the number of individuals who can promote program expansion and play an essential role in the continuous improvement of the overall quality and reputation of the MLC and the Seidel School of Education. The current council consists of nine individuals from various university programs, community organizations, and local school districts who are dedicated to education, social action, and equitable experiences for traditionally marginalized populations. Table 17.1 shows the membership of the Advisory Council.

The Advisory Council's bylaws state that members will advise the MLC Director and other MLC constituencies concerning programming, community outreach, and other pertinent issues likely to impact student success. At a recent council meeting, discussions centered on connecting with community partners that provide services to the Haitian Creole population, currently the fastest growing diverse people in our region. That conversation led to meetings with those community partners to determine how the MLC could help with literacy-based educational resources. Council members are also asked to help cultivate external support for the MLC, and the United Way did this by providing $1,200 to add a collection of health literacy books to our library, which included new children's books on nutrition, physical health, bullying, mental and emotional health, and language.

Table 17.1 Membership of the MLC Advisory Council

Advisory Council Member	Role of the Organization
Wicomico County Public School Elementary Teacher	A third-grade teacher and district diversity director from a partner school.
Horizons Delmarva	An organization that provides low-income, K-8 public-school students with intensive academic support dedicated to closing the achievement gap.
Wicomico Public Libraries: Project Read	Provides curriculum that seeks to improve relationships with, services to, and resources for youth of color and Native youth.
Wicomico Public Schools	Supervisor of Accelerated Learning Programs.
United Way of the Lower Eastern Shore	An organization dedicated to reducing the achievement gap between low- and middle-income students, financial stability by advancing the economic security of families and individuals, and good health by improving access to and awareness of local health and wellness services.
School of Social Work	A Salisbury University MLC partner that has helped to expand our programs to better assist caregivers and enhance community partnerships.
Educators Rising Collegiate (Salisbury University student organization)	President of Salisbury University's chapter of Educators Rising. Established to create a community within education majors while providing professional development, scholarship, and volunteerism opportunities.
Graduate student representative	M.Ed. Reading Specialist program at Salisbury University is a professional degree and certification program designed to prepare reading educators in instructional and leadership capacities for K–12 school settings.
Alumni	Graduates of our teacher preparation programs.

Alternative Tutoring

The MLC alternative tutoring program was established to provide one-on-one educational support in reading, writing, math, science, and/or homework support to local school children who were not enrolled in our traditional literacy tutoring program. Tutors were recruited from our undergraduate teacher preparation programs as volunteers eager to work with children in a non-virtual setting during the global pandemic to address learning gaps as a result of remote instruction. Research shows that volunteer tutoring services offered to children in educational settings have a positive academic impact in areas related to alphabetic principles, word work, oral fluency, and writing (Lindo et al., 2018; Ritter et al., 2009), which is the primary means of instruction we deploy at the MLC. We feel it is important to note that 100% of the students receiving services in this program come from diverse backgrounds. This alternative tutoring model provided us with the opportunity to expand programming and impact of the MLC.

Summer Film Camp

The MLC Film Camp was launched in 2021 and brought together young filmmakers from grades 5–9 to create and produce short action films on-screen. Children worked in small groups throughout the five-day camp to learn filmmaking, acting, camera shots and angles, and editing. Participants also had the chance to write, produce, and act in their short films. The live-action filmmaking camp culminated with a screening of their movies to friends and family.

Research of film camps shows that children engage in several aspects of literacy multimodalities through filmmaking processes (Kozdras, 2010; Schneider et al., 2020). Schneider et al. (2020) state that "a film is the result of composition across multiple modes such as a script, recorded scenes, actors' narration, and camera work" (p. 69). Therefore, film camp is a creative outlet for children with a solid educational foundation.

Creating Partnerships and Growing Our Mission

Internal Institutional Partnerships

Often, when university departments (i.e., education, business, social work) generate partnerships, they look to outside community agencies to collaborate, conduct research, and, most importantly, place the numerous interns preparing for careers in their respective field of choice. It is not often that schools/departments find opportunities for partnerships promoting internships within the institution itself. This section discusses newly formed partnerships between the MLC, the School of Social Work, and the English Language Institute. First, we show how a social work internship has enhanced our relationships with families and caregivers through new programming and learning experiences for the teacher candidates we serve.

Social work clinical placements are year-long internships for undergraduate seniors where individuals receive experiential activities essential to social work. Since the MLC is a literacy center, we did not have social work protocols in place. Yet, we knew we wanted to enhance the programs we offered to better impact the families we serve. Therefore, our first step was to work with our community partners – local schools and healthcare services – to generate a needs assessment that we distributed to the families of enrolled children.

The needs assessment data revealed that families wanted information on mental health and stress management, literacy tips for reading with their child at home, and information from outside agencies that provide family services. Therefore, we organized parent workshops that addressed these topics. The social work intern facilitated a partnership with Chesapeake Health Care. This organization provides "affordable, culturally competent patient and family-centered health care" (Chesapeake Health Care, 2021, para 2) through dental, adult medicine, pediatrics, mental health, obstetrics and gynecology, and pharmaceutical services. One outcome from this partnership was reconnecting a child attending MLC who received school-based services from Chesapeake Healthcare with the opportunity to receive the services at home during the COVID-19 school closures.

For our teacher candidates working with children at the MLC, we created social work-oriented workshops on communication with non-English speaking families, mental health and suicide prevention, and antiracism. At one such workshop, a participant commented that this was the first opportunity for a *real* conversation about racism and antiracism in her four years at the university. This unique in-house partnership provided a rich landscape for MLC program expansion and outside agency partnership possibilities.

High School Spanish Teacher Partnership

Due to the increased ELL population at the MLC, many of the tutees' caregivers have limited English proficiency, proving a unique challenge for teacher candidates during parent/caregiver conferences. It is important to note that tutors attempted to use Google Translate and parent-child interpretation to bridge this language barrier at the first conference, but these practices were not ideal. Parents and tutors were frustrated that the conversations lacked the personal elements that natural conversation evokes. These participants talked into an iPad and waited for a less-than-accurate interpretation that disrupted the authentic discussions, which could have led to more positive outcomes and emotional responses. Likewise, it was difficult for younger children serving as interpreters to express precisely the details associated with the educational plan and the tutee's progress.

With a second parent conference scheduled at the end of the tutoring sequence, we wanted to find a better way to facilitate positive conversations between parents and the tutors by finding a solution to the interpretation problem so that the parents in the community would observe that the MLC invests fully in their child's success. We decide to involve community members as interpreters for families to foster more productive conversations. Therefore, we contacted an advanced placement (AP) Spanish teacher at the local high school to see if students would be willing to serve as interpreters, which resulted in five students serving in this capacity.

The final conferences were a great success. Families were relieved and enthusiastic about the MLC's effort to meet their needs for the meetings. The parents were excited to have honest conversations with tutors. The information about the tutorial successes as received in real-time created an environment of celebration. Student successes were quickly and accurately discussed, and parents felt more comfortable sharing examples of the tutee's growth as they had seen at home and school.

English Language Institute

Another university-based partnership that enhances the work at the MLC is with the English Language Institute (ELI). The ELI's mission is to offer English language courses to international ESL students and to promote individuals' transition to U.S. culture. Now part of the MLC framework, ELI has participated in our parent workshops and provides four academic programs with a focus on language and culture. These programs include (a) the Academic English Program, offered both virtually and face-to-face, which helps students with their English academic skills and preparation for enrollment in U.S.-based universities; (b) the Summer English Program, which focuses on English language learning as students engage in campus activities, attend presentations by guest lecturers, and undertake regional travel; (c) the Online Oral English Program that improves students' English speaking and listening skills while they learn about U.S. culture; and (d) customized programs that tailor instructional programs to meet an organization's unique needs. This budding partnership with ELI enhances the programming at the MLC for a global population.

Beyond the Walls of the MLC

Pushing beyond the boundaries of the MLC, we sought a partnership opportunity with a local Title I public school. In creating this partnership, the school's administration and MLC staff looked at the needs of the students, parents, teachers, and staff. Through extensive planning, the administrative team implemented several changes to what is standard practice in local schools. For example, when working with interns, there was a shift away from supervisory practices toward a content coaching approach (Dennis, 2016) to enrich the mentoring relationships, and the MLC utilized university AmeriCorps student volunteers in classrooms to provide additional instructional support for teachers. Additionally, a multiyear restorative practice professional development (PD) initiative is now in place.

School data showed that, for the 2018–2019 academic year, 86% of the referrals to the MLC were Black or Multiracial students, and at the midpoint of the 2019–2020 academic year that number had already increased to 89%. The school's administration and staff believed that a primarily white instructional team was struggling to connect to the Black student population in the school. To address this issue, the MLC procured a small workforce development grant to provide a two-year restorative practice PD program to the school staff. Institutions that deploy restorative practices seek to repair damaged relationships, prevent relationship-damaging incidents from happening, and provide quick resolutions when these incidents occur while increasing school attendance, reducing exclusions, and improving achievement. By enriching this partnership, the MLC has created more opportunities to increase impact in the community.

As we continue to grow this effort, we are planning our next steps in this social justice-oriented endeavor. Therefore, our next step is to facilitate a year-long school-wide professional learning community (PLC) book study collaborative with the Seidel School of Education at Salisbury University. Williams' (2013) research shows "collaboration between university professors and a public-school district resulted in improved student achievement at three of the lowest-performing elementary schools" (p. 33). Therefore, this collaborative aims to place school staff, university faculty, and community members in PLC groups to conceptualize and enhance the socio-cultural, socio-emotional, socio-economic, and socio-political climate of the school, thus benefitting children and families served.

Predictions, Trends/Issues that Impact the Future

Literacy centers have always been at the forefront of helping an array of struggling readers. Through additional programming, the creation of an Advisory Council and partnerships with outside agencies, the School of Social Work, the English Language Institute, and our local school district, the MLC has made significant strides to improve the programs for the children and families we serve. Looking to the future, it is uncertain as to the magnitude of educational fallout that COVID-19 will have on children's reading and writing. Many children have missed critical literacy learning developmental milestones during the nearly two academic years of COVID-dominated educational practices (Bansak & Starr, 2021; Reich, et al., 2020). Yet, there is a growing consensus that tutoring will play a major role in overcoming pandemic-oriented learning loss. The MLC is ready to take up the challenge and serve our partners as needs are identified.

This chapter demonstrates how the MLC has expanded its services to become an important partner in the community of literacy providers. We hope this discussion provides insights for other centers seeking program expansion. Regardless of how much progress university-based literacy centers make to help teachers teach and children learn, the ever-changing educational environment, school demographics, and research-based literacy practices mean that centers will always make room for program enhancement.

References

Bansak, C., & Starr, M. (2021). Covid-19 shocks to education supply: How 200,000 US households dealt with the sudden shift to distance learning. *Review of Economics of the Household, 19*(1), 63–90. https://doi.org/10.1007/s11150-020-09540-9

Bond, G. L., & Fay, L. C. (1950). A comparison of the performance of good and poor readers on the individual items of the Stanford Binet scale forms L and M. *The Journal of Educational Research, 43*(6), 475–480. https://doi.org/10.1080/00220671.1950.10881801

Chesapeake Health Care. (2021, March 10). *Who we are.* Chesapeake Health Care. https://chesapeakehc.org/

Dennis, D. V. (2016). A teacher residency melds classroom theory with clinical practice. *Phi Delta Kappan, 97*(7), 14–18. https://doi.org/10.1177/0031721716641642

García, O., & Wei, L. (2012). Translanguaging. *The encyclopedia of applied linguistics,* 1–7. https://doi.org/10.1002/9781405198431.wbeal1488

Kozdras, D. (2010). *From real to reel: Performances of influential literacies in the creative collaborative processes and products of digital video composition.* (Publication No. 3425688) [Doctoral dissertation, University of South Florida]. ProQuest Dissertations and Theses Global.

Lindo, E. J., Weiser, B., Cheatham, J. P., & Allor, J. H. (2018). Benefits of structured after-school literacy tutoring by university students for struggling elementary readers. *Reading & Writing Quarterly, 34*(2), 117–131. https://doi.org/10.1080/10573569.2017.1357156

Martínez, R. A. (2018). Beyond the English learner label: Recognizing the richness of bi/multilingual students' linguistic repertoires. *The Reading Teacher, 71*(5), 515–522. https://doi.org/10.1002/trtr.1679

National Clearinghouse for English Language Acquisition. (2010). *The growing number of English learner students: 1997/98–2007/08.* www.ncela.us/files/uploads/9/growingLEP_0809.pdf

Pacheco, M. B., & Miller, M. E. (2016). Making meaning through translanguaging in the literacy classroom. *The Reading Teacher, 69*(5), 533–537. https://doi.org/10.1002/trtr.1390

Paris, D. (2012). Culturally sustaining pedagogy: A needed change in stance, terminology, and practice. *Educational Researcher, 41*(3), 93–97.

Pletcher, B., Robertson, P., & Sullivan, M. (2019). A current overview of ten university-based reading clinics. *Reading Horizons: A Journal of Literacy and Language Arts, 58*(3), 2.

Reich, J., Buttimer, C. J., Fang, A., Hillaire, G., Hirsch, K., Larke, L. R., & Slama, R. (2020). *Remote learning guidance from state education agencies during the covid-19 pandemic: A first look.* https://doi.org/10.35542/osf.io/437e2

Ritter, G. W., Barnett, J. H., Denny, G. S., & Albin, G. R. (2009). The effectiveness of volunteer tutoring programs for elementary and middle school students: A meta-analysis. *Review of Educational Research, 79*(1), 3–38. https://doi.org/10.3102/0034654308325690

Schneider, J. J., King, J. R., Kozdras, D., & Welsh, J. L. (2020). Fast and slow literacies: Digital and compositional conundrums in a post-truth era. *Literacy Research: Theory, Method, and Practice, 69*(1), 320–338. https://doi.org/10.1177/2381336920937275

Seidel School of Education. (2019, August 1). May Literacy Center. Retrieved from SU: Salisbury University: https://www.salisbury.edu/academic-offices/education/may-literacy-center/

Tompkins, G. (2015). *Literacy in the early grades* (4th ed.). Pearson.

Vygotsky, L. S. (1978). *Mind in society: The development of higher psychological processes.* Harvard University Press.

Wicomico County Public Schools (2019, August 1). Retrieved from Wicomico County Public Schools: https://www.wcboe.org/cms/lib/MD50000151/Centricity/Domain/108/Student%20Population%20Demographics.pdf

Williams, D. J. (2013). Urban education and professional learning communities. *Delta Kappa Gamma Bulletin, 79*(2), 31.

Part Four

Evaluating and Researching Community Literacy Programs

Chapter 18

Methods and Models for Literacy Program Evaluations

Vincent Genareo

> **Author Note**
>
> Vincent Genareo: https://orcid.org/0000-0003-3789-0118

About 20 first-grade students rush into classrooms while teachers and staff direct them to their tables. Each table has crayons, markers, and pencils, as well as printed, stapled books with prompts that allow students to complete a phrase about themselves. Today, students begin creating an autobiography with hand-written words, phrases, and drawings. At the end of the week, students will share their books by reading, explaining, and connecting their printed and artistic symbols to the class. This is the start of a new unit in a literacy and arts-integrated after-school program that takes place in three Title I elementary schools.

The teacher begins with an interactive read-aloud – a short, autobiographical children's book with simple, watercolor graphics. Some students appear disengaged, while others blurt out answers in excitement. The teacher then models her thinking about her own autobiographical book as she projects it

DOI: 10.4324/9781003228042-23

on the front screen and reads it to the class. Lastly, she leads students, page-by-page, to attempt creating the first four pages of their own autobiographies together. It is immediately clear that some students are challenged to even write their names. A few appear to have issues generating ideas. Others seem overwhelmed deciding the colors and drawings to include. Teachers and staff struggle to keep up with the number of students who need assistance, and their approaches differ across classrooms and schools of the same program.

In many ways, this may have been a strong literacy lesson, but was it successful? How do literacy programs define and measure their success? How do program managers understand if the programming is implemented correctly and consistently? How do they evaluate what is working along the way to make changes, let alone measure long-term outcomes to see if they were successful? They need a strong program evaluation.

The Need for Literacy Program Evaluations

Effective literacy programs provide vital contributions to helping children succeed, and they might have even greater power with low-income students. Literacy skills – both *outside-in* and *inside-out* – can predict later academic and personal success (Hemphill & Tivnan, 2008). Program quality, timing, and intensity can have a dramatic effect on student literacy outcomes (Dickinson & Neuman, 2007). But even the strongest literacy programs need evidence they are working. Even the strongest programs should be continuously examined for efficacy and consistency (Bowers & Schwarz, 2018). Students in effective programs can lose their literacy gains if the program staff's implementation fidelity begins to drift (Feldman et al., 2012). As such, program managers need data on the program effectiveness to inform and justify program changes, such as staffing, programming, and budget. This chapter provides an overview of program evaluation and will inform literacy practitioners about some forms of evaluation methods and models.

Purpose of Program Evaluations

Program evaluations serve many purposes. Program evaluations put data in the hands of the staff responsible for making program choices; informed choices often lead to better outcomes. Program evaluations also assess program success. Often, we think of success as outcomes: Is the program meeting, or did it meet, its proposed outcomes, whether those be student social skills, student academic gains, or family participation? But success can also be process-oriented: Do staff feel properly trained or supported? Do students enjoy their experiences? Is the programming operating as intended?

Each of these success markers needs appropriate methods, data, and interpretation to be utilized for decision-making. Evaluations provide these. However, it takes knowledge and skills to plan for the evaluation, facilitate the appropriate methods within allotted timelines, run data analyses, and provide reports or communications to and among stakeholders. Programs might choose a dedicated program staff member conducting the evaluation – an *internal evaluation* – or someone outside the organization – an *external evaluation*. Both have benefits and challenges.

If a program staff member conducts an internal evaluation, they likely have an intimate knowledge of the program's purpose, process, staff, and students. As such, they are able to have an insider perspective as they undertake the evaluation. They do not need to communicate to or rely on an external evaluator. But there are challenges with internal evaluations. First, programs may not have staff with technical expertise to conduct a quality evaluation (The Pell Institute, 2021). It takes a broad skill set, ranging from research knowledge, proposal writing, survey design, interview design, interviewing, communication, data software, data analysis, and report writing, among others. Next, internal evaluations may be – or appear to be – biased. People who are involved in a program want that program to be successful and could, even unintentionally, be subjective in reporting program successes and shortfalls. Finally, it becomes very difficult to conduct a quality internal evaluation because of relationships. An internal staff member, who may have a direct stake in the success of the program and friendships or working relationships with those they are asked to evaluate or report to, might have trouble asking difficult questions and reporting to program managers information such as staff unhappiness, staff inadequacies, or program failures (Conley-Tyler, 2005).

Although external evaluators might also carry some biases with them, they are generally viewed by the public and grant funders as being more impartial (Conley-Tyler, 2005). External evaluators can serve a number of roles in program evaluations. They can assist in selecting and planning evaluation methods and models. They collect and analyze data on the program's effectiveness and compliance with grant proposals or standards. They communicate between stakeholders to facilitate program improvement and understanding of concealed issues. They can assist in writing, publishing, and presenting program findings. They are typically also experts on a wide range of methods and analyses. If a literacy program decides to obtain an external evaluator, they should select one with a deep knowledge of education and literacy, as well as the quantitative and qualitative methods required to adequately evaluate it.

The costs of external evaluators are dependent upon location, experience, whether the evaluator is freelance or associated with a university or institute, and the methodology required of the evaluation. A grant program manager might expect to budget 5–10% of funding for an external evaluator, though those costs may increase substantially if more rigorous methods are required (Rutnik & Campbell, 2002) or if the grant specifies a certain amount dedicated for evaluation. It is good practice to interview evaluators if a program does not have any in mind and select one who appears experienced, knowledgeable, reliable, and personable. Decide on the scope and sequence of work and clearly write it into the contract. Many evaluators can consult on smaller portions of the evaluation plan if the budget restricts their full-scale evaluation, so talk with the evaluator about the amount and quality of work they can do within restricted budgets.

Evaluation Methods

Whether a literacy program chooses to design an internal evaluation or contract an external evaluator, decisions will need to be made to choose an evaluation model; decide on evaluation procedures, purposes, and timelines; select data analyses that will yield results to measure the goals; and ensure an alignment across methods and outcomes. If the methods cannot measure the program's outcomes, the methods or outcomes should be modified. Each outcome of the program must have data associated with it to ensure it can be measured and reported. If the program is currently operating and wants to begin an evaluation, these decisions can be made and formalized – written down and shared – during workshops or retreats. If a program is seeking funding, these decisions should all be clearly written into the proposal.

It is vital to be clear about the evaluation methods and models. Potential evaluation models that might be appropriate for literacy programs are described next. Evaluation methods might be included in the *formative evaluation* – which reports the progress of the program throughout the year so program managers can ensure it is implemented correctly and make appropriate changes – or *summative evaluation*, which reports whether the outcomes were achieved. Common methods include interviews, observations (notes, checklists), surveys, document or content analyses, and assessment data analyses, although this is not comprehensive.

Formative evaluation methods are driven by what the program managers want and need to know about the programming, staff, students, budget, and other issues that can be adjusted to make changes. Formative data reports should be provided to program managers to help them understand the findings and recommendations for improvement. Summative evaluation methods are driven by the outcomes. If an outcome states that gains will be made, then pre- and post-data must be available and analyzed. If they state significant improvements will be made, then statistical significance tests must be run. If they relate to participant attendance, then descriptive data – perhaps graphs of attendance rates – would suffice.

Evaluation Models

Selecting an evaluation model – or a combination of models – is a decision often made between the evaluator and the program planners or managers. Frequently, the evaluator can propose a model based on their belief in its appropriateness in assessing the program and on their expertise, personal experiences, and values. If an internal evaluation is being completed, the program staff might select a model they find most appropriate and feasible or may pay a stipend for an external evaluator to help them design or select a model in their planning stage. There are many quality evaluation models (Stufflebeam & Zhang, 2017), and none are perfect or free from valid criticism (Frye & Hemmer, 2012). One could further position the models into broader philosophical frameworks based on the models' values, key audiences, and preferred methods (Guyadeen & Seasons, 2018), but that is beyond the scope of this chapter. Next, four common models for educational program evaluation and their major components are presented.

Kirkpatrick Model

The Kirkpatrick is perhaps the most common model for educational training program evaluations. This model posits that training programs can be evaluated across four levels, each level progressively becoming more difficult, expensive, and data-generating. Level 1, *Reaction*, is based on evaluating the extent to which trainees believe the training is "favorable, engaging, and relevant" (Kirkpatrick Partners, 2021, para. 1). Level 2, *Learning*, evaluates the extent the participants "acquire the intended knowledge, skills, attitudes, confidence, and commitment" (para. 2). Level 3, *Behavior*, evaluates the degree to which the program participants apply their learning. Level 4, *Results*, measure the degree to which targeted program outcomes are met.

Literacy program evaluations can be based upon the Kirkpatrick model. Evaluators and program managers can discuss how they want to frame the *training*, whether that be framed as professional development provided to staff, educational opportunities provided to students through programming, or, most likely, both. If a literacy program provides training to its staff members and also attends to students' literacy development through programming, assessment, and/or curricular supports, the four levels might be applied in this way. Level 1 might assess participants' – staff and/or students' – ratings of their enjoyment and relevancy, as measured by surveys or interviews. Though some critics of this model find it weak as a tool for formative assessment (Saks & Haccoun, 2010), these types of data would likely provide information on opportunities for programmatic improvement.

Level 2, focusing on learning, might be measured through interviews and surveys, which would allow participants to rate their growth in a number of areas (reading or teaching skills, confidence, etc.) from beginning- to end-of-program. Level 3, which focuses on behavior, might also be self-reported data from the perspective of staff (self-report of application of teaching aspects relevant to the programming) or students (self-report of application of learning aspects necessitated by the program, such as time-at-home independent reading). These might also be observational data; the programming is observed and key aspects are noted and documented to ensure implementation fidelity of the programming. In organizational evaluations, the Level 4 outcomes are often financial targets. In educational program evaluations, the outcomes are often longer-term educational impacts such as quantitative growth in reading ability or graduation rates, although financial outcomes, such as cost-benefit analyses, are part of many educational evaluations and will continue to be so. The Kirkpatrick model is straightforward and provides some useful information to evaluators and program managers but often cannot answer questions about causality or variability of participants in outcome attainment, relationships between and among the aspects of the program, and other complex issues. It is often recommended it be used in conjunction with other evaluation models (Saks & Haccoun, 2010).

Outcome-Based Evaluation Model

The outcome-based evaluation (OBE) model originated from the Government Performance and Results Act of 1993 (GPRA, Pub. L. 103–62). This act required agencies to set goals, monitor progress, and record results of their outcomes. It was updated to the GPRA Modernization Act of 2010 to update how results are reported. The GPRA required agencies, including those receiving government funding – such as federal education grants – to prepare reports that review the success of the program's goals (most often, annually), evaluate the performance toward current and future goals, and explain when and why goals were not met (Sec. 116, D1–3).

The GPRA established an emphasis on outcomes, derived from management analysis in which strategic plans included specific, measurable goals that could be quantified and reported as an indicator of a program's or agency's effectiveness. The GPRA model, and the associated OBE model, operate similarly. *Inputs*, the resources available to carry out programming, produce *outputs*, the programming itself, which generate *outcomes*, measurable goals that reflect the services received by clients or students. Presently, some federal grants allow some qualitative goals, but most – nearly all – grants emphasize quantifiable goals be developed and analyzed in the evaluation efforts. Outcomes may include cost-benefit analyses, impact analyses, and numerous other quantitative (and, more rarely, qualitative analyses) methods designed to demonstrate that students have made gains in their abilities, knowledge, attitudes, or condition (Wang, 2010). Though other evaluation theorists have proposed methods to incorporate formative and process evaluations within OBE frameworks, the outcome evaluation is still foremost.

Funded literacy programs often operate within an OBE model. Plans for programming, curricula, staffing, training, site selection, participant recruitment, and evaluation procedures must be developed. Perhaps, due to low reading-based standardized test scores in a certain school, district, or population, an agency seeks funding to provide supplemental reading instruction. Goals and outcomes are developed, indicating the types of student growth expected each year, and the overall growth over a five-year funding cycle. Then, program managers and evaluator(s) might decide the best way to assess and analyze the reading tasks they intend to target, as well as the types of programming research indicates is likely to be effective. At the end of each year and often at mid-year points, the planning is described in reports, as well as data on outcome progress. If progress is sufficient, plans are developed for continuing the growth trend; if not, the plans explain the likely reasons why and give explanations of how they will make satisfactory progress the next year.

Critics of GPRA and the OBE model – and there are many – argue numerous points, including the burden placed on agencies and reviewers to create and review reports; the process and formative evaluations are, sometimes, entirely unimportant to the funders; that educational outcomes are a result of innumerable, sometimes uncontrollable, variables; and that the efficacy of an educational program often cannot be simply quantified by whether or not outcomes are achieved (Radin, 1998). Few educational program managers work in a laboratory-type environment. Naturally, literacy programming carries with it risks to implementation fidelity. Teacher participants get sick, go on leave, or quit; students drop out of programs; or the programming changes from the original plan. The COVID-19 school closures are one example. I evaluated six funded programs during 2020–2021, and none could carry out their plans as intended. Naturally, the outcomes were affected.

CIPP Model

The CIPP (Context/Input/Process/Product) evaluation model was designed to guide a wide range of program evaluations, from building-level to organizational systems (Stufflebeam, 1983). The core components of the CIPP model are understanding context, inputs, processes, and products of educational programs. The CIPP model is a holistic model with a focus on program improvement throughout the program, even starting with the program planning or proposal stages.

The *Context* evaluation assesses the program's strengths, needs, priorities, and goals. This portion is often done during program planning or proposal stages, which helps give the program planners a holistic view of the program's potential and needs. The *Input* evaluation is done in the planning stages and helps gather information on feasibility of the program, costs and benefits, and practicality of programming elements (Saks & Haccoun, 2010). The *Process* evaluation unobtrusively assesses the programming in action, providing formative data to program managers about the operations of the program. The *Product* evaluation determines the extent to which the program's objectives were met. Importantly, there are a number of considerations evaluators must make in their analyses, ranging from potential effects of program implementation on the outcomes to understanding how – and, if possible, why – subgroups of participants performed certain ways in relation to the outcomes.

It is highly recommended that an external evaluator be hired if a CIPP model is to be implemented in literacy program evaluations due to the complexity and breadth of the evaluation procedures and analyses, as well as the need to have a member without a direct stake in the program providing input on process and product evaluations (Stufflebeam, 1983). If a literacy evaluation were based on the CIPP model, there are a number of potential considerations that could prove beneficial. Through document analyses or interviews, the Context evaluation might provide insight into stakeholders and resources being underutilized, including community literacy partners or local resources, or it might shed light on program needs or problems that could be addressed through early planning, like inadequate leadership, curricula, or technology access.

The Input evaluation might be designed as a literature review, analysis of similar programs, or expert input to determine components that have promising efficacy evidence for students or subgroups of students. It can help inform decisions on curricula, pedagogies, program structure, partnerships, staffing, and budgeting. If an intended element of the program planning does not show evidence of effectiveness in the existing literature or in existing programs, decisions could be made to redesign how resources in the literacy program might better be allocated. The Process evaluation can be conducted through observations and interviews of participants. Evaluators can watch the programming and talk with students and staff to give input to program planners about whether they appear to be implemented well or as intended.

Finally, the Product evaluation can determine whether the students were effectively served by the program and if the outcomes of the program were achieved. Evaluators can analyze data in relation to participant subgroups. For example, in my own program evaluations, there are goals and outcomes that are set by the program planners and/or funders. Grant funders want to know if the program is successful. Though my literacy programs might not always meet the outcomes as stated – often, quantifiable achievement goals related to assessment data growth – I can statistically analyze whether the number of days students attend programming significantly affects their ability to meet the program goals. It might be that, as a group, the students were unable to meet the target growth. Looking at attendance gives a perspective that those who attended more often were more likely to meet the goals, which is a way to provide nuanced, more accurate ways to view the program outcomes. These types of analyses can help combat the limitations of the rigid, objectives-based evaluations (Stufflebeam & Zhang, 2017).

Logic Model

Partly based on the OBE model and the CIPP model, a logic model is now required by many grant funders. The logic model (see Appendix D) is a method for developing a program's implementation plan, goals, utilization of resources, and evaluation methodology, although it may not always be considered an evaluation model itself. Program planners and evaluators can generate planning based on four generally accepted components of the logic model: *Inputs* ◊ *Activities* ◊ *Outputs* ◊ *Outcomes* (Frye & Hemmer, 2012). If carefully designed, procedures can be developed to evaluate each of the components and make determinations of how the components interact (Ormsby & Morrow, 2019). The focus on the process of change – and making determinations about program effectiveness based on contexts in which the program is situated – separates the Logic Model from both the OBE and CIPP (Frye & Hemmer, 2012).

Inputs are the resources available to a program, both currently or as a result of the programming decisions. They might include facilities, policies, curricula, texts, faculty and staff, professional learning opportunities, or academic or social supports. In developing a literacy program logic model, all relevant resources related to programming should be considered inputs. In addition to the tangible resources, other resources probably exist that might affect the program's output later on, including administrative support, channels of communication, and procedures.

Activities are just that: Activities implemented by the program to strengthen literacy. They are a result of what a program does with the inputs. Each input is aligned with activities in a Logic Model. Activities are the proposed services to be offered by the program. These might include programming processes such as staff trainings and meetings; supports or scaffolds offered to students by the program; or events held throughout a year for staff, students, families, or communities. It is best to brainstorm a list of all available and proposed literacy activities to make the determination of what is missing or can be removed from programming. If a later outcome of the program is that students improve their reading of high-frequency words to select texts at a greater reading level, the program must ensure they have activities in place that would allow students to achieve that (The Pell Institute, 2021).

Outputs are the forms of evidence that result from activities. Multiple inputs may be tied to a single output (Ormsby & Morrow, 2019). For example, staffing and professional learning may be inputs. Activities were determined as the types of trainings that would be held for staff. The outputs associated with the activities might be the actual training procedures and subsequent implementation of the procedures with students, potentially with strategies recommended by the International Literacy Association (ILA). These might be evaluated through observational checklists that record the training itself or when these learned strategies are observed in practice during the programming.

Outcomes are the specific, measurable goals that result from changes due to program participation. These might relate to changes in students' attitude toward reading, literacy skills, knowledge changes within certain literacy standards, or behaviors, including attendance, time spent reading, and so on. Generally, outcomes are separated by short-term (achieved within one to three years) and long-term (achieved within four to six years) outcomes (The Pell Institute, 2021). A literacy program should consult literature to determine what reasonable growth can be expected within a given timeframe, and create measurable, observable, and specific outcomes to be evaluated, similar to the OBE model. Again, outcomes should be traced back through the outputs to the activities and through the original inputs. If designed and evaluated well, it is possible to connect and trace the result of each input all the way to the final outcomes to determine the program's specific strengths, needs, and function.

There is not a consensus on these four components. Sometimes, outputs and activities are considered an interactive unit; other times, outcomes are further divided into short-, mid-, and long-term outcomes. In some logic models, *Impact* is a fifth component, which looks at broader impacts of programming and is sometimes considered part of the Outcomes. Impacts might be outside the bounds of the funding and programming cycle and other times, may not be as directly or easily measured as traditional outcomes. Impacts are often considered those that can be achieved in 7–10 years (The Pell Institute, 2021), which may be after the programming has ended, so a literacy program may consider longitudinal evaluation plans to capture the long-term impacts of the program on students, families, or communities. With careful design, a literacy program may be able to trace the long-term impact on their student participants, such as increases in college attendance and employment or decreases in school attrition.

Conclusion/Summary

There are many decisions to be made in evaluating literacy programs. Who evaluates it, how, and the model(s) they follow must be firmly established in the early stages of literacy program planning, particularly if they are programs that must report to grant funders or other agencies demanding data on their efficacy. This chapter provided a number of evaluation criteria for literacy program managers, but specific programs will all have their unique, nuanced strengths and needs that should be considered when planning the evaluation. With a plan for an evaluator and firmly grounded evaluation methods and models, literacy programs will have the pieces in place to best understand the operations and impact of their work.

References

Bowers, L. M., & Schwarz, I. (2018). Preventing summer learning loss: Results of a summer literacy program for students from low-SES homes. *Reading & Writing Quarterly, 34*(2), 99–116.

Conley-Tyler, M. (2005). A fundamental choice: Internal or external evaluation?. *Evaluation Journal of Australasia, 4*(1–2), 3–11.

Dickinson, D. K., & Neuman, S. B. (Eds.). (2007). *Handbook of early literacy research* (Vol. 2). Guilford Press.

Feldman, J., Feighan, K., Kirtcheva, E., & Heeren, E. (2012). Aiming high: Exploring the influence of implementation fidelity and cognitive demand levels on struggling readers' literacy outcomes. *Journal of Classroom Interaction, 47*(1), 4–13.

Frye, A. W., & Hemmer, P. A. (2012). Program evaluation models and related theories: AMEE guide no. 67. *Medical Teacher, 34*(5), e288–e299.

Government Performance and Results Act of 1993, Pub. L. 103–62 (1993). https://www.dol.gov/agencies/eta/performance/goals/gpra

Guyadeen, D., & Seasons, M. (2018). Evaluation theory and practice: Comparing program evaluation and evaluation in planning. *Journal of Planning Education and Research, 38*(1), 98–110.

Hemphill, L., & Tivnan, T. (2008). The importance of early vocabulary for literacy achievement in high-poverty schools. *Journal of Education for Students Placed at Risk, 13*(4), 426–451.

Kirkpatrick Partners (2021). *The Kirkpatrick model.* www.kirkpatrickpartners.com/Our-Philosophy/The-Kirkpatrick-Model.

Ormsby, S. M., & Morrow, J. A. (2019). Development of a logic model for use in evaluation of learning support programs. *Journal of Student Success and Retention, 6*(1), 1–26.

Pell Institute (2021). *How to create a logic model.* Evaluation Toolkit. http://toolkit.pellinstitute.org/evaluation-guide/plan-budget/use-a-logic-model-in-evaluation/

Radin, B. A. (1998). The government performance and results act (GPRA): Hydra-headed monster or flexible management tool? *Public Administration Review, 58*(4), 307–316.

Rutnik, T. A., & Campbell, M. (2002). *When and how to use external evaluators.* Association of Baltimore Area Grantmakers. http://efc.issuelab.org/resources/11630/11630.pdf

Saks, A. M., & Haccoun, R. R. (2010). *Managing performance through training and development.* Nelson.

Stufflebeam, D. L. (1983). The CIPP model for program evaluation. In G. F. Madaus, M. S. Scriven, & D. L. Stufflebeam (Eds.), *Evaluation models: Viewpoints on educational and human services evaluation* (pp. 117–141), Kluwer-Nijhoff. Doi:10.1007/978-94-009-6669-7_7.

Stufflebeam, D. L., & Zhang, G. (2017). *The CIPP evaluation model: How to evaluate for improvement and accountability*. Guilford Publications.

Wang, V. X. (Ed.). (2010). Assessing and evaluating adult learning in career and technical education. IGI Global.

Chapter 19

Community-Based Qualitative Approaches to Studying Literacy

Methodological Issues and Concerns

Laura Johnson

Author Note

Laura Johnson: https://orcid.org/0000-0001-9629-9016

Background

Community-based Qualitative Research (CBQR) is rooted in participatory and collaborative approaches to research that challenge positivist views of research as a "value-neutral" endeavor in search of a single truth (Lather, 1986). It is an approach to research that seeks to build reciprocal relationships between academic researchers and community organizations and stakeholders, to conduct research studies that are rooted in the everyday experiences and processes of meaning-making of community members, and that aim to address local conditions and expand resources to improve learning for the community. CBQR projects have been conducted in a variety of disciplines

DOI: 10.4324/9781003228042-24

and do not follow a single methodological template but share a number of key elements. First, CBQR is inherently critical, in that it challenges status quo explanations related to the topic under study and is oriented toward social justice (Johnson, 2017). CBQR projects are collaborative – involving reciprocal and bidirectional processes of teaching and learning and transformative – with the goal of using research to change conditions and enact change (Freire, 1970; Johnson, 2017).

There is a robust body of research that has sought to better understand literacy development and practices in community settings (see Cushman, 1998; Farr, 2005; Guerra, 1998); however, most of these studies have used community settings as sites for investigation and data collection, with community members serving as research subjects or as primary informants, rather than as research team members (and the intention of these studies was not such). Community-based research studies aim to not just study within a community but to develop meaningful and rich research projects in collaboration with community organizations, leaders, and stakeholders. It should be noted that projects that describe themselves as "community-based" can vary in the degree to which communities are involved in the design and implementation of study. On one end of the continuum are projects in which community members serve as research assistants, helping with and participating in data collection; yet, the leader of the project is still the academic researcher, and relationships are largely asymmetrical, with academic researchers making the majority of decisions (Johnson & Rodriguez-Muniz, 2017). Within these models, there is limited accountability on the part of academic researchers to the community, in terms of the design and implementation of the study and the dissemination of findings.

Models that adopt a more reciprocal approach aim to build symmetrical relationships with community members, and community stakeholders are closely involved in the design and implementation of the research; academic researchers are fully accountable to community members and engage in ongoing dialogue about the study and evaluate participation in the project to ensure that it is equitable. Findings are shared with the community in a variety of ways and are focused on improving conditions and resources in ways that are meaningful and useful to the community. Some projects take the notion of reciprocity a bit further, purveying more weight to community knowledge and leadership. In these sorts of projects, community members are viewed not just as research partners but as theoretical interlocuters (Johnson & Rodriguez-Muniz, 2017). This model is premised on the notion of *Communities as Intellectual Spaces*, wherein communities are acknowledged as rich sites and contexts for intellectual and collaborative inquiry (Community as Intellectual Space, 2005). Such work entails a reversal of traditional research roles and requires that academic researchers cede a certain amount of power and authority within the project, which can be difficult and unsettling for university academics accustomed to serving as "experts" (Johnson, 2017; Spears Johnson et al., 2016). These sorts of asymmetrical relationships in favor of community knowledge "redistribute intellectual authority" (Campano et al., 2015, p. 30) and involve a repositioning of university-community relationships.

Community-based researchers also need to be mindful not to replicate the sorts of inequities found in more traditional, extractive research models (Strand et al., 2003); even projects that purport to be "community-based" can fall into more traditional, top-down research practices and approaches, leading community partners to feel divested from the project and, in the worst cases, exploited by researchers. Furthermore, the most productive community-based research projects involve forging and fostering sustained, continuous, and long-term relationships with community partners rather than short-term projects (Johnson, 2017; Spears Johnson et al., 2016). This allows for research teams to gain in-depth understanding of complex issues within the community and for projects to make more meaningful, impactful, and lasting change. Although community-based research projects can be quite time-consuming in terms of the planning and ongoing communication that is required, these projects often result in research findings that are more salient, as they are grounded in the knowledge and experiences of community residents and stakeholders instead of the interpretations of those who possess limited experiences within the community.

Design and Implementation of CBQR Studies for Examining Literacy

When designing and conducting community-based studies, in addition to considering the aforementioned elements and concepts, researchers should be particularly attentive to the different sorts of contexts existing within the community that might serve as settings for literacy development, as well as how the specific practices embedded and enacted within these contexts can offer insights on literacy within the community. Finally, I will discuss how the nature and strength of the collaborative relationships developed between academic researchers and community partners are important to the success of the project.

Spaces, Places, and Practices

When designing CBQR studies to examine literacy in community settings, researchers need to pay attention to the sorts of spaces and organizations that are engaged in work related to their phenomenon or topic of interest. These spaces might include organizations one might typically associate with literacy – such as schools, public libraries, and tutoring programs – but could also encompass unofficial educational spaces and places where individuals engage in informal learning processes, such as bike clubs, community gardening groups, and civic organizations. All too often, literacy researchers have taken presumptive and narrow stances regarding where literacy occurs and what form it should take, focusing on formal institutions as literacy gatekeepers while ignoring how informal organizations and settings can serve as contexts for literacy development. For example, in a community-based and participatory research class I instructed within a Puerto Rican/Latinx community in Chicago, a graduate student was interested in studying youth reading and literacy practices and was bothered by the lack of bookstores within the community and an apparent underutilization of the local public library by community youth. During a tour of the community, the class visited a community bike shop, which employed a lot of neighborhood youth. After talking to one of the staff members about her research interests, she learned that staff had noticed that youth needed a safe space to work on homework and thus created a sort of homework/social lounge in the back of the shop. The worker added that, in this space, older youth often helped tutor younger kids and commented that within the community "kids need more books." This interaction with a community member helped the student obtain a more expansive view of the community and provided her with ideas for establishing libraries within community spaces. This alternative space for literacy practices exemplifies the concept of community cultural wealth (Yosso, 2005), which challenges the deficit-oriented notions the student initially held about youth literacy within the community, based on a rigid view of what literacy settings should "look like," often adopted in more traditional approaches to literacy research.

When examining spaces for literacy, and the practices contained within these spaces, community-based researchers should be attentive to how these settings are shaped by larger sociohistorical factors and conditions. This sort of critical lens is a key feature of community-based studies and helps researchers better understand literacy behaviors and practices, by connecting patterns of experiences, behaviors, perspectives, and practices with broader factors and inequities, rather than viewing them as isolated examples or as individual characteristics or traits. For example, in the aforementioned Chicago community, the graduate student had also visited the local public library branch and conducted an informal interview with the director, from which she learned that the library was underutilized by area youth. By doing some research online and through discussions with staff, she attributed the underuse to a limited schedule. Although these limited hours across the system would impact all youth across the city, they could be especially cumbersome for youth in this area, the majority of whom were low-income and needed to work to contribute to family expenses. Furthermore, through discussions with community insiders, she also learned that the library location on one side of a large park entailed the crossing of gang lines for many community youth. Having an awareness of the social and economic realities of the local context and its residents assists researchers in more fully and accurately explicating research findings, as well as elaborating more meaningful practical implications and recommendations. The graduate student suggested conducting some focus groups with area youth to gain insights into programming and usage patterns. Although some of this contextual information could be supplied through area statistics and demographic information and within discussions and interviews with organizational staff, the multiple narratives, perspectives, and insights that can be elicited through talking to and collaborating with community insiders offer up "an epistemic good that can help all involved arrive at a deeper understanding of our shared social world" (Campano et al., 2015, p. 39).

Many community-based research projects involve developing partnerships with community-based organizations, as they often offer a range of education, health, housing, and cultural services, and exist outside of traditional institutions. For literacy researchers interested in community-based research, these organizations can offer the opportunity to examine literacy practices and programming among a variety of age groups, including adults, youth, and children, as well as work with populations and constituencies who are often not well served by traditional and more formalized educational institutions, such as immigrants, high school drop-outs, LGBTQIA+ youth, gang members, people with disabilities, and pregnant and parenting youth. Despite the rich and diverse settings and the innovative programming they can offer for literacy research, these organizations are not necessarily representative of all sectors of a community. Similar to other sites and institutions within a community, they are not neutral spaces but contested ones that reflect certain positions within and orientations toward the world and are influenced by the same hierarchies and inequities that exist in the broader community and larger society. Thus, community-based researchers need to be mindful of issues of power within the organization as well as among various institutions within the community. Within the community-based research literature, much attention has been paid to power between academic researchers and communities, with less focus on how power functions within the community, both between and within organizations and groups, to privilege certain experiences and perspectives over others.

Community-based researchers must avoid the tendency to homogenize and essentialize literacy practices and behaviors, ascribing to them a coherence or universality, and possibly ignoring the ways that certain practices might be "complicit in the fostering of oppressive relations" (Moje, 2000, p. 82). Furthermore, it is important to recognize that communities are multidimensional, dynamic, and complex, rather than monolithic, coherent, and static; communities are diverse places composed of individuals representing a variety of experiences, including educators, activists, students, artists, workers, entrepreneurs, tradespeople, and parents. Too often, the university and community are posed as mutually exclusive binaries, as oppositional entities to be "bridged" with the university acting as the imprimatur and broker of knowledge.

Literacy studies that adopt a more traditional or positivist perspective on research conventionally focus on particular literacy outcomes, as measured through test scores and literacy assessments, to evidence the effectiveness of a specific approach or program. This sort of emphasis on measurable outcomes often overlooks other forms of knowledge, skills, and practices that might be acquired and developed through certain community activities and processes. For example, there have been numerous studies that have attributed literacy and language "gaps" also referred to as "word gaps" for Latinx children to a lack of adequate literacy activities and materials in the home to prepare them for school, with the children's parents being blamed for engaging in "warm and fuzzy" social and cultural activities and routines at the expense of the promotion of academic literacy skills (Watanabe, 2015). What many of these studies miss are how a family or community's oral and literate traditions and practices – such as singing, rhyming, and proverbs – can contribute to a child's knowledge and skill development in ways not easily quantifiable. For example, studies that have been conducted within community contexts have documented the print-rich environments of urban Latinx communities (Orellana, 2016) and how graffiti functions as a literacy practice (Aguilar, 2000).

Moreover, studies that view literacy simply as the acquisition of a discrete set of skills ignore the many other forms and functions of literacy – or multiliteracies – and the ways that literacy can involve "reading the world" rather than just "reading the word" (Freire, 1970; New London Group, 1996). For example, a graduate student enrolled in one of my summer community-based research classes who was a reading specialist began the course excited for the "downtrodden" children she might work with in the community and hoped to help them improve their reading skills. However, she ended up working with a group of young women attending a summer youth program who were involved in civic engagement projects on the topic of gentrification, which was greatly impacting their community and displacing many longtime residents. Throughout the summer, her initial expectations of her role vis-à-vis students were challenged, and she found herself learning more from the students and about community issues than she believed she could ever possibly reciprocate (Johnson et al., 2019). Her views of literacy development were also expanded as she gained insight into how literacy might involve advocacy and activism on issues meaningful to students' lives and communities. In their project, the youth engaged in collective and collaborative literacy processes, ones that might not be captured by individual literacy assessments. These sorts of participatory and collective literacy cultures (see Jocson & Rosa, 2015) can help researchers and educators rethink notions of how and when literacy development occurs and the ways it might be assessed.

Relationships and Collaboration

As previously mentioned, in order to conduct this sort of research, academic researchers need to build relationships with community organizations and groups – which might entail multiple visits to the community, meetings with community members, and engagement in various orienting activities – and collaborate with partners throughout the research process, from design to dissemination (Johnson, 2017). Before research begins, academic researchers need to orient themselves to the community history and context, through activities such as community tours, readings, and discussion groups on salient issues, and then develop research questions collaboratively with community-based organizations and stakeholders. In some cases, community organizations might reach out to academic researchers for assistance addressing an issue or problem, whereas other projects are initiated by an academic researcher with an interest in working with the community around a specific issue; sometimes, academic researchers have an existing relationship with the community through their own role as a community member or because of some previous research projects. My own history as a community-based researcher stemmed from my role as a director of a community literacy program in a Puerto Rican community in Chicago and activist within the community; after attending graduate school, I conducted traditional ethnographic research within the community, gradually shifting to more collaborative and community-based approaches.

Building strong and equitable relationships with community partners at the outset of a project is especially essential, as these will provide a foundation for the collaboration required in the implementation process. Data collection and analysis within community-based studies should be bidirectional, involving the bringing together of knowledge and skills. Unfortunately, many projects that are labeled "community-based" tend to take a unidirectional approach, wherein academic researchers teach or train community members in research methods so that they can go out and conduct interviews and field work within their community, serving as research assistants rather than meaningful partners. Activities that are more bidirectionally collaborative include panels, where community members and stakeholders present/speak to research team members on a particular issue and engage in discussion about relevant research, such as youth sharing their experiences in local schools and educational and literacy resources in the community. Data collection tools should be developed collaboratively. For example, a project I was involved in – which brought together academic researchers who had conducted studies on civic engagement within a community-based alternative high school serving Latinx and African American youth with teachers and staff at the school, in order to better understand the design and implementation of civic and community engagement initiatives and activities at the school (Johnson & Rosario-Ramos, 2012; Rosario-Ramos & Johnson, 2013) – convened a number of sessions on developing interview guides. In these sessions, university faculty provided some presentations on writing qualitative interview questions, and teachers and staff from the school (many of whom were from the surrounding community) drafted questions for interviews with their students, using their firsthand and insider knowledge of and experience with their students to craft questions that could tap into youth's views and definitions of their communities and their role in civic engagement work. The process of creating the guides was facilitated by existing relationships of mutual trust and respect between the academic researchers and school staff, which allowed for differences of opinion to be aired and discussed in constructive ways. Rather than being viewed as hindrances within the research process, the inevitable tensions and disagreements that will arise in these sorts of studies can offer opportunities for reassessing project goals and negotiating relationships of research team members in important and insightful ways, akin to Larson's notion of "generative frictions" (Kinloch et al., 2016, p. 9).

Data collection and analysis activities should continue these collaborative relationships; for example, research team members could conduct collaborative interviews, with a community member and academic researcher teaming up to contribute their unique skills and knowledge to the interviewing processes. Insider and community knowledge are especially integral to the analysis of data, although in many community-based studies community members unfortunately play a peripheral role in the analysis phase. This limited involvement is particularly regrettable as community members and stakeholders possess semantic, semiotic, and lexiconic knowledge and skills for making sense of data and textual forms in ways not accessible to many academic researchers from outside of the community. Collective coding processes (see Johnson, 2017) allow for the convergence of theoretical and practical knowledge and various conceptual understandings. These collaborative research activities challenge notions of objectivity that predominate much research, instead demonstrating how certain lenses and cultural intuition (Bernal, 1998) can help researchers gain comprehensive insights and lead to richer and more meaningful findings.

Dissemination, Evaluation, and Credibility of CBQR Studies

Community-based qualitative studies emphasize using research findings to "take action" and enact transformations; thus, dissemination efforts within these studies look quite different than the traditional journal article or conference presentation, although articles and presentations might be included as part of the broader dissemination plan. In addition, community-based studies adopt certain standards to evaluate their quality that account for the authenticity of findings and the benefits of the project for various sectors of the community, rather than being concerned about generalizability of findings and the validity and reliability of the study, concepts prevalent within quantitative studies.

Dissemination

Many of the traditional ways that academic research findings are reported are quite limited in scope and audience, consisting of research articles that are usually addressed to a narrow audience of other academic researchers and published within expensive and exclusive outlets or publications that are not accessible without academic credentials. A primary goal of community-based qualitative projects is to make meaningful changes, hence findings are used to identify – and in many cases implement –– approaches and initiatives that might address a key issue or obstacle. Members of the research team might prepare a grant application to strengthen or expand needed programming and services or create unit or lesson plans focused on a specific topic or aimed at a specific group. Within community-based studies, dissemination efforts are aligned with the model's emphasis on collaboration and thus include opportunities for academic researchers and community partners to work together to share findings, possibly co-authoring articles or book chapters or co-presenting at academic conferences and community events or forums.

Community-based studies often employ creative and innovative approaches to report their findings that are geared toward activism and advocacy on particular issues and concerns. For example, youth researchers might wage a social media campaign to build awareness on an issue and connect with other activists, such as when pregnant and parenting youth employed the hashtags #noteenshame and #teenparentpride to tag posts of them holding signs with positive messages as a way of challenging the stigma and low expectations piled on young parents in the public media and discourse. They might organize protests and become involved in lobbying efforts to enact or influence policy. A goal in these efforts is to reach broader audiences and report findings in accessible venues, which might entail publishing findings as an op-ed piece or posting reports and pieces on social media sites such as Facebook and Twitter.

Evaluation of CBQR studies

A central question that community-based researchers should ask as they are evaluating the success of the project is how it is benefitting the community (Kinloch et al., 2016; Moje, 2000). Whereas the quality of most traditional research studies is assessed using concepts such as validity and reliability, community-based researchers ask questions about the credibility of the project, the types of relationships and roles developed in the project, and how the project contributes to the amelioration of certain problems and issues at the heart of the study. Critics of this sort of fine-grained collaborative and participatory work often fault it for its lack of generalizable findings; however, community-based researchers are more concerned with the concept of *particularizability* (Erickson, 1985) and the discovery of "universals as manifested concretely and specifically" (p. 130) within local and particular contexts. Furthermore, community-based studies are judged in terms of their authenticity and the extent to which they bring together individuals with a variety of skills and expertise related to the phenomenon of interest to collaboratively and collectively make sense of data (Fine, 2008).

Throughout the project, community-based researchers should be accountable to other members of the research team, ensuring that relationships are equitable and that there is space for multiple voices and divergent perspectives, what I have referred to as *dialogic accountability* (Johnson et al., 2019; Johnson & Rodriguez-Muniz, 2017). Other questions that may arise during a project might be related to the sustainability of the project: "When does the project end? When is the research 'over'?" Some of the more successful community-based projects build on existing projects and attempt to develop long-term and sustained relationships and research initiatives to enact more meaningful and lasting change. Thus, there is often no end point or "exit strategy," as in more traditional research studies (Kinloch et al., 2016). The astute advice of Kinloch and colleagues (2016) regarding the lifespan of community-based studies, is in line with the model's emphasis on the needs and interests of the community: "The project at the heart of the partnership lives for as long as the community it serves believes it is needed" (p. 15).

References

Aguilar, J. A. (2000, April). *Chicano street signs: Graffiti as a public literacy practice*. Paper presented at the Annual Meeting of the American Educational Research Association, New Orleans, LA.

Bernal, D. D. (1998). Using a Chicana feminist epistemology in educational research. *Harvard Educational Review, 68*(4), 555–579.

Campano, G., Ghiso, M. P., & Welch, B. (2015). Ethical and professional norms in community-based research. *Harvard Educational Review, 85*(1), 29–49.

Community as Intellectual Space. (2015). *Preliminary program*. Symposium held in Chicago, IL. https://conferences.illinois.edu/cis/cis.program.draft7.pdf

Cushman, E. (1998). *The struggle and the tools: Oral and literate strategies in an inner city community*. SUNY Press.

Erickson, F. (1985). Qualitative methods in research on teaching. In M. Wittrock (Ed.), *Handbook of research on teaching* (pp. 119–161). Institute for Research on Teaching.

Farr, M. (Ed.). (2005). *Latino language and literacy in ethnolinguistic Chicago*. Lawrence Erlbaum.

Fine, M. (2008). An epilogue, of sorts. In J. Cammarota & M. Fine (Eds.), *Revolutionizing education: Youth participatory action research in motion* (pp. 213–234). Routledge.

Freire, P. (1970). *Pedagogy of the oppressed*. Continuum.

Guerra, J. C. (1998). *Close to home: Oral and literate strategies in a transnational Mexicano community*. Teachers College Press.

Jocson, K., & Rosa, J. (2015). Rethinking gaps: Literacies and languages in participatory cultures. *Journal of Adolescent & Adult Literacy, 58*(5), 372–374.

Johnson, L. R. (2017). *Community-based qualitative research: Approaches for education and the social sciences*. Sage.

Johnson, L. R., & Rodriguez-Muniz, M. (2017, November). *Community as intellectual space: Reflections from research on Puerto Rican Chicago*. Paper presented at Annual Meeting of American Studies Association, Chicago, IL.

Johnson, L. R., & Rosario-Ramos, E. M. (2012). The role of educational institutions in the development of critical literacy and transformative action. *Theory Into Practice, 51*(1), 49–56.

Johnson, L. R., Stribling, C., Rivera, N., Preissner, K., Hsu, C. P., Jones, A., & May-Schroeder, A. (2019). "Earning the Right": Conducting community based research. *Critical Questions in Education, 10*(3), 161–179.

Kinloch, V., Larson, J., Orellana, M. F., & Lewis, C. (2016). Literacy, equity, and imagination: Researching with/in communities. *Literacy Research: Theory, Method, and Practice, 65,* 1–19.

Lather, P. (1986). Research as praxis. *Harvard Educational Review, 56*(3), 257–277.

Moje, E. B. (2000). Circles of kinship, friendship, position, and power: Examining the community in community-based literacy research. *Journal of Literacy Research, 32*(1), 77–112

The New London Group (1996). A pedagogy of multiliteracies: Designing social futures. *Harvard Educational Review, 66,* 60–92.

Orellana, M. F. (2016). A different kind of word gap. *Huffington Post.* www.huffpost.com/entry/a-different-kind-of-word_b_10030876

Rosario-Ramos, E. M., & Johnson, L. R. (2013). Communities as counter-storytelling (con)texts: The role of community-based educational institutions in the development of critical literacy and transformative action. In J. C. Zacher-Pandya & J. A. Avila (Eds.). *Moving critical literacies forward: A new look at praxis across contexts* (pp. 113–126). Routledge.

Spears Johnson, C. R., Kraemer Diaz, A. E., & Arcury, T. A. (2016). What does it mean for something to be "scientific"? Community understandings of science, educational attainment, and community representation among a sample of 25 CBPR projects. *Health Education & Behavior, 44*(2), 271–277.

Strand, K., Marullo, S., Cutforth, N., Stoeker, R., & Donahue, P. (2003). Principles of best practice for community-based research. *Michigan Journal of Service Learning, Spring 2003,* 5–15.

Watanabe, T. (2015, April). Literacy gap between Latino and white toddlers starts early, study shows. *Los Angeles Times.* www.latimes.com/local/lanow/la-me-ln-latino-literacy-20150401-story.html

Yosso, T. J. (2005). Whose culture has capital? A critical race theory discussion of community cultural wealth. *Race, Ethnicity, & Education, 8*(1), 69–91.

Chapter 20

Quantitative Methods for Examining Community Literacy

Janet K. Holt and Diana J. Zaleski

Author Note

Janet K. Holt: https://orcid.org/0000-0003-2468-8148

Diana J. Zaleski: https://orcid.org/0000-0002-0846-2125

Quantitative Methods for Examining Community Literacy

Quantitative methods have been foundational in describing the nature of literacy in the home and community. Some of the more well-known experimental and quasi-experimental studies include randomized controlled trials (RCTs) for project REAL (Raising Early Achievement in Literacy) in the UK, which indicated significant early literacy gains by the age of 5 after 18 months of a parent literacy intervention (Nutbrown et al., 2005) and the PEEP (Peers Early Education Partnership) intervention, which demonstrated that a comprehensive parent literacy program helped 3- and 4-year old children make significant gains in several areas of literacy development, as well as self-esteem (Evangelou & Sylva, 2007). Although experimental methods are a desired way

DOI: 10.4324/9781003228042-25

to show causal effects, they are not always practical in education and community settings, and quantitative survey research has provided valuable information about literacy in community settings as well. For instance, survey analyses of prison populations have demonstrated the importance of literacy activities among inmates and parolees (Harlow et al., 2010; Zhang et al., 2006).

A community literacy perspective assumes that literacy development occurs across the complex set of interactions that a person has with the world around them and the community in which they live. As people become literate, the emerging reader or writer receives information from the community around them, which is processed and folded into their literacy schema. Hence, literacy development is contextualized based upon the cultural, socio-economic, school, and other environments in which the emergent reader interacts with and lives within. As such, there are many social and environmental interactions that need to be considered in order to develop a theoretical model of literacy development within the community. Fortunately, there are many quantitative data analysis methods that can model community context and myriad personal, social, and community influences that comprise that context. However, many of these methods require fairly large sample sizes, so they are particularly suited to the analysis of large-scale data and longitudinal research designs with data collection over time.

Contextual Effects Models

The value of using multilevel modeling methods to take into account school and classroom effects is well known. Yet, community, family, and other contexts also impact literacy development and can be measured and accounted for with multilevel modeling (aka general linear mixed models [GLMM], or hierarchical linear modeling). In one example, variations in adult literacy skills and practices by neighborhood were studied using the National Adult Literacy Survey (NALS; Sheehan & Smith, 1997) to examine adults' engagement in a variety of self-reported reading practices for work, school, and leisure to address the research questions: (a) Does the average poverty level and education level of the neighborhood contribute to adults' literacy, beyond one's individual poverty and education level? and (b) Do neighborhood characteristics moderate the effect of an individual's poverty and education level on their literacy? Sheehan and Smith used a contextual-effects multilevel model (Raudenbush & Bryk, 2002) to address these questions. To assess neighborhood effects, household-level-variables were aggregated to the neighborhood level to measure neighborhood poverty level and neighborhood education level. In contextual effects studies, both the individual effect (e.g., family poverty) and the aggregated effect (e.g., poverty of the neighborhood) are included as predictors in the model. The difference between the two effects is the compositional or contextual effect (e.g., the effect of neighborhood poverty between two individuals with the same family poverty level). In this study, there was a significant contextual effect of neighborhood income on adult literacy proficiencies (Sheehan & Smith, 1997) indicating that there is a combined effect of one's individual poverty level *and the poverty level of the neighborhood* on adult literacy.

There may also be instances in which neighborhood effects might be the focus of the research, yet there is not a clear nested design. For instance, children from the same neighborhood may enroll in different schools, or, conversely, children from a given school may come from different neighborhoods confounding the effects of school and of neighborhood. In these cases, one can use cross-classified multilevel models to study the effects of both neighborhood and school contexts on language and literacy development (Beretvas, 2004; Raudenbush & Bryk, 2002). For instance, multilevel cross-classified modeling was used to answer the research question: What community-, district-, and school-level factors are related to third grade literacy, as measured by state reading assessment scores? (Vagi et al., 2017). Because the community factors (e.g., percent of preterm births) were measured within a community metric (i.e., primary-health care unit) and schools and districts were not precisely nested within community areas, the researchers used a cross-classified model to partition the school, district, and community sources of variance and study the effects at each of these levels on third-grade literacy outcomes. For additional resources for contextual-effects and cross-classified analyses, see Table 20.1.

Table 20.1 Research Scenarios: Contextual Effects and Cross-Classified Models

Example Study	Example Research Question	Additional Resources
Contextual Effects and Cross-Classified Models		
Vagi et al. (2017) used cross-classified analysis within a multilevel modeling framework to partition sources of overlapping variance into school, district, and community sources and study their effects on third-grade literacy outcomes.	What community-, district-, and school-level factors are related to third-grade literacy, as measured by state reading assessment scores?	Beretvas, 2010. Raudenbush & Bryk, 2002.

Randomized Studies

The gold standard of causal analysis is to employ randomized controlled trials in which different individuals are randomly assigned to different treatment regimens or treatment "arms" to infer causality to a particular treatment regimen. This typically results in strong causal inferences because any confounding variables should be equally dispersed among the treatment arms because of the randomization. Randomized controlled trials are often employed in community health research, with the goal of implementing educational interventions to increase general health literacy or specific disease-related literacy. Careful planning goes into the research design, but analyses tend to be simple comparisons among treatment arms, because the control for extraneous effects is done experimentally, not statistically. For example, Smith et al. (2019) studied: What is the difference in the effectiveness of a complementary medicine educational intervention to increase older adults' decision self-efficacy, decision making preparedness, and health literacy with different modes of delivery? They recruited older adults through community settings, and after examining multiple metrics at baseline, determined the samples were very similar except on internet usage, so they adjusted for baseline internet usage in their analyses. Participants were randomly assigned to receiving content via a website/ DVD or a booklet. Analyses of variances at post-test revealed no differences in changes from baseline to two-month follow-up across the treatment arms in decision-making self-efficacy or in nine health literacy domains. However, there were improvements in several domains in both arms indicating similar engagement with the content across the different delivery modalities.

However, in community-based research, often the treatment cannot be randomized at the individual level because it would result in significant cross-contamination, so the treatment group is randomly assigned at the community level, such as health clinics or community centers using a cluster randomized trial (CRT). For example, several studies have randomly assigned churches to health-based education interventions, and participants within a particular church received the same intervention (e.g., Sattin et al., 2016; Schoenberg et al., 2016). However, treatment assignment to clusters complicates analysis methods because errors are not independently distributed, e.g., health literacy scores are expected to be more similar among individuals in a particular community. The influence of the cluster effect on statistical estimates is related to the intraclass correlation (ρ) or the proportion of total variance in the outcome that is between clusters. When there is much difference across clusters or communities in the outcomes, the intraclass correlations are higher. Consequently, the standard error estimates will be underestimated in standard statistical analyses and will result in higher levels of Type I errors. Therefore, to analyze such data, the intraclass correlation needs to be accounted for in the analytic method such as with GLMM or generalized estimating equations (Hayes & Moulton, 2017). GLMM provides robust estimates of standard errors and accurate, unbiased estimates of effects by accounting for the cluster variance with a multilevel model that has both individual-level and cluster-level equations. However, these designs require more clusters to reach adequate power, which often results in higher research costs.

To illustrate, suppose researchers create an intervention to address the question: Does a diabetes health education intervention provided at community health clinics increase diabetes literacy and diabetes referrals among participants? To conduct this study, researchers employ a CRT in which half of the enlisted community health clinics are randomly selected to receive the educational intervention and the other half receive a control condition. Every enlisted participant within a particular health clinic would receive the same assignment to treatment group. This design allows the researchers to make strong causal inferences because of the random assignment to treatment group and it also controls for cross-contamination of individuals within the same health clinic. However, because the assignment of treatment is by community health clinic, an appropriate statistical analysis would be GLMM. Cluster randomized trials are common in community health research because patient outcomes are often the observational unit of interest, but the treatment is assigned to schools, worksites, clinics, or whole communities (National Institutes of Health, n.d.). For additional resources of analyses for CRTs, see Table 20.2.

Large-Scale Survey Analyses

National and international surveys provide easily accessible data for the study of literacy (e.g., Head Start Family and Child Experiences Survey, the Early Childhood Longitudinal Study (ECLS), National Assessment of Adult Literacy (NAAL), and the International Adult Literacy Survey). These surveys provide researchers with the opportunity to examine various contexts (e.g., homes, neighborhoods, prisons, healthcare environments), as well as a variety of demographic characteristics related to community literacy. In addition, large-scale surveys often utilize multistage probability sampling designs that organize populations into groups and then sample data from within these

Table 20.2 Research Scenarios: Cluster Randomized Trials

Example Study	Example Research Question	Additional Resources
Cluster Randomized Trials		
Price-Haywood et al. (2014) implemented a continuing medical education (CME) intervention to physician primary care providers (PCPs) to teach methods of cancer risk communication and shared decision making to patients with low health literacy. Patient health literacy was assessed using the Rapid Estimate of Adult Literacy in Medicine (REALM) instrument. Outcomes included knowledge of cancer screening and standardized patient ratings. This cluster randomized controlled trial was administered to clinics, and data was collected from patients within the clinics, hence a multilevel design was employed, and analytic methods took into account the clustering effect.	Does the CME program improve physician communication behaviors and increases patient receipt of breast/cervical/ colorectal cancer screening to a greater extent than audit-feedback alone in patients with limited health literacy?	Campbell et al., 2012. Davis et al., 1993. Hayes & Moulton, 2017. https:// researchmethodsresources. nih.gov/methods/grt

groups. Because of this sampling complexity, responses are not independent on many variables of interest (e.g., children from one school may have more similar academic outcomes than children from other schools due to school policies and practices and the neighborhoods that the schools draw upon). Due to the violation of the assumption of independence of errors because of nested designs and sampling methods, analytic methods such as GLMM are necessitated.

For example, Durham and Smith (2006) analyzed ECLS data with a multilevel modeling approach to examine the research question: Do beginning kindergarteners vary in early literacy readiness according to their county's metro/non-metropolitan status, county-level economic and social characteristics, individual demographic characteristics, family social capital resources, and preschool childcare? They constructed extensive models predicting initial kindergarten literacy from individual-level variables (e.g., socio-economic status

[SES]), demographic characteristics, family and parent characteristics, type of preschool childcare, and county variables (e.g., metropolitan or non-metropolitan county). They were able to identify several individual-level variables related to initial kindergarten literacy ability, such as SES, ethnicity, single-parent households, and family vs. center-based childcare environments. At the county level, rural counties had significantly lower literacy scores, but this variance was largely accounted for by county poverty and minority concentration in the county. They also found cross-level interactions, such as the negative effect of SES on literacy decreased for kindergartners from rural counties. Testing extensive models of the relationships of level-1 variables, level-2 variables, and the interaction of the two on outcomes is a hallmark of multilevel modeling.

In another study, data from the Programme for International Student Assessment (PISA) survey, GLMM was used to ascertain the individual, country, and community factors that influence scientific literacy skills for migrant children (Meyer & Benavot, 2013). Because migrants move from various origin countries to various destination countries, a cross-classified analysis was used to parse out the sources of variance in scientific literacy due to origin country, destination country, and pairing of origin and destination country (i.e., migrant community). In this innovative design, the authors determined, among other findings, that the socio-economic and cultural capital of the community were important correlates of later scientific literacy of the children, and, although much of the variation in student scientific literacy was attributed to individual factors, origin, destination, and community were also influencers of migrant children's later scientific literacy. For additional resources for large-scale survey analyses, see Table 20.3.

Table 20.3 Research Scenarios: Large-Scale Survey Analyses

Example Study	Example Research Question	Additional Resources
Large-Scale Survey Analyses		
Durham and Smith (2006) analyzed ECLS data using a multilevel modeling approach. They constructed models predicting initial kindergarten literacy from individual-level variables and county characteristics.	Do beginning kindergarteners vary in early literacy readiness according to county-level economic and social characteristics, individual demographic characteristics, family social capital resources, and preschool childcare?	Lee & Forthofer, 2005. Raudenbush & Bryk, 2002. Singer & Willett, 2003. https://nces.ed.gov/surveys/

Models with Multiple Literacy Outcomes

Research suggests that literacy occurs within a larger community context including schools, neighborhoods, diverse contexts, as well as community resources and programs. Traditional quantitative models such as multiple regression analyses cannot easily accommodate such a wide range of empirically related variables. However, more advanced multivariate models have gained popularity for their ability to accommodate such complexity.

Structural Equation Models (SEM) refer to a family of related procedures for developing measurement models, testing theoretical models that include relationships among variables and constructs, and for other applications that are best described by a system of equations rather than a single regression model. This flexibility results in the ability to define and measure constructs from a set of indicators, estimate measurement error, estimate correlations among errors and among constructs, and use variables and constructs in one model that may act as both a predictor of and as a criterion.

Structural equation models consist of a structural model representing the relationship among the unobserved or latent variables in the model and a measurement model representing the relationships among the latent variables and their observable indicators. A comparison of the model to empirical data assesses the model fit. If the fit is acceptable, then the proposed relationships between latent and observed variables, as well as the assumed dependencies between the various latent variables, are viewed as supported by the data. Some applications of SEM only use the measurement model (e.g., confirmatory factor analysis), and other applications involve relationships among observed variables only (e.g., path analysis), but many applications of SEM involve both a measurement and a structural component.

For example, Storch and Whitehurst (2001) developed a model that answered the research question: What is the role of home environment in the development of emergent literacy and subsequent literacy development? Structural equation modeling allowed the researchers to define constructs such as home literacy environment using multiple home and family variables This model accounted for 40% of the variance in emergent literacy skills. In this example, researchers were able to examine a variety of environmental factors, as well as their influence over time, to clarify the relationship between the environment and child language and literacy development.

It is important to note that a limitation of SEM is that it may produce models without substantive meaning if researchers do not base their models on sound empirical evidence, such as relationships suggested by prior research. The model also assumes linear relationships and data without outliers. The accuracy of SEM results depends on the sample size and the number of variables; the smaller the sample and the larger the number of variables, the less accurate the model estimates will be. Applications of SEM in literacy research include refining measurement models of the indicators that underlie literacy, determining if theoretical models fit across different samples; comparing different populations at a single point in time in cross-sectional studies; and examining literacy trends over time in longitudinal research (Lomax, 2004; Nachtigall et al., 2003). For additional resources regarding SEM, see Table 20.4.

Longitudinal Research of Language and Literacy Trends

Various longitudinal research designs are used to measure change over time. When making inferences from large-scale surveys, data can be compared across different cohorts using a time-lag design, in which same-aged individuals are sampled over time but the cohort and the time period change. The goal is often to make inferences about change over time; however, this can be

Table 20.4 Research Scenarios: Structural Equation Models

Example Study	*Example Research Question*	*Additional Resources*
Models with Multiple Literacy Outcomes, Mediating, and Moderating Effects		
Storch and Whitehurst (2001) used SEM to map the relations between home and family factors, language development, emergent literacy skills, and reading achievement.	What is the role of home environment in the development of emergent literacy and subsequent literacy development?	Byrne, 2016. Stevens, 2012.
Foster et al. (2005) hypothesized and tested a mediation model using structural equation modeling to examine the relationships between family variables and children's emergent literacy competence and social functioning.	What are the relationships between family variables (SES, social risk factors, and home learning variables) and children's emergent literacy competence and children's social functioning?	MacKinnon, 2008.
Alvernini et al. (2011) developed a model comprising school, teachers, parents, and pupils' variables. The influence of curriculum policies in various European countries was tested in terms of an interaction effect by means of multiple samples using SEM.	What are the relationships among educational policy; school, teacher, family, and student factors; and their relationships to reading literacy?	Hayes, 2018.

confounded with cohort effects. In one example, the Black-White literacy gap in prose, document, and quantitative literacies was compared using data from the 1992 NALS and 2003 NAAL to determine literacy trends over an eleven-year period to address (a) whether the size of the Black-White literacy gap changed from 1992 to 2003, and (b) if so, what are the sources of those changes with a specific emphasis on how they relate to educational attainment? (Cohen et al., 2012). The researchers noted that the Black-White literacy gap decreased on all three literacy scales over time. However, literacy trends within education level were relatively flat while literacy among Black adults had grown over time in tandem with increased educational attainment. By relating the literacy trend with the historic trend in educational attainment, the authors provided evidence that the findings were not just a cohort effect but likely resulted from changes in education among Black adults during that period.

Developmental changes are often assessed with the longitudinal cohort design when data are collected on the same individuals over time. The cohort is held constant, but as age progresses trends can be attributed to age-related development within a cohort. Using multilevel growth modeling (MLGM), both the growth trajectories of individuals, as well as the predicted average growth over time, are estimated (Holt, 2008; Raudenbush & Bryk, 2002). In a series of studies, Hadley and colleagues (2014) investigated early grammatical development in children at 3-month intervals between 21 months and 3 years of age (Hadley & Holt, 2006; Rispoli et al., 2009). Growth models included an individual-level equation that assessed changes in each child's tense and agreement productivity (TAP) score over time and a between-child equation that assessed differences among children in their TAP growth trajectories. Linear and quadratic growth models were tested to determine the most parsimonious growth model that best fit the data. In some cases, a curvilinear model was the best fit – i.e., adding a quadratic component to measure acceleration or deceleration over time or adding a cubic term to measure the change in acceleration or deceleration over time. This procedure was used to examine research questions such as (a) Are there individual differences in the onset of tense marking in young children with slowly developing language abilities? and (b) Is lower-than-expected performance in tense marking at 30 months related to slower growth over time? (Hadley & Holt, 2006).

Time-varying predictors, measured at the same intervals as the outcome measure, can be entered in the level-1 model to predict the relationship of the predictor to the outcome over time. For instance, Hadley and Holt (2006) controlled for the child's utterance length and child vocabulary by entering these variables in the level-1 model, since they changed over time as the child's language exposure and verbal ability grew. Variables that were only measured at one point in time, because either they were not expected to change over the study period (e.g., child gender, maternal education, family history of language impairment) or due to a treatment condition, were inputted as time-invariant variables in the level-2 models to allow prediction of growth curve variation based on these factors.

If growth is expected to predict or impact later development, individual growth curves can be outputted and used as predictors of later outcomes. For instance, to address the question: Does tense and agreement growth between 21 and 30 months predict accuracy of finiteness marking at 36 months?, a predictive validity study was designed in which children's individual TAP growth trajectories from 21–30 months (i.e., average TAP at 21 months, linear growth in TAP at 21 months, and acceleration from 21–30 months) were outputted and used in a separate analysis to predict accuracy at 36 months (Hadley et al., 2014).

Table 20.5 Research Scenarios: Longitudinal Designs

Example Study	Example Research Question	Additional Resources
Longitudinal Research of Language and Literacy Trends		
Hadley, Rispoli, and colleagues (Hadley & Holt, 2006; Hadley et al., 2014; Rispoli et al., 2009) studied developmental trends in early grammatical development in young children. By analyzing data on tense and agreement productivity (TAP) in children as young as 21 months, they captured the onset of TAP and modeled developmental growth of TAP as children aged. They created trend lines for typically developing children and children with specific language impairments. They used features of growth modeling and correlated both time invariant variables – e.g., maternal education, family history of language impairment – and time varying variables, e.g., mean length of utterance and other early language measures, to determine how these variables related to the onset of TAP and to the trend lines.	1) Are there individual differences in the onset of tense marking in young children with slowly developing language abilities? 2) Is lower-than-expected performance in tense marking at 30 months related to slower growth over time?	Holt, 2008. Holt, 2009. Raudenbush & Bryk, 2002. Singer & Willett, 2003.

The flexibility of MLGM makes it feasible to consider research scenarios that would not meet the more restrictive assumptions of repeated measures analyses, such as when the structure of time and time-varying covariates vary across persons. Further, time-invariant covariates do not have to be consistent across the level-2 equations. This flexibility results in models that can be readily adapted to various longitudinal models that occur in language and literacy across different community settings and during different developmental periods. See Table 20.5 for additional resources for investigating developmental change through longitudinal growth modeling.

Summary

When studying language and literacy in community settings in which parents, neighbors, child-care providers, workplace colleagues, and others interact and influence our evolving language and literacy profile, traditional bivariate analyses or least-squares regression may not be sufficient to capture the rich influences on language and literacy development. Sociocultural influences are important to model, as well as other environmental and maturational factors that influence mature language and literacy development. The advancement of statistical modeling methods provides a broader array of approaches to model language and literacy in these contexts. The methods discussed in this chapter provide a wide array of methodological tools for modeling language and literacy proficiency in informal learning settings such as the home and the community. As such, statistical modeling can be a powerful complement to ethnographic and case study research to uncover the rich array of influences and moderators of language and literacy development.

Statistical Support

The methodological tools discussed in this chapter are appropriate for organizations interested in evaluating the impact of their community literacy programs. Not all organizations have staff that are familiar with quantitative data analysis. In those cases, local universities are excellent resources. Many universities have formal statistical consulting programs that match faculty and advanced graduate students with local organizations. In addition, organizations might also reach out to literacy centers at local universities. These centers engage in community literacy programming, research, and advocacy and are often looking for affiliates within the local community. Current examples include the Center for Literacy at the University of Illinois Chicago, the Stevens Literacy Center at Ohio University, and the Center for the Interdisciplinary Study of Language and Literacy at Northern

Illinois University. These programs and centers are ideal for organizations looking for additional support when evaluating the effectiveness of their programs.

References

Alvernini, F., Lucidi, F., Manganelli, S., & Di Leo, I. (2011). A map of factors influencing reading literacy across European countries: Direct, indirect, and moderating effects. *Procedia Social and Behavioral Sciences*, *15*, 3205–3210. https://doi.org/10.1016/j.sbspro.2011.04.272

Beretvas, S. N. (2004). Using hierarchical linear modeling for literacy research under No Child Left Behind. *Reading Research Quarterly*, *39*, 95–99.

Beretvas, S. N. (2010). Cross-classified and multiple membership models. In J. Hox & J. K. Roberts (Eds.), *The handbook of advanced multilevel analysis* (pp. 313–334). Routledge.

Byrne, B. M. (2016). *Structural equation modeling with Amos: Basic concepts, applications, and programming* (3rd ed.). Routledge. http://dx.doi.org/10.4324/9781315757421

Campbell, M. K., Piaggio, G., Elbourne, D. R., & Altman, D. G. (2012). Consort 2010 statement: extension to cluster randomised trials. *BMJ*, *345*.

Cohen, D. J., White, S., & Cohen, S. B. (2012). Mind the gap: The Black-White literacy gap in the National Assessment of Adult Literacy and its implications. *Journal of Literacy Research*, *44*, 123–148. https://doi.org/10.1177/1086-296X12439998

Davis, T. C., Long, S. W., Jackson, R. H., Mayeaux, E. J., George, R. B., Murphy, P. W., & Crouch, M. A. (1993). Rapid estimate of adult literacy in medicine: A shortened screening instrument. *Family Medicine*, 391–395.

Durham, R. E., & Smith, P. J. (2006). Nonmetropolitan status and kindergartners' early literacy skills: Is there a rural disadvantage. *Rural Sociology*, *71*(4), 625–661. https://doi.org/10.1526/003601106781262052

Evangelou, M., & Sylva, K. (2007). Evidence on effective early childhood interventions from the United Kingdom: An evaluation of the Peers Early Education Partnership (PEEP). *Early Childhood Research and Practice*, *9*(1). https://ecrp.illinois.edu/

Foster, M. A., Lambert, R., Abbott-Shim, M., McCarty, F., & Franze, S. (2005). A model of home learning environment and social risk factors in relation to children's emergent literacy and social outcomes. *Early Childhood Research Quarterly*, *20*, 13–36. https://doi.org/10.1016/j.ecresq.2005.01.006

Hadley, P., & Holt, J. (2006). Individual differences in the onset of tense marking: A growth curve analysis. *Journal of Speech, Language, and Hearing Research*, *49*, 984–1000. https://doi.org/10.1044/1092-4388(2006/071)

Hadley, P., Rispoli, M., Holt, J., Fitzgerald, C., & Bahnsen, A. (2014). The growth of finiteness in the third year of life: Replication and predictive validity.

Journal of Speech, Language, and Hearing Research, 57, 887–900. https://doi.
org/10.1044/2013_JSLHR-L-13-0008

Harlow, C. W., Jenkins, H. D., & Steurer, S. (2010). GED holders in prison
read better than those in the household population: Why? *The Journal of
Correctional Education, 61*(1), 68–92.

Hayes, A. F. (2018). *Introduction to mediation, moderation, and conditional process
analysis: A regression-based approach* (2nd ed.). The Guilford Press.

Hayes, R. J., & Moulton, L. H. (2017). *Cluster randomized trials* (2nd ed.).
Chapman and Hall/CRC Press.

Holt, J. K. (2008). Modeling growth using multilevel and alternative
approaches. In A. A. O'Connell & D. B. McCoach (Eds.), *Quantitative
methods in education and the behavioral sciences* [Issues, Research and Teaching
Series: Vol. 3, Multilevel Analysis of Educational Data] (pp. 111–159).
Information Age.

Holt, J. K. (2009). Analyzing change in adulthood with multilevel
growth models: Selected measurement, design, and analysis issues. In M.C.
Smith & N. DeFrates-Densch (Eds.), *Handbook of research on adult learning
and development.* (pp. 137–161) Routledge. http://dx.doi.org/10.4324/
9780203887882

Lee, E. S., & Forthofer, R. N. (2005). *Analyzing complex survey data* (2nd ed.).
Sage. http://dx.doi.org/10.4135/9781412983341

Lomax, R. G. (2004). Whither the future of quantitative literacy research?
Reading Research Quarterly, 38(1), 107–112.

MacKinnon, D. P. (2008). *Introduction to statistical mediation analysis.* Routledge.
http://dx.doi.org/10.4324/9780203809556

Meyer, H. D., & Benavot, A. (Eds.). (2013, May). *PISA, power, and policy: The
emergence of global educational governance.* Symposium Books Ltd.

Nachtigall, C., Kroehne, U., Funke, F., & Steyer, R. (2003). (Why) should
we use SEM? Pros and cons of structural equation modeling. *Methods of
Psychological Research Online, 3*(2), 1–22.

National Institutes of Health (n.d.) *Research methods resources.* https://research-
methodsresources.nih.gov/methods/grt

Nutbrown, C., Hannon, P., & Morgan, A. (2005). *Early literacy works with families: Policy, practice and research.* Sage.

Price-Haywood, E. G., Harden-Barrios, J., & Cooper, L. A. (2014). Comparative
effectiveness of audit-feedback versus additional physician communication
training to improve cancer screening for patients with limited health literacy. *Journal of General Internal Medicine, 29*(8), 1113–1121.

Raudenbush, S. W., & Bryk, A. S. (2002). *Hierarchical linear models: Applications
and data analysis methods* (2nd ed.). Sage.

Rispoli, M., Hadley, P., & Holt, J. (2009). The growth of tense productivity. *Journal of Speech, Language, and Hearing Research, 52*, 930–944. https://doi.org/10.1044/1092-4388(2009/08-0079)

Sattin, R. W., Williams, L. B., Dias, J., Garvin, J. T., Marion, L., Joshua, T. V., & Narayan, K. V. (2016). Community trial of a faith-based lifestyle intervention to prevent diabetes among African-Americans. *Journal of Community Health, 41*(1), 87–96. http://dx.doi.org/10.1007/s10900-015-0071-8

Schoenberg, N. E., Studts, C. R., Shelton, B. J., Liu, M., Clayton, R., Bispo, J. B., & Cooper, T. (2016). A randomized controlled trial of a faith-placed, lay health advisor delivered smoking cessation intervention for rural residents. *Preventive Medicine Reports, 3*, 317–323. http://dx.doi.org/10.1016/j.pmedr.2016.03.006

Sheehan, J. K., & Smith, M C. (1997, March). *Hierarchical linear modeling of contextual effects on literacy proficiencies: An analysis of NALS*. Paper presented at the annual meeting of the American Educational Research Association, Chicago.

Singer, J. D., & Willett, J. B. (2003). *Applied longitudinal data analysis: Modeling change and event occurrence*. Oxford University Press. http://dx.doi.org/10.1093/acprof:oso/9780195152968.001.0001

Smith, C. A., Chang, E., Gallego, G., Khan, A., Armour, M., & Balneaves, L. G. (2019). An education intervention to improve decision making and health literacy among older Australians: a randomised controlled trial. *BMC Geriatrics, 19*(1), 1–12. http://dx.doi.org/10.1186/s12877-019-1143-x

Stevens, J. P. (2012). *Applied multivariate statistics for the social sciences* (5th ed.). Routledge. http://dx.doi.org/10.4324/9780203843130

Storch, S. A., & Whitehurst, G. J. (2001, Summer). The role of family and home in the literacy development of children from low-income backgrounds. *New Directions for Child and Adolescent Development, 92*, 53–71. http://dx.doi.org/10.1002/cd.15

Vagi, R. L., Collins, C., & Clark, T. (2017). Identifying scalable policy solutions: A state-wide cross-classified analysis of factors related to early childhood literacy. *Education Policy Analysis Archives, 25*(9). http://dx.doi.org/10.14507/epaa.25.2686

Zhang, S. X., Roberts, R. E. L., & Callanan, V. J. (2006). Preventing parolees from returning to prison through community-based reintegration. *Crime and Delinquency, 52*(4), 551–571. http://dx.doi.org/10.1177/0011128705282594

Appendices

Within this section the reader will find a collection of documents that can serve as useful draft policy documents, checklists for practice, and job descriptions. These resources may be used exactly as presented in this section or can serve as useful examples (prototypes) that can be customized to meet the immediate needs of a specific community literacy program. A list of the specific documents follows.

A) Planning for a Community Literacy Program Audit
B) Checklist for Planning and Implementing a Community-Based Literacy Program
C) Procedural Policies Manual for Community Literacy Program Outline
D) Program Logic Model Example: Community Literacy Center
E) Community Awareness Plan
F) The Grant Readiness Assessment
G) Key Steps in Approaching Grant-Seeking Activities for Community Literacy Programs
H) Rights of Community-Based Literacy Volunteers
I) Responsibilities of Literacy Volunteers
J) Job Description: Literacy Program Coordinator
K) Job Description: Adult Literacy Tutor
L) Key READ ENC Community Solutions Action Plan Excerpts

Appendix A

Planning for a Community Literacy Program Audit

Initial Stage: Identify a Diverse Team of Community Members

Each team member (10–12 individuals) should maintain an active role in the audit process from planning through implementation to formal reporting. Team members should bring diverse perspectives from a variety of stakeholder groups and be representative of the target community or region (e.g., faith leaders, educators, healthcare workers, civic leaders, business owners, local advocates, non-profit sector, law enforcement, neighborhood representatives, etc.).

Stage 1: Developing a Strategy

Goal Setting and Decision Making

At the initial team assembly, roles and responsibilities should be identified based on the skills and expertise of each team member. Together, the team should complete the following components to develop a strategy for the audit:

- Identify the scope of the audit (e.g., neighborhood, community, geographic region) and target population (e.g., early childhood, adolescent, adult, homeless, low-income, etc.).
- Set SMART goals (Specific, Measurable, Achievable, Relevant, Time-Bound).
- Identify existing data and how to compile it into a usable form.
- Determine what data will be collected, how, and by whom.
- Select data collection methods (e.g., interviews, focus groups, surveys, etc.).
- Determine data sources.
- Select collection tools to be used (e.g., Excel spreadsheet, Google form, Word document, paper-based logs, etc.).
- Assign tasks to team members based on skills and expertise.
- Establish a realistic timeline for each stage of the process.

Stage 2: Conducting the Audit

Data Collection and Formative Review
   Team members engage in an iterative process of data collection and review to determine quality of the data and when enough data has been collected.

- Designate one team member to serve as the data manager.
- Begin data-collection process.
- Record and review consolidated data periodically.
- Summarize the data to determine if additional data is needed.

Stage 3: Developing a Community Action Plan

This stage focuses on the identification of effective programs and gaps or additional needs that exist.

- Identify the programming strengths that exist in the community.
- Identify areas for growth within current programs.
- Identify gaps in programming and what services are not provided.
- Prioritize the needs based on the set goals of the audit (Stage 1).
- Set short term (annual) and longer term (5 year) strategies to eliminate the gaps.
- Summarize the impact factors of successful implementation.
- Identify available resources to carry out the plan (i.e., fiscal, personnel, etc.).

Stage 4: Action Plan Implementation

Once the action plan is developed, implementation and progress tracking ensue. This includes an evaluative component to capture successes, document obstacles or challenges, and communicate to the broader stakeholder groups.

- Develop a logic model (see Appendix D) to help guide the implementation of the action plan.
- Work with a program evaluator to ensure data and progress metrics are collected.
- Create a strategic communication plan to share the progress and accomplishments with the broader community and organizations or individuals who assisted with the audit.
- Celebrate accomplishments in a public venue.

Adapted from the Community Needs Assessment. Atlanta, GA: Centers for Disease Control and Prevention (CDC), 2013.

www.cdc.gov/globalhealth/healthprotection/fetp/training_modules/15/community-needs_pw_final_9252013.pdf

Appendix B

Checklist for Planning and Implementing a Community-Based Literacy Program

1. Does the community really want you there? How do you know such is the case?
2. Is everyone who will be involved in the program or who will be affected by it participating in the planning and design (i.e., community members, representatives from kindred agencies, volunteers, faculty doing service-learning, or school representatives)?
3. Do the potential program leaders accurately estimate their ability to deliver on the goals and objectives developed by the stakeholders?
4. Will important areas such as orientation, training, supervision, and evaluation be undertaken by individuals with the appropriate training and experiential backgrounds? Will these individuals be part of the formative planning activities for the program?

5. Are the stakeholder groups part of the decision-making process such that trust, and the sense of participation and responsibility are maximized?

6. What organization (or who) is providing the financial or material resources for the program? What is expected of the program in return? Is the program leadership prepared to meet these expectations? Are there other resources that might be explored?

7. Is there a provision for conducting ongoing outreach to the community to fully gauge its changing literacy needs?

8. Will the program be dependent upon volunteers (from the community or from other sources)? Will the leadership of the program rest with the community, or will the volunteers subsume this role?

9. Will the volunteers get appropriate rewards for their work? If service-learning is an intricate component, will the students be receiving course credit for a course? If so, to what degree does a course instructor have influence upon the program's direction?

10. If the larger community or college campus has a volunteer bureau, what is the relationship between the community program and volunteer bureau? What contacts have been made? What arrangements have been developed?

11. Is there to be a permanent paid program director? What are the qualifications for this position? To whom does the individual report? How is the individual evaluated? In what manner is the individual remunerated for the services rendered?

12. What is the plan for summative evaluation of the program? How is this drawn out of the formative design efforts?

Original author: Stahl, N. (2022). Appendix B: Checklist for planning and implementing a community-based literacy program.

Appendix C

Procedural Policies Manual for Community Literacy Programs Outline

Mission of the Program
(i.e., history, purpose, function, clientele)

Goals of the program

Staff roles, administrative, service
(Including volunteers and/or interns)

Administration of the program
1) Staff administration
   a) Person(s) responsible (titles)
   b) Qualifications
   c) Duties of administrative position (job classification)
   d) Budget allowance
   e) Supervision and accountability
2) Volunteer and intern administration

      a) Coordinator
         i. Responsibilities
         ii. Qualifications
         iii. Duties
         iv. Supervision received
         v. Accountability
3) Advisory committee
      a) Membership
      b) Responsibilities
      c) Relationship
         i. To staff
         ii. To volunteers and interns
         iii. To community stakeholders
4) Communication
      a) Internal: between staff, committees, volunteers
      b) External: community, organizations, other stakeholders
      c) Modes: electronic, postal, signage
5) Guidelines for volunteers and interns (service-learning)
      a) Rights
      b) Responsibilities
      c) Supervision
      d) Accountability
6) Job classification for volunteers and interns (multiple as necessary by role)
      a) Description
      b) Recruitment
      c) Qualifications
      d) Orientation
      e) Evaluation
7) Training
      a) Staff
         i. Orientation
         ii. Professional development
      b) Volunteers and interns
         i. Orientation
         ii. In-service
      c) Advisory board
         i. Orientation
         ii. On-going development

8) Program Evaluation
   a) Formative and summative
   b) Annual reporting
   c) Fiscal responsibility
9) Other

Adapted from Swanson, M. T. (1970). Your volunteer program: Organization and administration of volunteer programs. Des Moines Area Community College. Office of Education.

https://files.eric.ed.gov/fulltext/ED052414.pdf

Appendix D

Program Logic Model Example: Community Literacy Center

Inputs	Activities	Outputs	Outcomes		
			Initial	Intermediate	Long-term
Staff Project Director Tutorial Coordinator Volunteer Coordinator Volunteers Resources $350,000 grant Program Office Tutorial Room Training Library Community Community Advisory Group University Evaluator Local school district	Volunteers Recruitment Orientation Training Placement Supervision Evaluation After school tutoring Summer tutoring and enrichment Drop-in tutoring Parent and caregiver workshops Interactions with community partners, schools, and community college	# of volunteers recruited, trained, serving, and effectiveness # of tutees served (biweekly) in after school program # of tutees served daily in summer program # of tutees served through drop-in program # of parent workshops # of outreach activities with community, schools, and community college	# and % of tutees with positive dispositions toward literacy practices # and % of tutees demonstrate greater competency with literacy practices # and % of parents and caretakers attending workshops to support tutees' literacy development # and % of teachers attending professional development activities to work with volunteer tutors	# and % of teachers reporting tutees have demonstrated more positive attitudes toward literacy practices # and % of tutees improving performance on informal and state required standardized test # and % of teachers reporting parents or caregivers are more involved in tutee's education # and % of parents taking an active role in their tutee's literacy development	# and % of tutees reading at grade level or above # and % of tutees with improved end of semester GPA # and % of tutees with increased school attendance rates

Original author: Henry, L. (2022). Appendix D: Program logic model example: Community Literacy Center.

Appendix E

Community Awareness Plan

A key requirement for any community literacy program is that it be a well-known and fully respected entity within the target community. Holding such status in a community does not simply happen based on the good works undertaken by the program. A program must have a Community Awareness Plan. This requires a concerted and well-planned messaging effort delivered on a continuing basis. Such work draws from the field of public relations.

The Public Relations Society of America (PRSA) defines *public relations* as follows: "Public relations is a strategic communication process that builds mutually beneficial relationships between organizations and their publics." As such, it focuses on "influencing, engaging and building a relationship with key stakeholders across numerous platforms in order to shape and frame the public perception of an organization" (www.prsa.org/about/all-about-pr). What follows is a Community Awareness Plan checklist (questions) that has been drawn from resources provided by a number of community agencies.

First Steps

Is the leadership of the literacy program convinced of the importance of and need to develop an ongoing Community Awareness Plan?

Has the program's leadership and members of the Advisory Committee identified appropriate individuals, including a public relations professional, to serve on a Community Awareness subcommittee?

Will the members of the Advisory Committee (Board of Directors) take an active role in promoting the literacy program in the community? Is this the reason why such individuals are recruited to serve?

Has the leadership prepared information to be disseminated (printed or digital) that details the program's purposes, goals, accomplishments, and relationship to the community?

Has there been a line item added to the budget for the ongoing work associated with the Community Awareness Plan?

Does the program have a public relations program, or will the program develop one that covers a fiscal year?

Are the endeavors of those individuals who serve the literacy program and the clientele, particularly those volunteers and interns, acknowledged and recognized on a regular basis?

Community Membership

Have you assessed the attitudes of the individuals and organizations in the community toward the literacy program?

What is the image in the community of the literacy program? Is it positive, or has a problem been identified? Has the program developed a plan to overcome any problems with the image held by members of the community?

Is the community, including the leaders within it, well informed of the mission and goals of the community literacy program?

Are the members of the Advisory Board, leaders of other community service providers, members of the education and church community, and media outlets updated regularly about the literacy program's activities and accomplishments via press releases and direct notifications whether by traditional text or digital sources?

Do stakeholders, other community service providers attached to agencies, schools and churches, and members of the local media have the necessary information to make direct contact with the literacy program?

Is your recruitment plan successful in reaching out to potential clientele as well as potential volunteers? How might it be improved?

Does the leadership of the community literacy program adhere to the principle of being a contributing and supportive neighbor (i.e., sensitive to their needs) by serving on advisory and institutional boards, attending other groups' outreach meetings, and partnering with other agencies on kindred projects?

Does the leadership team have regular contact with education providers in the community such as public, private, and charter schools as well as other extra educational organizations and agencies?

Is the literacy program receptive to and supportive of both established programs and emerging service providers?

Program Publicity

Has the leadership team (communications committee) for the community literacy program made direct contact and maintained regular communication with appropriate members of the media such as newspaper and digital source editors, education beat reporters, radio and television station managers, local bloggers, etc.?

Has the literacy program provided media contacts with information about the program on a prompt basis when such requests have been received?

Do the media sources receive regular press releases about the literacy program's special projects as well as ongoing needs or activities (i.e., volunteer recruitment, new or ongoing service cycles, seminars and workshops, exhibits, awards, and recognitions)?

Do the other community service providers and public educational agencies in the community receive regular updates about the literacy program's special projects as well as ongoing needs or activities (i.e., volunteer recruitment, new or ongoing service cycles, seminars and workshops, exhibits, awards, and recognitions)?

Does the communications team for the community literacy program provide suggestions for feature stories about the program's accomplishments and future plans to local media contacts on a regular basis?

Has the leadership approached individuals from local businesses, faculty from postsecondary business programs, PRSA chapters, etc. for assistance in developing an outreach and dissemination program?

Does the literacy program have a Speakers' Service that can provide speakers for various community functions?

Original author: Stahl, N. (2022). Appendix E: *Community awareness plan.*

Appendix F

The Grant Readiness Assessment

Ranking of criteria: 0–4 points

0: We don't fit at all or deal breaker

1: This would be a stretch for us

2: We could do this with a little outside help or internal support

3: Right up our alley

4: We were made for this, or the funder asked/invited us to apply

Foundations	Rank	Comments
Grant applicant eligibility		
Project intent vs. funding priorities		
Funder mission and focus		
Collaboration requirement		

Foundations	Rank	Comments
Monetary: Funding level; match; payout timeline; allowable focus and expenses; appropriate ask level		
Management capability: Deadline vs. staff time and resources to complete; implementation process; staff capacity; reporting/evaluation requirements and costs; history on similar projects		
Feasibility of getting award: # grants to be awarded; # of prior awards in your region; local or regional competition		
Agency strengths: Sustainability plan; compelling case for this agency to get this funding; agency connections with the grantor's decision-makers		
Potential obstacles: Uncommon requirements of proposal or implementation; collaborative process; online technical issues; grant delivery details		
Total points available for foundations: (36 points)		
Suggested point levels foundations: 30–36: Go for it 25–29: Address the issues and proceed 20–24: Build a fabulous narrative to compensate Below 20: Search for better fit		

Government	Rank	Comments
Grant applicant eligibility		
Project intent vs. funding priorities		
Funder mission and focus		
Collaboration requirement		
Monetary: Funding level; match; payout timeline; allowable focus and expenses; appropriate ask level		
Management capability: Deadline vs. staff time and resources to complete; implementation process; staff capacity; reporting/evaluation requirements and costs; history on similar projects		

Feasibility of getting award: # grants to be awarded; # of prior awards in your region; local or regional competition		
Agency strengths: Sustainability plan; compelling case for this agency to get this funding; agency connections with the grantor's decision-makers		
Potential obstacles: Uncommon requirements of proposal or implementation; collaborative process; online technical issues; grant delivery details		
The number of times this specific funding opportunity has been awarded in your Congressional district over the past five years		
Project in need of funding is documented as a priority in local and state plans related to government Single Point of Contact approval		
Congressional composition – Favorable		
Congressional advocacy history for previously requested grants and funded projects		
Total points available for Federal Grants: (52 points)		
Suggested point levels for Federal Grants: 44–52: Go for it 38–43: Address the issues and proceed 30–37: Build a fabulous narrative to compensate Below 30: Search for better fit		

Author: Browning, B. (2022). The grant readiness assessment. (See also Chapter 9)

Appendix G

Key Steps in Approaching Grant-Seeking Activities for Community Literacy Programs

- Researching Potential Corporate and Foundation Funders – Learn how to identify the right funders for your organization.
- Funder Relationship-Building Processes – Practice the relationship building approach internally before picking up the telephone to call a funder or email them a brief overview of your organization and its needs.
- Preparing for Accountability Questions from the Funder's Staff – Be prepared for a barrage of questions from potential funders.
- Point of Entry Protocol for Private Sector Funders – Pay special attention to your communications with potential funders. They should be well-planned and executed with confidence.
- Invitation to Submit a Grant Proposal – Learn what to expect when you have made a convincing introduction to potential funders.

- Required Corporate and Foundation Grant Proposal Components – Begin writing with a structured outline and then flesh out the information for each section of the proposal.
- Researching Government Grants – This process can be daunting; however, one federal grant award can bring millions into your non-profit organization.
- Focusing on a Government Grant Funding Opportunity – Learn how to read a grant funding opportunity synopsis.
- Politics Matter – Your Congressional team members' staff are the key to getting your elected officials to act as your advocate from submission to a funding award.
- Government Grant Writing Expectations – Writing a federal government grant application is not a piece of cake. It's a complicated, laborious, research-based process.
- The Not-Funded Follow-Up Process – Obviously, private sector and federal grantmaking agencies cannot fund every grant request. When you're not funded, knowing the next steps is critical to building deeper relationships with funders and preparing your application for the next funding cycle.
- Myths About Federal Grant Funding – There's a lot of misinformation floating around about how getting a federal grant award (think millions of dollars) can help the grantee cover all their operating expenses. This is a myth!
- The Grant Readiness Test – Before you and your work team can jump into writing a grant request, it's important to apply the grant readiness assessment to the type of funder (foundation or federal) and the grant applicant organization's capability to implement and track expenses and outcomes for a federal grant-funded project.

Author: Browning, B. (2022). Key steps in approaching grant-seeking activities for community literacy programs. (See also Chapter 9).

Appendix H

Rights of Community-Based Literacy Volunteers

The Rights of Literacy Volunteers include the right to be:

- Treated in a professional, courteous, and collegial manner that respects a volunteer's ethnicity, race, gender, sexual orientation, religion, national origin, age, disability, and/or economic status during all stages of association with the program.
- Assigned to a volunteer project, role, or task that is appropriate for the individual's training, prior experiences, and interests.
- Provided with a thorough and precise job description and a volunteer policy manual that details the tasks, responsibilities, roles, and hours/days of service to be undertaken.
- Provided with appropriate mentorship, guidance, supervision with feedback, and tangible recognition from an appropriately trained designated supervisor.
- Given an honest and accurate orientation about the mission and goals of the program and targeted training for any assigned task.

- Presented with ongoing professional development associated with assigned volunteer duty or to develop advanced competencies to serve the organization and its clientele in new ways.
- Furnished with a healthy and safe environment appropriate for volunteer activities.
- Furnished with suitable materials and tools appropriate for the assigned volunteer literacy tasks or other volunteer task.
- Not asked to perform roles previously held by a paid staff member or a staff member who might be part of a work stoppage (strike).
- Permitted to participate in planning and development activities for new projects and revision of active programs.
- Covered adequately by insurance.
- Conferred grievance and dispute resolution procedures as well as competent guidance/support throughout the process.
- Reimbursed for out-of-pocket expenses when prior approval was obtained.
- Respected and supported by other volunteers and program staff.
- Granted a verbal or written reference as appropriate.

Original author: Stahl, N. (2022). Appendix H: Rights of community-based literacy volunteers.

Appendix I

Responsibilities of Literacy Volunteers

Responsibilities of literacy volunteers include:

- Provide accurate background information and respond honestly to questions asked during any intake interview.
- Participate in background checks that might be required when working with children.
- Inform supervisor of any pre-existing medical conditions or special needs that might influence one's ability to undertake any tasks associated with the volunteer assignment.
- Keep the program current with all personal and emergency contact information.
- Commit to and regularly prepare for any assignment; be reliable and punctual.
- Maintain confidentially about and respect for individuals receiving program services.
- Support and demonstrate collegiality with all program staff members and volunteers.

- Accept guidance, supervision, and evaluation of duties from those providing oversight.
- Participate actively in any orientation and appropriate training programs offered.
- Complete all volunteer duties in an efficient and honest manner.
- Notify one's supervisor if unable to provide literacy services at any point, inability to attend required training, or upon decision to leave the program.
- Ask for assistance whenever necessary.
- Adhere to all of the program's policies and procedures and one's job description.
- Observe all safety rules so as to not endanger the health and safety of others and report immediately any injuries or workplace hazards.
- Address grievances or complaints according to procedures and polices set by the program.
- Provide representatives of the program with honest feedback and suggestions about the services rendered by the organization.
- Not spending program funds or ordering materials without prior approval of the organization's fiscal officer.

Original author: Stahl, N. (2022). Appendix H: Responsibilities of literacy volunteers.

Appendix J

Job Description: Literacy Program Coordinator

Duties: The Coordinator organizes and directs the overall literacy program for the Bayview Community Center Literacy Program. This individual works with the Center's staff in planning, developing, and supervising a tutorial program staffed by college students and community volunteers. The Coordinator works with community partners including agencies and school systems to maximize the effectiveness of the literacy program.

Requirements: The individual serving as the Coordinator must demonstrate tact, initiative, and good judgement in working with staff, recipients of services, volunteers, and the public at large. The individual must demonstrate a firm understanding and support for the mission, goals, and objectives of the Bayview Community Center as well as the ability to interpret and convey them to staff, volunteers, and community members. A history of responsibility along with the ability to organize effectively are required.

Professional Qualifications: The applicant for this position should have a college degree or its equivalent in experience, with a focus on pedagogy and human behavior. Training or strong experience in personnel administration along with general knowledge of office procedures and technologies are desirable. Knowledge of the Bayview community and the service agencies and local schools serving the locale is recommended. Past experience working with the public is desirable as is past experience as a tutor.

Working Conditions: The Coordinator is provided with an office, standard resources to accomplish the job, and up-to-date technology. Clerical support to an equivalency of ten hours per week is provided.

The Coordinator works under the general supervision of the Director of the Bayview Community Center. Overall Literacy Program oversight is provided by the Bayview Community Center Advisory Committee.

Specific Duties and Responsibilities:

1. Orients the Center's staff for the tutorial program.
2. Arranges for the necessary equipment, technology, supplies, instructional resources, and space for program activities.
3. Drafts the job description for each staff member and volunteer tutorial positions.
4. Plans the overall literacy program.
5. Recruits and interviews staff and volunteers.
6. Selects, orients, and places staff and volunteers.
7. Provides or arranges for initial training and professional development of literacy program staff and volunteers.
8. Supervises and evaluates the staff members and volunteers within the literacy program.
9. Keeps staff members and volunteers informed of new policies and procedures and promotes a collaborative work environment.
10. Motivates and recognizes the endeavors of both staff and volunteers.
11. Undertakes periodic evaluation of the program including the effectiveness of the pedagogical programming provided to clients.
12. Undertakes public relations and publicity for the program for various stakeholder audiences.
13. Administers the program office, including keeping records, preparing reports, and preparing and maintaining a budget.
14. Prepares grant proposals and engages in fundraising to support programming.
15. Attends meetings and conferences that pertain to the work of the literacy program.

Contact:

Jacob Peterson, Director
Bayview Community Center
Phone: (555) 555–1212
Email: petersonj@email.org

Original author: Stahl, N. (2022). Appendix J: Job description: Literacy program coordinator.

Appendix K

Job Description: Adult Literacy Tutor

Job Description: The adult literacy tutor provides instruction to adults who have below average literacy skills as determined by the program's diagnostic procedures. The tutor will work with one student for an hour each week for a period of one year.

Duties: Responsibilities include diagnosing, placing, tutoring, and assessing the tutee's progress. The tutor will select the methods and materials of instruction. Periodic assessments of tutee's growth will be filed with the program coordinator. Attendance at a three-hour program orientation followed by nine hours of instructional training is expected. Additional professional development via individual meetings with the supervisor and advanced training sessions are required on a quarterly basis.

Qualifications: The tutor should possess: (a) desire to help; (b) enthusiasm and respect for all people regardless of economic background, gender, sexual orientation, age, ethnicity, or culture; (c) positive attitude and self-confidence; (d) willingness to learn and take direction; (e) commitment in time and energy to meet the goals of the program and needs of the tutee; and (f) dependability and responsibility. Willingness to learn appropriate technology is required. Experience in educational settings is desirable but not required.

Working Conditions: The tutor will provide tutoring services within the literacy resource room of the Bayview Community Center during the designated hour each week. Instructional materials will be provided by the center, and these are found within the library section of the resource center. A supervisor will be available for counsel as needed. Appropriate technology is available for instructional purposes and record keeping.

Contact:

Ms. Janae Hopkins
Literacy Coordinator
Bayview Community Center
Phone: (555) 555–1212
Email: hopkinsja@email.org

Original author: Stahl, N. (2022). Appendix K: Job description: Adult literacy tutor.

Appendix L

Key READ ENC Community Solutions Action Plan Excerpts

Full version available at: https://readenc.org/csap/.

READ ENC Vision Statement (p. 3–4)

Due to our location and collaboration with regional partners such as ECU, Vidant Health Systems, and Martin-Pitt Partnership for Children, READ ENC seeks to serve as a hub for literacy resources, support, and collaboration across Eastern North Carolina. We hope to unify parents, teachers, childcare professionals, non-profit agencies, business, industry, government, academia, faith-based communities, and surrounding Grade-Level Reading Campaigns to ensure that *every* child is surrounded by people and programs needed to assure their 0–5 development, support their school success, and instill a lifelong passion for reading and learning. Doing so will improve our schools, build hope and possibility within our children, and ensure our continued growth and advancement. Over time, the region will become known for its collective passion and efforts in support of community literacy, kindergarten readiness, and school success. A specific commitment is made to helping all children read at or above grade level by the end of third grade due to the importance of this benchmark as a critical predictor of high school graduation and career success. Due to our community-wide investment in early literacy, we will be a destination for teachers, families, businesses, and industries who seek access to world-class schools and workforce. We will know we are successful when we have significantly increased the number of children who enter kindergarten "ready for school learning," who experience learning-filled summers, who attend school regularly, and, ultimately, who are reading at or above grade level by the end of third grade.

READ ENC Goals, Targeted Outcomes and Dates, Strategies, and Tactics (pp. 12–19)

Overall READ ENC Goal *All children will read at or above grade-level by the end of third grade.*			
Targeted Outcome	End of Year Targets		
	2017–2018	2020–2021	2023–2024
Increase the percentage of all students who are reading at or above grade level by the end of third grade	49.2%	51.2%	53.2%
Increase the percentage of economically disadvantaged students who are reading at or above grade level by the end of third grade	35.8%	37.8%	39.8%
Overall Strategy, Tactics, and Responsible Parties Through the collaborative efforts of community partners and READ ENC leadership, Pitt County and the surrounding Eastern North Carolina region will mobilize to increase the number of children reading at or above grade level by the end of third grade. The collective impact efforts of READ ENC community partners will focus on (a) community-wide literacy engagement; (b) school readiness; (c) summer learning; and (d) school attendance in order to accomplish this overall goal.			

Goal #1: Community-wide Literacy Engagement *100% Literacy through 100% Community Engagement*
Targeted outcome
Cultivate literacy as a crucial attribute for our community's vitality and economic development.
Strategies
S1: Formalizing and Growing the READ ENC S2: Developing and launching a Community Literacy Awareness/Engagement Campaign S3: Developing and launching a Pledge and Take-Action Campaign
Tactics, responsible parties/community partners, [Responsible parties include: READ ENC Leadership Council (LC), READ ENC Executive Director (ED), Sheppard Memorial Library (SML), United Way (UW), Martin-Pitt Partnership for Children (MPPFC), Action Volunteers (AV), Research & Measurement Group (RG), Pitt County Schools (PCS)]

Goal #2: School Readiness *All children will enter kindergarten ready for school learning.*			
Targeted Outcome	End of Year Targets		
	2017–2018	2020–2021	2023–2024
Increase the percentage of kindergartners who are assessed as proficient or above on the beginning of the year literacy assessment.	49%	51%	53%
Strategies			

S4: Increase book access and opportunities for shared book reading through:
    S4.1: Dolly Parton Imagination Library (DPIL)
    S4.2: Baby & Me and other early literacy events at Sheppard Memorial Library branches and other public libraries
    S4.3: Community book sharing opportunities
S5: Supporting parental engagement
S6: Expand childcare provider literacy-focused training and develop linked READ ENC literacy certification/recognition			

Tactics, responsible parties/community partners, [Responsible parties include: READ ENC Leadership Council (LC), READ ENC Executive Director (ED), Sheppard Memorial Library (SML), United Way (UW), Martin-Pitt Partnership for Children (MPPFC), Action Volunteers (AV), Research & Measurement Group (RG), Pitt County Schools (PCS)]			

Goal #3: Summer Learning *All children will experience a learning-filled summer.*			
Targeted Outcome	End of Year Targets		
	2017–2018	2020–2021	2023–2024
Decrease the percentage of students in kindergarten through third grade who demonstrate summer reading loss.	70% proficiency pre summer 63% proficiency post summer 7% difference	<6% difference	<5% difference
Strategies			
S7: Increase summer literacy learning awareness S8: Increase and improve summer literacy learning opportunities for K–3 students S9: Provide summer learning opportunities for hard-to-reach populations			
Tactics, responsible parties/community partners, [Responsible parties include: READ ENC Leadership Council (LC), READ ENC Executive Director (ED), Sheppard Memorial Library (SML), United Way (UW), Martin-Pitt Partnership for Children (MPPFC), Action Volunteers (AV), Research Group (RG), Pitt County Schools (PCS), Oakwood School (OS)]			

Goal #4: School Attendance *All children will attend school regularly.*			
Targeted Outcome	End of Year Targets		
	2017–2018	2020–2021	2023–2024
Decrease the number of students chronically absent among all kindergarten through third grade students.	9% (approximate data)	Decrease # of students chronically absent by 5%	Decrease # of students chronically absent by 5%
Strategies			
S10: Increase parental awareness about the importance of school attendance S11: Support families to overcome barriers to regular school attendance S12: Provide student, classroom, and school attendance strategies and incentives			
Tactics, responsible parties/community partners, [Responsible parties include: READ ENC Leadership Council (LC), READ ENC Executive Director (ED), Sheppard Memorial Library (SML), United Way (UW), Martin-Pitt Partnership for Children (MPPFC), Action Volunteers (AV), Research & Measurement Group (RG), Pitt County Schools (PCS), Pitt County Schools Committee (PCSS), Parents for Public Schools (PPS)]			

Adapted from READ ENC: Community Solutions Action Plan.
Atkinson, T. S., Anderson, K. L., Swaggerty, E. A., and Rowe, M. W. (2022). Key READ ENC community action plan excerpts. (See also Chapter 8)

Resources

Quick Guide to Community Literacy Needs Assessments

This guide, developed by Connie Jones, Adult Literacy Coordinator with the Saskatchewan Literacy Network, provides strategies for planning a community needs assessment.

http://en.copian.ca/library/learning/sln/lit_needs_assessments/lit_needs_assessments.pdf

Grants

Writing grants can be tricky and time consuming. It is best to find a colleague experienced in obtaining grants. Federal grant opportunities can be found at www.grants.gov

Writing Mission Statements

An organization's mission statement provides a concise yet broad explanation of an organization's purpose, goals, and/or primary focus. The following resource serves as a brief guide for writing mission statements.

https://assessment.uconn.edu/wp-content/uploads/sites/1804/2016/06/HowToWriteMission.pdf

501(c)(3)

A 501(c)(3) is a non-profit designation recognized by the federal government. Visit the IRS.gov website.

www.irs.gov/charities-non-profits/charitable-organizations/exemption-requirements-501c3-organizations

W. K. Kellogg Foundation Logic Model Development Guide

A logic model development guide designed for planning, evaluation, and action.
https://wkkf.issuelab.org/resource/logic-model-development-guide.html

SMART Goals

A how to guide for writing SMART Goals provided by the University of California.

https://www.ucop.edu/local-human-resources/manager-resources/performance-management-corrective-action/overview.html

Community Research Collaboratives

York, A., Valladares, S., Valladares, M.R., Snyder, J., & Garcia, M. (2020).
Community Research Collaboratives. Boulder, CO: National Education Policy Center. Retrieved October 6, 2021 from http://nepc.colorado.edu/publication/crc

Augustine Literacy Project

115 West 7th Street, Charlotte, NC 28202
Serves first- and second-grade students with a one-on-one tutor to improve literacy skills partnering with more than 20 elementary schools.
https://alpcharlotte.org/

Fill My Cup! Adult Literacy and Basic Education Services

PO Box 480301, Charlotte, NC 28269

Serves adult residents of Mecklenburg County who are over the age of 16, do not have a high school diploma or are not functionally literate, and who would like to learn how to read or improve their reading skills.

www.fillmycupliteracy.org/volunteer-1-1

Freedom School Partners

1030 Arosa Ave., Charlotte, NC 28203

Promotes the long-term success of children by preventing summer learning loss through igniting a passion for reading and inspiring a love of learning. Serves youth in 18 partner schools.

https://freedomschoolpartners.org/

International House

1817 Central Ave #215, Charlotte, NC 28205

Provides services to immigrants and foreign-born residents in the community through cross-cultural connections that foster understanding and inspiration. Programs help immigrants settle and succeed in the region.

www.ihclt.org/about

Northern Illinois University Jerry L. Johns Literacy Clinic

Provides an impressive array of programs to meet the varied literacy needs of children in the community. Their America Reads program is an after-school program for K–5 students struggling readers. This program also offers summer camp options and the Raising Readers You Tube Channel video series about fostering literacy at home.

www.cedu.niu.edu/literacy-clinic/

Salisbury University May Literacy Center

Provides one-on-one tutoring to children from grades K–8. This center's homepage contains resources for teachers and parents, the Advisory Council's bylaws and configuration, applications for admission, and the description of the May Literacy Center Film Camp.

www.salisbury.edu/academic-offices/education/may-literacy-center/

University of Kentucky Literacy Clinic

Serves readers with reading difficulties from first grade to high school. This program provides assessment (e.g., tests, observations) and instruction for readers in an after-school setting while working with parents and caregivers on literacy learning.

https://education.uky.edu/edc/literacy/clinic/

The University of Oregon Center on Teaching and Learning

This center recently partnered with Florida State University's Florida Center for Reading Research and RMC Research Corporation to help improve literacy through evidence-based interventions and assessments. This partnership was awarded a five-year, $7.5 million grant from the U.S. Department of Education.

https://around.uoregon.edu/content/uo-lead-national-comprehensive-literacy-center

National Comprehensive Center to Improve Literacy for Students with Disabilities

Florida Center for Reading Research, University of Oregon, and RMC Research Corporation partnered to create the National Comprehensive Center to Improve Literacy for Students with Disabilities. The main focus is on identifying and disseminating research-based materials such as assessment tools, literacy instructional strategies, technologies, and professional development materials for parents, teachers, and paraprofessionals.

www.fcrr.org/news/news_comp_center.html

National Center for Families Learning (NCFL)

NCFL works to eradicate poverty through education solutions for families by partnering with educators, literacy advocates, and policymakers.

https://www.familieslearning.org/

National Center for Improving Literacy (NCIL)

NCIL is a U.S. Department of Education funded partnership between literacy experts and university researchers whose mission is to increase access and use of evidence-based approaches to screen, identify, and teach children with exceptionalities.

https://improvingliteracy.org/about

Editor Biographies

Laurie A. Henry is Professor of Literacy in the Department of Literacy Studies and Dean of the Seidel School of Education at Salisbury University in Maryland. Her research interests focus on the new literacies of internet-based reading, writing, and communicating and social equity issues related to the digital divide. She has extensive knowledge in adolescent and adult literacy and was the 2011 recipient of the J. Michael Parker Award for contributions in adult literacy research from the Literacy Research Association.

Norman A. Stahl is Professor Emeritus of Literacy Education at Northern Illinois University. He has been President of the Literacy Research Association, the Association of Literacy Educators and Researchers, and the College Reading and Learning Association, and Chair of the American Reading Forum. He is a CLADEA National Fellow and the President of the Reading Hall of Fame. Scholarly interests include literacy history, postsecondary literacy, and research methods.

Contributor Biographies

Kimberly L. Anderson is Associate Professor in the Department of Literacy Studies, English Education, and History Education at East Carolina University. She is a former school psychologist and reading specialist with more than 20 years of experience working with teachers in public school settings. Her current research projects focus on improving literacy achievement through community engagement; the long-term impacts of shared book reading in the preschool years; the impact of professional development for kindergarten teachers on their students' literacy learning; and the use of digital resources to improve early literacy instruction in face-to-face and virtual contexts.

Terry S. Atkinson is Associate Professor in the Department of Literacy Studies, English Education, and History Education, at East Carolina University in Greenville, NC where she has taught graduates and undergraduates since 2001. Prior to that she served as a classroom teacher, reading specialist, and principal in both public and independent schools. Atkinson has served as Executive Director of READ ENC Community Literacy Coalition since summer 2018. She has been actively involved in early planning and ongoing implementation of community birth through grade three literacy initiatives within this role and is actively engaged in community-engaged scholarship.

Ann M. Bennett earned her PhD in education from The University of Tennessee. She joined the faculty at Kennesaw State University in 2015 as Assistant Professor of Educational Research in the Department of Secondary and Middle Grades Education. Bennett's research focuses on countering dominant and mainstream deficit discourses and perspectives affecting marginalized and minoritized communities through the use of Photovoice and experimental and progressive ethnographic methods. In 2018–2019, she served as the Diversity Faculty Fellow in the area of disability with KSU's Center for Diversity Leadership and Engagement in the Office of Diversity and Inclusion.

Karabi Bezboruah is Associate Professor of public administration and planning in the College of Architecture, Planning, and Public Affairs (CAPPA) at the University of Texas at Arlington. She teaches courses in public and non-profit administration and directs the PhD programs and the non-profit management certificate in CAPPA. Her research includes cross-sector collaboration, non-profit management and leadership, strategic management, community development, NGOs – organizational behavior, gender roles, leadership, and NGO effectiveness. Bezboruah received the 2020 USDLA Award for Teaching Effectiveness and UTA President's Award for Transformative Online Teaching in 2017 and 2021.

Beverly Browning has been awarded both an MPA and a DBA. She is a grant writing consultant and course developer who has been consulting in the areas of grant writing, contract bid responses, and organizational development for over four decades. She has assisted clients throughout the nation in receiving over 750 million dollars in grants and contract bids. Browning is the author of the multiple editions of the best-selling text *Grant Writing for Dummies* as well as hundreds of grant-related publications.

Candace Chambers is the CEO of Educational Writing Services, LLC, where she provides college admissions and scholarship coaching to high school students, conducts college readiness and scholarship essay writing workshops, and provides editorial services to students and professionals. Chambers is a PhD candidate in Curriculum and Instruction at the University of North Carolina at Charlotte. She earned her master's degree in English composition from the University of Alabama and bachelor's degree in English education from Jackson State University. She teaches college English courses in the Correctional Education program at Ashland University in Ohio and at Central Piedmont Community College in Charlotte.

Gemma Cooper-Novack is a writer, arts educator, writing coach, and doctoral candidate in Literacy Education at Syracuse University. Her research focuses on the affective experiences of young writers, particularly adolescent writers from LGBTQ+ communities, the intersections of distinct models and theories of writing education, and community building and engagement in and through theater and writing.

Joshua Cramer has spent more than 20 years working in non-profit and public school administration roles including his current position as Senior Vice President at the Nebraska Children and Families Foundation. He has designed and supervised a plethora of programs and initiatives for families and children, including social, educational, and federally funded programs based on research and best practices. He has considerable experience writing competitive federal, state, and private grants and managing philanthropic partnerships. Cramer holds a BA in Political Science, MA in Education Curriculum and Instruction, and EdD in Educational Leadership and Higher Education.

Susan Cridland-Hughes is Associate Professor of English Education at Clemson University. Her research interests include critical literacy and critical pedagogy in and out of school literacy spaces. Recent publications include the article "Fostering critical participatory literacy through policy debate" in the journal *English Teaching: Practice and Critique* and "Debate as a tool to develop disciplinary practices and student agency" in the journal *Teaching and Teacher Education*.

Spy Dénommé-Welch (Algonquin-Anishinaabe) is an interdisciplinary scholar, educator, composer, librettist/playwright, and producer. His research focuses on Indigenous arts, music, performance, and education. He is Associate Professor and Canada Research Chair in Indigenous Arts, Knowledge Systems and Education in the Faculty of Education at Western University, London, Ontario, Canada.

Brian M. Flores is Assistant Professor at Salisbury University in the Department of Early and Elementary Education and Director of the May Literacy Center. He earned his PhD at the University of South Florida. He teaches about literacy education, and his research interests include literacy practices, identity, and culturally sustaining pedagogical practices.

Vincent Genareo is Associate Professor and Assistant Dean for Program Assessment at Salisbury University in Maryland. Genareo specializes in assessment and program evaluation. He earned his PhD from the University of North Dakota and served in a postdoctoral research associate position at Iowa State University. He has evaluated over a dozen grant-funded programs, many of which he helped plan and write. Genareo serves multiple roles as an assessment specialist across SU, local schools, and in collaborations with other universities across the country. He also prepares teachers to understand assessment and student learning.

Stanley R. Henry is a citizen of the Gayog̲o̲hó:nǫ' (Cayuga) Nation, member of the Ball Deer Clan, and member of the Six Nations of the Grand River Territory community. He is a learner and speaker of the Gayog̲o̲hó:nǫ'néha (Cayuga language). Henry is an assistant professor in the Faculty of Education, Brock University, St. Catharines, Ontario, Canada. He researches the reclamation/regeneration/restoration of Indigenous languages in general and Gayog̲o̲hó:nǫ'néha specifically, Hodinohsyo:ni' Culture-Based Education systems, and teacher education.

Janet K. Holt is Professor Emeritus (Educational Leadership) at Southern Illinois University Edwardsville (SIUE) and serves as an academic researcher in the College of Nursing at Florida Atlantic University. Holt's previous positions include Executive Director of the Illinois Education Research Council at SIUE – which produced research reports to inform Illinois P20 education policy – and Professor and Program Coordinator of Educational Research and Evaluation at Northern Illinois University. Her scholarship includes education policy, inequities in degree persistence and completion, and methods of multivariate analyses and growth modeling, as well as multiyear collaborations in early grammatical growth in young children and adult literacy.

Megan Hughes is Dean of Allied Health and Emergency Services at Prairie State College. She has a research interest in health literacy and community literacy. She was previously Assistant Professor of Reading and English and Coordinator of Adult Literacy, both at community colleges. Her experiences also include working as an EMT.

Kim Jacobs is a retired Senior Director of Education and Curriculum Development at the National Center for Families Learning (NCFL) where her expertise in education publications, evidence-based content development, and digital classroom and family engagement tools lives on. Her work at NCFL centered around early childhood education, language/literacy development, and family engagement. She is the former Director of the Family and Child Education (FACE) program, and she garnered many publication credits. Jacobs came to NCFL as a 20-year public education veteran, including classroom teaching from preschool to high school, program management, and working with teenage parents and immigrant families.

Erik Jacobson is Associate Professor in the Department of Teaching and Learning at Montclair State University. Over his career in adult basic education, he has worked as a teacher, a researcher, and a consultant. His research focuses on adult literacy practice and policy, in the United States and in Japan. He is particularly interested in the political economy of adult education and how students and teachers make connections between their classrooms and their own social justice work.

Laura Johnson is Associate Professor in the Department of Educational Technology, Research and Assessment at Northern Illinois University where she teaches courses in qualitative research methods, including ethnographic research, interview methods, and community-based/participatory action research. Her research focuses on civic engagement, community involvement, and advocacy among Latinx and African American youth, with an emphasis on pregnant and parenting youth, as well as on community-based qualitative research methods and the development of equitable university-community partnerships. She is the author of *Community-based qualitative research: Approaches for education and the social sciences* (2017, SAGE Publications).

Katherine Marsh is a tutor and school consultant in the northeast United States. She holds a master's degree in special education and is a Fulbright Scholar who studied inorganic chemistry in West Germany before the fall of the Berlin Wall. She is currently pursuing a doctoral degree in reading education. She has worked as a teacher and a tutor in such diverse learning environments as gifted classrooms, multiage science classes, and museum-based programs, as well as in guiding middle and high school students back into school-based programs. She enjoys adapting her teaching strategies to fulfill individualized student needs at all age levels.

Dixie Massey is a lecturer at Seattle Pacific University. Her research interests include pedagogies of reading comprehension and the history of literacy. She is author and coauthor of the curriculum series *Comprehension Strategies for World History and U.S. History in the Social Studies; Targeted Vocabulary*

Instruction and the Seeds of Inquiry series published by The Social Studies School Services.

Amber Meyer is Assistant Professor at Salisbury University in the Department of Literacy Studies. She earned her PhD from Michigan State University with a specialization in language and literacy. Her research interests include teacher learning and professional development of early and elementary education teachers across the developmental spectrum, supporting teachers in developing and refining high-leverage practices and serving ELL students through research-based practices in literacy instruction.

M. Kristiina Montero is Professor of Social Development Studies and Culture and Language Studies at Renison University College, University of Waterloo, Canada. Her research and practice are framed in community-engaged scholarship that aims to use the space of research to engage with practical problems defined by community stakeholders. One of her overarching goals is to give voice to marginalized individuals and communities. Her more recent work examines the impact of culturally responsive early literacy instructional practices on the language and literacy development of adolescent English Language Learners with limited prior schooling and exploring the use of decolonizing pedagogies in teacher education.

Wendee Mullikin, Publications Manager at the National Center for Families Learning, uses her 26 years' experience as an educator; editing certification; and diversity, equity, and inclusion in the workplace certification to provide comprehensive editorial review of professional development and training, publications, and Wonders of the Day® on NCFL's award winning website, Wonderopolis®. Before joining the team at NCFL, Wendee taught K–12 music, 6–12 English/language arts, and collegiate-level composition; provided K–12 special education services; and worked with adjudicated youth. She holds bachelor's degrees in music and English as well as a master's degree in special education with supervisor coursework completed.

Brice Nordquist is Associate Professor of Writing and Rhetoric and Dean's Professor of Community Engagement in the College of Arts and Sciences at Syracuse University. He researches relations among language and literacy practices across media, context, material and digital spaces, and cultural and geopolitical borders. He directs the College's Engaged Humanities program, which seeds and cultivates interconnected projects focused on the cocreation of public goods based on community assets, needs, and interests.

Kristen H. Perry is Professor of Literacy Education at the University of Kentucky and earned her PhD at Michigan State University. Her work focuses primarily on literacy and culture in diverse communities, investigating everyday home/family and community literacy practices, particularly among immigrant and refugee communities. She also researches educational opportunities with respect to literacy for adult refugees. She is Codirector of Project PLACE, a federally funded program that provides intensive professional development to support K–8 teachers' ability to support English learners' academic language and literacy development. Perry was the 2012 recipient of the Literacy Research Association's Early Career Achievement Award and their 2007 J. Michael Parker Award for contributions to research in adult literacy.

Marjorie W. Rowe is Assistant Professor in the Department of Literacy Studies, English Education, and History Education at East Carolina University where she joined the faculty in 2020. She is a former elementary classroom teacher, reading specialist, and literacy coach who studies the intersection of orality and literacy in early literacy, particularly as it manifests in classroom discourse. Her current research focuses on teacher socialization of beginning writers into awareness of academic discourse expectations during writing instruction and the use of arts-integrated, participatory storytelling to promote preschoolers' narrative comprehension.

Mary-Celeste Schreuder is Assistant Professor of Education at Lander University in South Carolina. Her research explores the intersection of gender identity and critical feminist pedagogy in out-of-school writing spaces. Recent publications include the article "Safe spaces, agency, and resistance: A meta synthesis of LGBTQ language use" in the *Journal of LGBT Youth*.

Peggy Semingson is Associate Professor of TESOL in the Department of Linguistics and TESOL at The University of Texas at Arlington. She received her MEd in reading education from Texas State University, San Marcos and her PhD in curriculum and instruction with specializations in language and literacy studies from The University of Texas at Austin. Her research interests include digital pedagogies, media-based learning, online learning, and digital approaches to TESOL. She was awarded the 2013 USDLA Best Practices

Platinum Award for Excellence in Distance Learning Teaching and was the recipient of the prestigious UT System Regent's Outstanding Teaching Award.

Elizabeth A. Swaggerty is a former elementary teacher and current Associate Professor in the Department of Literacy Studies, English Education, and History Education at East Carolina University in Greenville, NC. She is an educator and scholar interested in linking theory and practice in literacy education, literacy teacher preparation, and community literacy initiatives.

Annette Teasdell is a social justice change agent. She is Assistant Professor of Curriculum and Instruction at Clark Atlanta University and serves as coordinator of the Master of Arts Program in Special Education. Her research agenda is driven by her commitment to meeting the needs of students with disabilities and improving academic outcomes for students in urban schools and communities. She holds a doctorate in curriculum and instruction from the University of North Carolina at Charlotte. Her research is centered on the fundamental belief that culturally responsive pedagogy combined with a curriculum that is accurate, relevant, and appropriate and whose educational processes are humane can yield improved student outcomes.

William Tignor is a primary grade teacher, currently in his seventeenth year in public education. He has been a Salisbury University PDS Outstanding Mentor Teacher and has mentored over 30 preservice teachers. He spent the last five years as an adjunct professor working with preservice teachers in the May Literacy Center at Salisbury University, focusing on community, reading instruction, and reading assessment. Tignor has a bachelor's degree in elementary education, a master's degree as a reading specialist, and is currently a doctoral candidate, working toward an EdD in contemporary curriculum theory and instruction.

Chad H. Waldron is Assistant Professor of Literacy Education, at the University of Michigan-Flint. At the university, he works with undergraduate, graduate, and doctoral candidates within literacy and educator preparation. He also serves in a leadership role as the Director of CAEP (Council for the Accreditation of Educator Preparation) Accreditation. Waldron's research work centers upon literacy educator preparation, community literacy, and family literacy practices within early childhood settings and elementary school contexts.

Laura Westberg, Director of Education and Evaluation Initiatives at the National Center for Families Learning, supports research and evaluation, contributes to evidence-based publication and training, and advises for messaging related to research. She started her career as an early childhood educator and program administrator within a variety of contexts – Head Start, childcare, preschool, and early childhood special education. Westberg has delivered collegiate instruction, provided training, managed projects, delivered conference presentations, and published research and instructional materials. She served as Director of the National Early Literacy Panel. Westberg has a BS in early childhood education and a MS in language education from Indiana University.

Tara Wilson is An Assistant Professor of Literacy at The University of Texas – Permian Basin. She teaches literacy courses for undergraduate and master's students. Prior to working in higher education, Wilson taught in Texas public education for 11 years. She presents at the local, state, regional, national, and international levels, as well as publishes in literacy and early childhood journals. Wilson received her EdD in literacy from Sam Houston State University. In her "free" time she enjoys reading and spending time with her fur babies and husband.

Mary Yee grew up in Boston's Chinatown, a daughter of working-class immigrants. A founder of Asian Americans United and Yellow Seeds, two Asian American organizing and advocacy organizations, she has worked extensively in Philadelphia with BIPOC, immigrant, and refugee communities. Yee's experience includes working at the School District of Philadelphia as an administrator around ESOL/bilingual education, family engagement, and language access. Her background is in East Asian studies, urban planning, TESOL, and critical literacies. Yee's research interests focus on educational issues in immigrant communities, youth activism, university-community partnerships, and health and educational disparities.

Diana J. Zaleski is Instructional Resource and Professional Development Director for the Illinois Education Association and an Instructor at the University of Illinois Springfield in the Department of Psychology. She is an educational psychologist who specializes in program evaluation and the design and delivery of learner-centered training programs for educators. Zaleski also serves as an educational policy and accountability expert on regional and national committees.

Index